Religion in Development

Religion in Development
Rewriting the Secular Script

Séverine Deneulin
with
Masooda Bano

Zed Books
London & New York

Religion in Development: Rewriting the Secular Script was first published in 2009 by Zed Books Ltd, 7 Cynthia Street, London N1 9JF, UK and Room 400, 175 Fifth Avenue, New York, NY 10010, USA

www.zedbooks.co.uk

Designed and typeset by Kate Kirkwood
Cover designed by Rogue Four Design
Printed in the UK by the MPG Books Group

Distributed in the USA exclusively by Palgrave Macmillan, a division of St Martin's Press, LLC, 175 Fifth Avenue, New York, NY 10010, USA

A catalogue record for this book is available from the British Library
Library of Congress Cataloging in Publication Data available

ISBN 978 1 84813 000 5 hb
ISBN 978 1 84813 001 2 pb

Contents

Acknowledgements

In March 2006, I received an email from Susannah Trefgarne of Zed Books: could I write an introductory book on the topic of religion and development? It was not something I had in mind to do at the time but it was an opportunity to clarify some thoughts regarding the recent surge in interest in religion in development studies.

I had been introduced to the subject of 'religion and development' almost twenty years ago when I met a missionary who had spent her life as a nurse in Madagascar. Many encounters followed with people who deepened my interest in the subject. It would be impossible to name them all here, but there are some people who have played a significant role in shaping the arguments I put forward. Sabina Alkire has been a constant interlocutor in exchanging ideas about how religion and development relate, and should relate, to each other. Scott Thomas has been another invaluable source, not only of dialogue but also of information. He helped guide me through the literature, carefully commented on the manuscript, and shared opinions and concerns regarding the treatment of religion in the social sciences. Many conversations with Nick Townsend on the place of religion in public life have helped shape my discussion of the political dimensions of religion. Joe Devine, Ian Linden, Jonathan Warner and an anonymous referee carefully revised the manuscript, saved me from many errors, and improved its structure and clarity. Monika Chmelova, in addition to designing a draft book cover, provided many opportunities for exchanging thoughts and experiences.

Finally, this book would never have seen the light without the help of Masooda Bano. She readily accepted my invitation to underpin the approach taken here from within the Islamic tradition. She played an essential part in refining the arguments advanced and situating them within the reality of life in developing countries.

Instances of the presence and influence of religion in the reality of development are extremely diverse. The Iranian revolution of 1979 saw the overthrow of a development model based on the pursuit of economic growth and Western modernization by forces favouring one arranged around the teachings of the Qur'an. The Christian churches had a significant role in the resistance against apartheid in South Africa and Buddhist monks in the resistance against the military dictatorship in Burma. The Hindu caste system is reported to have a negative impact on poverty reduction among the scheduled tribes in India. The Catholic Church's official prohibition of condoms and artificial contraception is held responsible for the spread of HIV/AIDS, as is the advocacy of abstinence by other Christian faith-based organizations. On the other hand, the same organizations account for an astonishing proportion of health services in certain parts of the world, especially weak African states. According to World Bank estimates, 50 per cent of health and education services in sub-Saharan Africa were provided by faith-based organizations in 2000. Islam, too, is vilified for its conservatism, yet Islamic organizations are one of the major providers of health and social services.[1] While religion is accused of bringing conflicts, it has also been an invaluable instrument of peace.[2]

It is a daunting task to write a monograph that covers, as exhaustively as possible, the state of the field regarding the relationship between 'religion and development'. If this relationship is mapped across time, space and religious traditions, the combination of possible connections becomes almost limitless. It would range from the early Protestant missionaries in Africa in the eighteenth century to the Buddhist-inspired Sarrodaya movement of empowerment in Sri Lanka, the impact of the preaching of Muslim mullahs on the lives of women in Somalia, or the influence of evangelical churches on politics in Latin America.

The aim of this book is two-fold. First, it tries to provide as extensive a survey as possible of the state of the field by describing numerous instances of how religious activities on the one hand and development activities on the other interact. It reports a great variety of case studies that take the reader beyond the existing development studies literature on the subject to illustrate the complex interplay between religion and development. Its second aim is to offer an analytical approach for dealing with religion in development processes. While the literature on religion and development is burgeoning fast, there has been no attempt yet to offer an analytical grid for understanding the role of religion in development, to conceptualize it, and to provide a framework for the growing partnerships that are observed between development donors and religious communities.

A number of studies already contain rich case studies illustrating the influence of religion, positive or negative, on development activities and poverty and equity outcomes. A series of books published by the World Bank under the lead authorship of Katherine Marshall give an account of a large variety of empirical examples of the work of faith communities and faith-based organizations engaged in development-related work, such as HIV/AIDS prevention, health care, education, environmental protection and conflict resolution.[3] Another collection of stories compiled by Wendy Tyndale (2007) relates the work of the World Faiths Development Dialogue, a World Bank initiative led by its then president, James Wolfensohn, and the then Archbishop of Canterbury, George Carey.

In a volume entitled *Religion and Development: Conflict or Cooperation?*, Jeff Haynes examines the constructive and destructive roles of religion in development processes by focusing on four major world religions – Islam, Christianity, Hinduism and Buddhism. Organized around key development themes including economic growth, environmental sustainability, health and education, the book documents the dominant development approaches within these fields, the initial resistance of development actors to acknowledging the potential of religious forces to advance development ends, and examples of the contribution of faith-based organizations in these areas. Though the book touches on broader theoretical debates on the role of religion in society and its links with development, its primary focus remains the documentation of approaches and the practical contributions of the four religions under study. Our attempt is thus quite distinct in approach from that of Haynes, as it addresses broader concerns around the role of religion in development rather than focusing on the contribution of selected religions to specific development sectors. Theoretically and empirically, the ambit we have chosen is much broader.

The Religions and Development Research Programme at the University of Birmingham is another source of studies on the relationship between religion and development.[4] The programme aims to understand three core questions: (1) How do religious values and beliefs drive the actions and interactions of individuals and faith-based organizations? (2) How do religious values and beliefs, and the religious organizations that espouse these, influence the relationships between states and societies? (3) In what ways do faith communities interact with development actors, and what are the outcomes with respect to the achievement of development goals? Drawing on empirical research in four focus countries – India, Nigeria, Pakistan and Tanzania – the programme is producing a series of working papers on issues emerging from these three core questions. These working papers will later be converted into book volumes and journals articles. While the strength of the programme is its empirically driven research studies testing theoretical concerns in specific settings, the contribution of this book is to imbed these debates in broader arguments. Conversely, the numerous publications that should result from the programme have the potential to elaborate on various dimensions of the interface between religion and development as analysed in this book. These two attempts at studying religion in development thus neatly complement each other.

At a more general level, Alkire (2006) offers a brief but compact survey of the literature on this subject. She has arranged the literature around ten issues: the intrinsic value of religion as part of people's wellbeing; the specific way in which religions conceive of development; the resurgence of religion against the prediction of the secularist assumption; the role of faith-based organizations in development processes and outcomes; the religious motivation of staff working in development organizations; inter-faith initiatives in the efforts to overcome poverty; the potential conflict between so-called religious values and those of development; religious groups as civil society actors; religious extremism and violence; and the recognition by religion of human fallibility.[5]

In *Development, Civil Society and Faith-Based Organizations*, Clarke *et al.* (2007) provide a broad overview of the role of faith-based organizations (FBOs) in development. They use the term FBO 'in reference to any organization that derives inspiration and guidance for its activities from the teachings and principles of the faith or from a particular interpretation or school of thought within the faith' (p. 6). Clarke (2006, 2007b) offers a five-fold classification of FBOs: (1) faith-based representative organizations which govern the faithful; (2) faith-based charitable or development organizations which are running projects and providing services for marginalized people; (3) faith-based socio-political organizations which mobilize the faithful politically; (4) faith-based missionary organizations which promote the faith; and (5) faith-based illegal or terrorist organizations which engage in armed struggles in the name of religion. The volume gathers a mine of information on numerous FBOs across the religious spectrum, with a wide geographical coverage.

This present monograph does not complement the above reviews by examining yet more case studies of religious influence in development processes and outcomes. For example, we do not set out to examine how various FBOs in each of the above categories participate in the development process, for better or for worse; we do not describe how Christian democratic parties emerged from the Church's teaching on social issues at the end of the nineteenth century; we do not consider the impact of religion on the reognition of labour rights and the emergence of social democracy; we do not enquire into how and why the missionary activities of Pentecostals and Wahhabi Muslims may be leading to conflict in some regions of Africa.

Nor does it complement them by reviewing various development issues, such as health, education, gender, corruption, governance, peace and environmental care, and examining the role of religious beliefs and faith-based organizations in each one of these areas. This would have involved, among other things, reviewing the influence of religion on people's behaviour: whether holding religious beliefs makes people more honest and reduces corruption; whether adhering to a religion makes non-governmental organization (NGO) staff more motivated and more willing to work for less; whether religious organizations are more efficient than non-religious ones in advancing key development aims.

This monograph attempts to offer a unique contribution to the existing literature by providing a conceptual framework, indeed another 'script', for understanding the role of religion in development processes and outcomes. Relying on a large variety of empirical material, the book advances the key argument that there is no separation between religion and development. Development is what adherents to a religion do because of who they are and what they believe in. The engagement of religious communities in development activities derives from their core beliefs and teachings. It is not easy to separate the development activities (schools, hospitals, political protests, and so on) from the religious activities (such as prayer and worship). For example, Hamas is as much a charitable organization delivering social services to the marginalized as a political organization seeking control of Palestine through armed struggle against Israeli occupation. A church or a mosque may have on its premises a place of worship, a legal aid service, an infirmary, a primary school, and a hall used for social events or meetings with political dimensions (such as preparing a demonstration against the government).

FBOs are not mere civil society or non-governmental organizations which happen to draw their inspiration from religious teachings instead of some form of humanistic philosophy. The development work of religious traditions is part of what being a good Christian or a good Muslim is all about, together with prayer and worship. The 'spiritual' and 'temporal' activities are deeply intertwined. Moreover, the distinction between 'faith-based' and 'secular' is often not straightforward (Linden, 2007). Oxfam, a secular NGO, started as an initiative by the vicar of Oxford University to help Greek Cypriot civilians in the Second World War (the Oxford Committee for Famine Relief).[6] Another UK secular NGO, VSO (Voluntary Service Overseas), started out as the vision of two committed Anglicans, with the support of the then Bishop of Portsmouth.[7] Amnesty International also emerged from the vision of a Christian layman whose religious commitment led him to help prisoners of conscience under dictatorships.[8]

A consequence of this for development theory and practice is that each religion needs to be studied in its entirety. By segmenting elements of a religion that are good or bad for 'development', those who study religion within the disciplinary boundaries of development studies often ignore this comprehensiveness. They also ignore a religion's potential for internal dynamic change – for central teachings, or at least their interpretations, constantly evolve in response to the socio-economic and political contexts in which adherents live and in which they embody these teachings.

That is why this book does not review the impact of religion and religious organizations on development topics such as health, education, humanitarian aid, political advocacy, civil society, safety net mechanisms and many others. Such an approach compartmentalizes religion-based organizations into different sectors and does not render account of the holistic nature of their activities. Observing that a 'secular Christian' NGO is purely involved in disaster relief and that a 'militant Christian' NGO uses disaster relief for winning souls by distributing bibles alongside food or tents[9] misses the fact that how various Christian NGOs act is linked to how the faith community they represent understands what living a good Christian life is about. For some, living the fundamentals of the Christian faith is about giving water to the thirsty, food to the hungry and health care to the sick, whoever they are. For other Christians, it is about changing the economic, social and political structures that make people thirsty, hungry and sick. For others, it is about professing faith in Jesus Christ as the only saviour and trying to make others endorse the same beliefs and vision of life.

Our book argues that development theory needs to rewrite its dominant script regarding its treatment of religion, a script which so far has been heavily inscribed in the secular tradition. One of the assumptions of secularism is that religion should be kept in the private sphere (see Chapter 3). In contrast, the reality of life in developing countries shows that religion has a public face that can neither be ignored nor contained within certain boundaries. This has implications for development theory and practice. Since the secularist assumption that religion can be kept private cannot be sustained, another mode of engagement with religion is required.[10]

Religion is not to be considered only as a significant force in development – the position adopted in the existing development studies literature – but has be engaged with in its entirety and not only to the extent that is conducive or detrimental to pre-defined development goals. For its adherents, religion infuses all aspects (and decisions) of their lives, and this has implications for the way they understand what development processes and outcomes ought to be. Development donors, such as governments and multilateral agencies, need to have a basic understanding of the religious context if their partnership with religious communities is to be successful. It is critical therefore to encourage dialogue between different worldviews – especially between those who see the world through secular eyes, without reference to a transcendental source of value, and those who see it through the eyes of a religion. This dialogue, however, has to be conducted with a view to respecting rather than winning over the other standpoint. This is an attitude essential for developing a mutually agreed consensus and forms of living together.

For the sake of analytical clarity and depth of arguments and illustrations, we have limited our study to the Abrahamic religions of Islam and Christianity. Adherents to these two religions constitute nearly half of the world's population. While we have not dealt with Judaism, Buddhism, Hinduism and others, we maintain that the basic analytical grid for understanding the role of religion in development proposed in this book could apply beyond the Islamic and Christian traditions. These religions are based on a set of core teachings embodied in people's lives and constantly reinterpreted in the light of the context in which they are lived. Because such teachings express certain views about how to live well and what development ought to be, the potential for conflict with non-religious understandings of development exists, prompting a need for dialogue and greater mutual understanding.[11]

In order to provide a new analytical grid for studying religion in development, we start by discussing five core questions that development practice confronts in the reality of developing countries: (1) Is religion still a powerful force in the public sphere, worthy of serious academic engagement, or is it bound to disappear as societies reach higher levels of economic and social development? (2) Can religion be confined to the private sphere and be prevented from overflowing into the public domain, or does it escape control? (3) Are religious precepts archaic, homogeneous and resistant to change, or do they have an internal dynamic of reasoning, argument, controversy and change? (4) Can dialogue and mutual understanding evolve when differences between the religious and secularist positions on certain development issues seem irreconcilable, or are they irresistibly heading towards violent clash? (5) Given the nature of irreconcilable differences over certain critical development issues, can religious teachings and practices be selectively endorsed, depending on their affinity with secular positions, or do they have to be recognized in their wholeness? The first chapter illustrates numerous case studies from both the developed and developing worlds that illustrate the importance of each one of these questions in reaching a comprehensive understanding of the role of religion in development processes.

The second chapter reviews how religion has been treated in the history of development thought since the 1950s. Given the scope of such a survey, we have chosen to discuss five core texts, each high-lighting a key theme. Arthur Lewis's *Theory of Economic Growth* illustrates Max Weber's work on the 'Protestant ethic'. This approach maintains that religious beliefs affect attitudes and behaviours, which influence the development process instrumentally. The second text selected is the Universal Declaration of Human Rights of 1948, which acknowledges the need to respect the right to religious freedom. Development policies ought to respect that right and people should not be discriminated against because of their religion. The third text discussed is a special issue of *World Development* published in 1980 and which advanced the debate by arguing that religious beliefs do not work in isolated ways but act as a moral basis of society and provide the set of norms under which to assess the legitimacy and validity of the development process. The gradual understanding of poverty as being a multi-dimensional phenomenon also led to the recognition of the central importance of religion in the wellbeing of people in developing countries, as documented in our fourth text, the World Bank's study *Voices of the Poor*. Finally, Amartya Sen's *Development as Freedom* provides our fifth theme, that development is value-based and that religion infuses the values that guide the development process, including the behaviour and decisions of actors in the political sphere, such as political parties and civil society organizations. Within the human development paradigm, religion has ceased to be an insignificant factor and become an essential part of the development process. Moreover, the role of religion is no longer viewed instrumentally but recognized as shaping people's moral values and what they see as desirable and worthy of pursuit. In other words, in this view religion may define the very ends and means of the development process itself.

In the third chapter, we examine three major concepts which deeply influenced development thinking and practice, but which have been subject to wide contestation: the secularization thesis, the definition of religion as a set of private beliefs, and the links between religion, fundamentalism and violence. Defeating the predictions that it would disappear as societies modernized, religion remains a living force in both the developed and developing worlds. It maintains its public significance because of its inherently political nature. Religion is political because it provides a framework for how to live well in society (according to God's command). It therefore penetrates the political sphere, characterized by a search for laws and policies that provide the conditions enabling people to live well together. Thus religion cannot be reduced to a set of private beliefs; instead it is best defined as a tradition of thought or inquiry guided by fundamental premises. A good life is one which abides by God's law, but religion never ceases to redefine and reinterpret that fundamental agreement in the light of the specific social and historical contexts in which it is lived.

Although religion shares many similarities with culture, such as providing norms and codes of conduct and meaning for what people are and do, it cannot be equated with culture because it rests on transcendental teachings (the fundamental agreement) which have authority for believers. We conclude the third chapter by discussing fundamentalism and violence. We argue that the risk of religion-based behaviours turning violent is real. However, these are often responses to the sacred and how to live well according to God's commands. We contend therefore that an internal change, within a religious tradition itself, of the leadership's interpretation of the tradition's teachings is a better strategy for curtailing religious-inspired violence than secular attempts to privatize religion and eliminate it from the public sphere.

Chapter 4 analyses some positive influences of religion in the practice of development. We describe examples of religiously inspired development activities, which illustrate that development work is not an addendum that the post-war development age has entrusted to religious communities, but is intrinsic to the fundamental agreement of these religions. This is why this book is entitled 'religion *in* development' and not 'religion *and* development', which implies two separate variables – note that this distinction is reminiscent of the shift from the 'women and development' to the 'women in development' approach to gender in development studies. Development work and the pursuit of social justice is part of what many adherents to a religion understand as the best embodiment in social practices of its fundamental teachings in specific social, economic and political environments. We examine in detail four development manifestations of religious traditions: (1) the Christian missions and Da'wa groups in Islam ('those who respond to God's call'); (2) the evangelistic nature of Christianity and the central precepts in Islam regarding charity and social welfare; and finally (3) the different modes of engagement with politics in Christianity and Islam.

The fifth chapter analyses how religious and non-religious worldviews may come into conflict with regard to how to live well, and the practices and institutions which secure a good life. The chapter highlights some significant overlaps between the religious and secular traditions on development issues. Both are committed to human dignity, social justice, poverty relief, concern for the earth, equality and freedom. Yet a religious tradition cannot be reduced to a mere humanistic moral framework cut off from its divine or transcendental roots. We focus on four areas of conflict: women's reproductive rights, liberal education, political authority and the epistemological foundations of the social sciences. These areas reveal irreconcilable differences between understandings of how to live well, and they highlight the need to develop a framework for mutual agreement and coexistence. For example, in the area of education, the tensions visible between those who advocate educating children into a certain way of thinking and living from a religious perspective and those who oppose this need to be bridged.

The concluding chapter documents the constantly evolving nature of religious traditions in response to the socio-economic and political realities. We argue that this changing internal dynamic represents a potential for secular-based development theory and practice to engage in a genuine dialogue with religion. The chapter focuses attention on the non-homogeneous character of religion and its vulnerability to abuses of power. There always remains the danger that one group may impose on the whole community of believers its own interpretation of a religion's central teachings. We cite some examples of a tradition's reinterpretation of how to live and embody its fundamental teachings: the Second Vatican Council in the Catholic Church and its impacts on development and social justice; the response of the Islamic tradition to capitalism; and the practice of *itjihad* in Sunni Islam, which focuses on constant reinterpretation in response to the needs of the time.

Two solutions for progressing towards a consensus when faced with irreconcilable positions are proposed. First, no powerful leader should be allowed to hijack interpretations of religious precepts. Second, there is a need for generating dialogue, as traditions are not homogeneous. The chapter proposes some guidelines inspired from the practice of inter-faith dialogue. Despite the difficulty of genuine understanding of another tradition and its mode of thinking and practices, such exercise of dialogue is essential to development practice. Unless this happens, a development process based on the premises characteristic of the secular tradition risks alienating religious communities and creating further conflict and clashes.

This book is primarily directed at undergraduate and postgraduate students in the social sciences, as well as at development practitioners, who wish to understand better the role of religion in development processes and outcomes. While our task has been to provide an introduction, we also offer further references for interested readers who wish to deepen their understanding of specific topics. While not containing primary empirical research material, the book hopes to be equally useful to academics in the field by providing an analytical framework for conceptualizing the role of religion in development. Last but not least, the book aims to offer religious groups who are actively engaged in development activities a detailed analysis of how their work is understood within the discipline of development studies.

Notes

1 Harb (2007) describes the role of Hizbullah in Lebanon as a faith-based organization delivering widespread social services.

2 For the well-documented case of a religious community's role in ending the civil conflict in Mozambique, see Appleby (2000) and Johnston (2003).

3 Marshall and Marsh (2003); Marshall and Keough (2004); Marshall and Van Saanen (2007). Belshaw *et al.* (2001) examine the partnership between the World Bank and churches in Africa.

4 The website of the programme is <http://www.rad.bham.ac.uk> (accessed November 2008).

5 For another general survey article on the role of religion in development, but with reference to Africa, see Ter Haar and Ellis (2006). They examine the role of what they call 'religious resources', such as religious ideas, practices, organizations and experiences, in promoting development.

6 See <http://www.oxfam.org.uk/oxfam_in_action/history/index.html> (accessed November 2008).

7 See <http://www.vso.org.uk/about/> (accessed November 2008).

8 The obituaries of Peter Benenson, who died in February 2005, reported that Amnesty International emerged from his reading a newspaper article in the London tube in 1960. The article was about two Portuguese students who had been jailed for raising a toast to liberty in a Lisbon pub. Disturbed by the article, Benenson entered the church of St Martin's-in-the-Fields in Central London to pray about how to act. He responded to the article by launching a campaign to help free prisoners of conscience, which later evolved into Amnesty International.

9 See Beneditti (2006).

10 Our use of the term 'secular' is thus not to be conceived as opposite to 'sacred', for we hold that religion cannot easily be separated from the economic, social, cultural and political world in which it is lived.

11 See, for example, Bradley (2006), who discusses how the Hindu tradition contains its own understanding of women's empowerment, which can fruitfully be engaged by secular feminist organizations.

In February 2008 the Archbishop of Canterbury, Dr Rowan Williams, became immersed in an intense controversy. There were calls for his resignation, with some calling him a 'disaster for the Church of England'. The critics came not only from the ranks of the liberals but also from among the conservatives in the Anglican Communion, all three leading political parties, fellow Christians in other denominations, Jews, and even some Muslims. At the heart of the controversy was the Archbishop's speech to the legal community in the UK in which he had argued for adoption of parts of Sharia – Islamic law – in Britain. For a book which aims at proposing an analytical grid for studying and understanding the role of religion in development, an examination of the Archbishop's proposal and the ensuing critiques illuminates the challenges development theory and practice confront in accommodating religion within their ambit.

In his speech,[1] the Archbishop tried to address what to him was an important modern-day challenge: how to accommodate the demands of minority religious communities who want to exercise the option to be ruled on certain issues by their religious legal systems? Drawing on the case of some members of the Muslim communities in the UK who argued for freedom to live under Sharia law, he addressed the generic question of what level of public and legal recognition, if any, might be allowed to the legal provisions of a religious group.[2]

While acquiescent to the fact that there are no easy solutions, he proposed a 'transformative accommodation' between secular and religious legal systems enabling the two to coexist. This, in his view, did not imply setting up a parallel legal system to British law. Rather it entailed formulating a scheme in which individuals retained the opportunity to choose the jurisdiction under which they would seek to resolve certain carefully chosen matters. The Archbishop maintained that this would force the religious and secular leaders to compete for the loyalty of shared constituents. The proposal involved accommodating religious law on a case-by-case basis where the legally recognized religious precepts did not interfere with the liberties guaranteed by state law in the society in question.

The justification for such a proposal was the recognition that social identities are not constituted by one exclusive set of relations or mode of belonging; people have multiple identities and affiliations. The modern secular state, when assuming a monopoly in terms of defining public and political identity, creates as serious a problem as do religious communities in viewing religious identity as the only significant category. For the Archbishop, it is unrealistic to believe that to be a citizen is essentially and simply to be under the rule of the uniform law of a sovereign state. The secular position, which holds that any other relations, commitments or protocols of behaviour belong exclusively to the realm of the private and of individual choice, is untenable (see Chapter 3):

> It would be a pity if immense advances in the recognition of human rights led, because of a misconception about legal universality, to a situation where a person was defined primarily as the possessor of a set of abstract liberties and the law's function was accordingly seen as nothing but the securing of those liberties irrespective of the custom and conscience of those groups which concretely compose a plural modern society. (Archbishop's lecture, February 2008)

The Archbishop, in simple words, was arguing for respecting people's religious commitments and carving out greater spaces to accommodate religious precepts within the secular system if the secular state was to win the full allegiance of religious communities.

For his critics, however, the proposal, or even the mere discussion of such demands, was outrageous. For them, the mention of Sharia raised instant references to repression of women, archaic and brutal physical punishments and a pre-modern system with no human rights. How could the Archbishop argue for tolerance of such values within a progressive Western society, inquired over 17,000 hostile viewers flooding the BBC's online message board?

Michael Nazir Ali, the Pakistan-born Bishop of Rochester, on the other hand, noted the practical challenge to such a proposal: 'Every school of Shariah law would be in conflict with British law on matters like monogamy, provisions for divorce, the rights of women, the custody of children, the laws of inheritance and of evidence so how would consensus be evolved?'[3] The toughest challenge to the Archbishop's proposal came from a group of columnists in *The*

Times online edition, who questioned whether Sharia was something that could be cherry-picked. Can we say that we will engage with certain aspects of Sharia, or any religious system, and not with others? And, if yes, which criteria should we use to distinguish the religious precepts that we see as 'good' to engage with from those that are 'bad'?

The issues raised by the debate between the Archbishop and his furious critics do not relate only to how Western societies are to accommodate the public presence of religion in their midst; they also arise in developing countries and especially in their relation to Western donors. As this book will illustrate, there are many parallels to be drawn between the above story and the reality of development practice in developing countries, such as the controversy surrounding secular and religious understandings of women's empowerment or the controversy surrounding religious education and its rejection of non-religious subjects.

In its essence, the Sharia law controversy in Britain captures the Gordian knot that needs to be untangled in order to find ways for development theory and practice to deal with the presence of religion in the public sphere. In the Introduction we identified five questions that the reality of development work in developing countries confronts (see p. 7). This chapter briefly examines each of these questions as they relate to development theory and practice. Our purpose here is not to put forward a set of satisfactory responses that can be accepted by all, for disagreement is a characteristic hallmark whenever the subject of the appropriate role of religion in the public sphere is concerned. Instead, our purpose is to demonstrate, through a variety of examples, that the reality of development work makes these questions unavoidable. They have to be addressed. The fact that they lack straightforward answers is not a sufficient warrant for not asking them. Some case studies help us illuminate the terms of debate. They also point out that, given the empirical reality, some answers to the above questions are more appropriate than others.

Is religion relevant?

Is religion still a powerful force in the public sphere, worthy of serious academic engagement, or is it bound to disappear as societies reach higher levels of economic and social development? If what the foundational texts of the social sciences said about religion were correct, religion would long have become an irrelevant phenomenon in our world of material affluence, an archaic need bound to disappear with the rise of modernity. The social sciences, born at the end of the nineteenth century as heirs of the Enlightenment, viewed religion as incompatible with the demands of rationality and human reason. The public domain was assumed to be guided by collective reasoning free of transcendental concerns. Religion was a force to be marginalized from the public sphere, and so its eventual disappearance was assumed. The fathers of sociology, Emile Durkheim and Max Weber, both established an inverse relationship between modernity and religion: as societies modernize, they may be expected to rely less on the sacred to interpret events around them or seek solutions. This is known as the secularization thesis. As a growing stream of literature within sociology now contends, the thesis has failed (see Chapter 3). Religion continues to be of significance in the lives of many people in both the so-called developed and developing worlds. Rather than being confined to the private sphere, religion continues to register its presence and is observed to have both positive and negative influences on development processes in developing countries, as the forthcoming chapters will document.

On the positive side, religion remains the source of inspiration for much welfare and humanitarian work (see Chapter 4). Religion-driven charitable contributions remain a critical source of welfare work in many countries, and faith-based organizations (FBOs), which exist in all religious traditions, remain the most significant non-state providers of basic social services to the poor in many developing countries. The notion of social justice has been critical to the work of Christian and Muslim missionary groups. Both have placed high emphasis on improving the living conditions of the communities within which they work as part of their concern with propagating the word of God. Beyond welfare activities and the provision of social services, many of these groups have also engaged in radical political activism. In terms of civil society engagement, a large number of churches and faith-based organizations have participated in advocacy campaigns on justice issues, and are contributing to changing economic, social and political structures.

Religion thus provides a unique opportunity to mobilize resources for promoting development outcomes, such as poverty reduction and improved health and education. Yet it presents at the same time some of the toughest challenges. Examples are not difficult to find. In many societies, women are prohibited by religious decrees from working outside the home; religion is often a cause of sectarian and communal violence; or religious beliefs are interpreted so that women whose partners are HIV-positive are denied the use of contraception on moral grounds. There are many cases where religion appears to be undermining basic human rights – such as the right to dignified work, freedom from discrimination and hatred, and the freedom to escape an easily preventable death. The rising tide of religion-based militancy witnessed internationally pushes the destructive potential of religion to the forefront.

Militancy based on religious precepts has become a serious international concern. The inability of the 'War on Terror' to curb it, despite major financial investment in counter-militancy strategies, highlights the need to understand better the religious phenomenon if effective strategies are to be devised to limit the negative consequences of this rising religion-based militancy for the social order. The War on Terror has led the United States to violate human rights principles in its dealings with prisoners held at Guantánamo Bay, has led to civil liberties being curtailed within US borders and those of its allies, and has led to large parts of Afghanistan and Iraq being destroyed and many civilians being killed. Further, these measures have entailed high costs for American taxpayers. But, despite current strategies to control it, religion-based militancy still remains unchecked.

Being blamed for training and supporting the Taliban and for harbouring pro-Al-Qaida sentiments, the government of Pakistan has followed closely the strategies advised by the US to curtail alleged Taliban and Al-Qaida militants in its tribal areas in the North West Frontier Province (NWFP). These have included, first, performing military operations in the tribal belt to cleanse the area of suspected foreign and local militants; and, second, handing over militant suspects to the US without trial.[4] Dialogue with the militants in order to reach peace agreements, though attempted, was not seriously pursued. The military operations led to many undesirable consequences, including deaths of innocent civilians, major displacement of the local population, and destruction of infrastructure. In October 2006, a military strike on a madrasa in Bajaur killed 82 people, many of whom were students under 18, some reportedly as young as 6 years of age.[5]

Reliance on force has proved of limited effectiveness in dealing with religion-based militancy. In the tribal areas repeated military operations have failed to displace militant groups. Rather, after four years of operations, the militant resistance has spilled out of the tribal belt right into the heart of Islamabad and other peaceful places such as the Swat Valley, formerly a popular tourist resort but now under siege by the militants. At the same time, suicide bombing has become an increasingly common phenomenon in Pakistan – it only started after the declaration of the War on Terror. The reactive nature of these attacks is clear. The first lethal suicide attack, which killed 40 soldiers at a military base in NWFP, was carried out just days after the missile attack in Bajaur.

Religion-based militancy remains strong despite attempts to contain it. One could even argue that the greater the number of strategies to curb public expressions of religion, the more strongly religious people react to maintain its public presence. As the forthcoming chapters will illustrate with examples from Islam and Christianity, religion remains an important force shaping the public sphere in developing countries. Rather than sweeping it under the carpet or explaining it as ideological indoctrination, it is important for development theory and practice to understand how religion works.

Can religion be controlled?

Can religion be confined to the private sphere and be prevented from overflowing into the public domain, or does it escape control? The strategy of confinement is proving to be of limited effect. As will be discussed in Chapter 3, one of the basic assumptions of the secularization thesis is that religion should not be in the public domain and influence political processes. But the reality of political life in developing countries does not match these aspirations. Instead, it bears testimony to the influence of religion on the political, social and economic spheres, and its resistance to confinement in the private sphere. The continued presence of religious political parties in many developing countries, such as the Muslim Brotherhood in Egypt and Jama'at-i-Islami in Pakistan and Bangladesh, testifies to the inherent political nature of religion.

The Society of the Muslim Brothers, or the Muslim Brotherhood, originated in 1928 in Egypt and was founded by Islamic scholar Hasan al-Banna as a network of Islamic organizations engaged in charity work among the poor. Its aim was to build progressively an alternative Islamic society based on Islamic values which would stand in stark contrast with the values imposed by the colonial power, such as secularism, individualism and economic liberalism. In the 1950s, some members of the Brotherhood started to resort to violent means to achieve their aim of establishing an Islamic society. They attempted to assassinate President Nasser, who was perceived as an instrument of Western domination in the region. The Society was thereafter forbidden and its leader executed, but the popularity of the Society among the Egyptian population remained strong.

After the 1992 Cairo earthquake, the Brotherhood emerged as a credible institution that was much more effective in delivering aid and social services than the government was. The Society demanded its legalization as a political party but it was refused. In the September 2005 elections, some members of the Muslim Brotherhood stood as independents and won 20 per cent of seats to become the main opposition group. It seems only a matter of time before the Muslim Brotherhood becomes a political party in Egypt, given its widespread support among the population.[6]

Jama'at-i-Islami, an Islamic political party established in 1941 by Mawlana Sayyid Abu'l-A'la Maududi (1903–79), one of most influential Muslim intellectuals of the twentieth century, continues to exert its influence in the political sphere in Pakistan and Bangladesh. The party propagates the philosophy that religion cannot be followed in parts but is a complete way of life, giving clear guidelines for individuals as well as collective behaviour. The party also advocates that Sharia should shape the entire working of Muslim societies. It argues that while the ultimate goal of every believer is indeed to find salvation in the other world, this objective cannot be achieved without attempting to establish the religion of God in this world first. Jama'at maintains that this requires the exercise of political power.[7]

In the 1958 elections in Pakistan, Maududi summed up the Jama'at-i-Islami plan of action as follows: 'First of all it brings intellectual change in the people; secondly [it] organizes them in order to make them suitable for a movement. Thirdly, it reforms society through social and humanitarian work, and finally it endeavors to change the leadership.'[8] The idea is that once the leadership has been won over to Islam, the society will be Islamized and cleansed of all socio-economic diseases. Jama'at-i-Islami remains actively engaged in electoral politics in Pakistan and Bangladesh, as well as in social action. It was part of the four-party alliance that formed the government of the Bangladesh Nationalist Party (BNP) after the 2001 elections. It had also been influential throughout the 1990s in the Awani League. In Pakistan, it was one of the two main leading parties which led the opposition in the National Assembly and formed the government in the NWFP.

Jama'at has complemented this struggle for control over the political space with a strong tradition of social service. It states that welfare work is one of its core functions. In Pakistan, Jama'at runs numerous welfare organizations working in the fields of education, health, water and sanitation, and poverty relief. Many of these organizations specialize in specific sectors: for example, the Al-Hira Trust and the Al-Ghazali Trust focus exclusively on education. The Jama'at flagship welfare organization remains the Al-Kidmat Foundation, which operates across all social sectors. Jama'at was banned in Bangladesh as a political party for some years after the war of liberation, owing to its alleged support for the Pakistani army. Given this past, Jama'at's involvement in welfare work in Bangladesh is more informal but still significant: Jama'at members sit on boards of directors in many Islamic welfare institutions. They closely supervise the Islamic Bank Foundation, the welfare arm of the Islamic Development Bank in Bangladesh, in selecting and executing its projects. In both countries Jama'at maintains extensive networks for undertaking disaster relief work.

Within Christianity, one also finds many examples of the political influence of religion. Christian organizations have often spoken on behalf of their faith in the public sphere of developing countries and seek to influence the political process, as will be discussed in greater detail in the fourth chapter. One of the most recent occurrences of such political pronouncements by religious bodies has been the case of the Zimbabwean Catholic Bishops' Conference; its public stance led to a direct confrontation between 'church and state'.

At Easter 2007, the Conference issued a pastoral letter to be read at all Catholic churches in the country. The letter, entitled 'God hears the cry of the oppressed', was an explicit condemnation of the human rights abuses committed by Robert Mugabe's government. It called on all Christian churches to resist the political regime and advocated the immediate resignation of Mugabe. The letter exposed the violence committed by Christians against other Christians:

> They are all baptised, sit and pray and sing together in the same church, take part in the same celebration of the Eucharist and partake of the same Body and Blood of Christ. While the next day, outside the church, a few steps away, Christian State Agents, policemen and soldiers assault and beat peaceful, unarmed demonstrators and torture detainees.[9]

The letter is reminiscent of statements by the Catholic Bishops' Conference in El Salvador at the end of the 1970s, which condemned the atrocities committed by a political regime that called itself Catholic. As in El Salvador, the political authorities in Zimbabwe accused the bishops of 'improper' mixing of church affairs with politics and urged them to be pastors of people's souls and to leave the care of the body to the state.[10] In El Salvador, the confrontation between the church and the state led to the assassination of the Archbishop, Oscar Romero, in 1980. In Zimbabwe, the life of the Archbishop was spared but Mugabe nonetheless silenced him on the grounds of alleged immoral behaviour – Mugabe accused Archbishop Pius Ncube of breaching his celibacy vows and Ncube was forced to resign as a consequence of these allegations.

As the above examples from Islam and Christianity illustrate, religion is a public force that has to be reckoned with in developing countries – as it is in developed countries, too. It cannot be controlled by pushing it into the private sphere. How to accommodate the presence of religion in the public sphere is another question that has received many different answers (see the section on democracy in Chapter 5). The irrepressibility of political expression by religious bodies leads us to inquire how religions work so that their public role can be better understood.

How does religion operate?

Are religious precepts archaic, homogeneous and resistant to change, or do they have an internal dynamic of reasoning, argument, controversy and change? The world is not lacking in examples to support the belief that religions are archaic, homogeneous and opposed to reason. In 2007, the story of a Saudi woman who was raped made international headlines. She was sentenced to prison and a hundred lashes as punishment because, at the time of the rape, she was in the company of another man who was not her *mahram* (a male relative which Islam approves as guardian of a woman, such as her father, son or brother-in-law). Given the international outcry, her sentence was revoked – but not without strong initial resistance within the Saudi Islamic leadership.

A few months later, a similar case of apparent religious intolerance erupted in Sudan. A British schoolteacher allowed her pupils to name a teddy bear Mohammad, the name of the Prophet. When some parents of the pupils heard this, the news spread throughout the country, and demonstrations emerged to call for tough sanctions against the schoolteacher – including lashes, while some people even demanded the death penalty. Intense British diplomatic intervention eventually resolved the crisis and the woman was flown back to the UK without her sanction being carried out. In the eyes of many people living in secular societies, such public expressions of religious faith – exacerbated by the international political situation linked to the presence of British troops in some Muslim countries – seem irrational and misplaced.

Christianity, too, has its share of manifestations which may appear irrational or archaic to the modern eye. While all modern states have buried divinely ordered absolute monarchies long ago, the Catholic Church still functions in its internal structures as an absolute monarchy, with its absence of democratic decision-making mechanisms. Decisions made by the Pope are binding on all the faithful. This was dramatically manifested in the case of the encyclical *Humanae Vitae*, whose teaching on contraception was not supported by the majority of the laity, as will be documented in Chapter 5. Moreover, while women are now given equal opportunities to men in the economic, political and social spheres, they are still banned from certain positions of authority and from making decisions that affect the institution of the Catholic Church as a whole.

Behind the apparent irrationality and archaism of certain practices found in religions, there is either an alternative interpretation of what is the desirable end result or the presence of vested political interests rather than religious principles. For example, the role of women in social, economic and political life remains one of the most contested areas of debate between secular and religious traditions. Closer examination reveals that specific notions of appropriate women's actions in Islamic and Christian traditions are heavily influenced by the patriarchal structures of the surrounding society in which these religions emerged and developed rather than commended in the religious texts themselves. (The influence of patriarchy in Christianity is further discussed at the end of the section on liberation theology in Chapter 6.)[11]

Fatima Mernissi (1993b), a prominent Muslim scholar from Morocco, demonstrates this point through her scholarship. She establishes that if women's rights are a problem in Islam, it is not due to the Qur'an or the Prophet, but because those rights conflict with the interests of the male elite. Prophet Mohammad gave a major place to women in his public life. At the age of forty, when he received his first revelation, the person in whom he immediately confided and sought comfort from was Khadija, his first wife. He ensured the equal status of women by ensuring that the women fleeing from the tribal Mecca and entering Medina, the Prophet's city in the seventh century, gained access to full citizenship and were awarded the status of a *Sahabi* ('Companion of the Prophet'). During military expeditions he preferred to take his wives as companions. They acted not just as background figures but shared with him his strategic concerns. With two of his wives, Aisha and Umm Salama, he had a strong intellectual relationship. Aisha led an armed opposition against Ali, the fourth Caliph.[12] Before Islam, only men were assured the right of inheritance in Arabia and women were usually part of the inherited goods. Islam gave them the right to inherit. Prophet Mohammad was also known to be very responsive to the demands of his wives.

The period after the Prophet, however, saw a serious shrinking of public space for women, which, as Mernissi demonstrates, had to do with the patriarchal structures inherited from the pre-Islamic period. Since religion was the main source of political legitimacy in Muslim societies in the seventh century, a tendency emerged to fabricate sayings that served the interest of those in power and appropriate them to the Prophet for moral legitimacy. Thus, sayings with little authenticity became part of established tradition. Examples include circulation of such *Hadith* (prophet's sayings) as: 'Three things bring bad luck: house, woman and horse'. Similarly, it became accepted knowledge that during the time of menstruation women were not allowed to touch the Qur'an or go near places of worship because they were considered impure during this period. In contrast, according to one of the Prophet's wives, Umma Maymuna: 'It happened that the Prophet recited the Koran with his head on the knee of one of us while she was having her period. It also happened that one of us brought his prayer rug to the mosque and laid it down while she was having her period.' The fabrication of *Hadiths* had become such an obvious problem a century after the Prophet's death that scholars of that time started to establish a science for the detection of fabricated *Hadiths*.

These examples show that how a religion interprets its fundamental teachings is intertwined with the socio-economic and political contexts in which it is lived. This is why paying attention to the task of interpretation, and who has the authority to interpret, is crucial for analysing the role of religion in development. Giving a full account of the complexity of how Islam and Christianity operate goes beyond the scope of this book. However, a minimal knowledge of how religions operate, and especially recognition of their non-homogeneous and dynamic character, is essential for fruitful engagement between religions and development agencies.

Is dialogue possible?

Can dialogue and mutual understanding evolve when differences between the religious and secularist positions on certain development issues seem irreconcilable, or are they irresistibly heading towards violent clash? Often conflict seems unavoidable between those who hold a religion-based worldview and those who do not. In late 2006, the decision of a Danish newspaper to publish a selection of cartoons depicting the Prophet Mohammad unleashed protests throughout the Muslim world and sparked an animated debate regarding the boundaries of freedom of expression. Within the Muslim religious tradition, representing the Prophet constitutes blasphemy. In addition, the way the Prophet was depicted – one of the cartoons portrayed him as a terrorist with a bomb – was found to be highly offensive.

Two different responses divided the community of Muslim believers. One strand chose to exert pressure on the publisher to retrieve the cartoons by taking to the streets and staging demonstrations, many of which turned violent – Danish embassies were attacked in Syria and Jordan. The other strand also argued for extracting an apology from the publisher but emphasized the use of logical reasoning and intellectual engagement with those holding a secular worldview in order to determine the limits of the right to freedom of expression. What followed was an interesting discussion between those who tended to interpret the right to free expression as boundless – that is, in a liberal democracy, one should be allowed to say whatever one wishes to say, independently of how offensive this can be – and those who interpreted the freedom of expression as limited by religious teachings.

Another area of apparent conflict between religious and secular worldviews has been the visibility of religious symbols in the public sphere. In France, Muslim women wearing headscarves have generated a hostile reaction from the defenders of the secular French Republic, which forbids any religious expression in state schools and buildings. Religious groups have found the secular position entirely unsympathetic and non-accommodating of their religious rights. The secular Republic of Turkey is also currently under pressure to allow public expression of religious symbols. In Qatar, the state forbids any public expression of religions other than Islam. However, the Catholic Church has recently secured a deal with the Qatari authorities to build a church to cater for the pastoral needs of the important immigrant community. The church was built entirely underground in the rock so that the law that forbids non-Muslim religious symbols in public spaces was not violated. In exchange, the Roman authorities have granted Muslims permission to build a large mosque in Rome provided that the height of the mosque does not exceed that of Saint Peter's.

The tensions between different worldviews are thus very real, as the above examples illustrate. Yet, there is often scope for dialogue and for reaching consensus when conflict emerges. Rather than being a source of conflict, divergent views make the need for active dialogue between different positions even more salient. Three key factors facilitate such dialogue: genuine openness to the other position, an ability to identify the multiple voices within the opposing traditions, and an openness to revise one's own worldview in the light of the encounter with others (see Chapter 6).

Can dialogue be a menu of choice?

Within development discourse and practice, recent years have witnessed a growing recognition of the importance of religion for designing development programmes and projects. The process of this engagement, however, remains highly selective. Instead of mainstreaming religion in all development interventions, it is called upon only for sectors viewed to be primarily the domain of religion. For example, owing to recent concerns about links between religion-based militancy and madrasas (schools of Islamic education), many development agencies are exploring means to reform the madrasa education system where subjects such as mathematics, science and social studies are incorporated in the curriculum. Instances include Pakistan, Nigeria, Bangladesh and Afghanistan. Other attempts at engaging with religions revolve around *ad hoc* projects involving ulama (religious leaders in Islam) in family planning programmes or HIV/AIDS interventions. There is, however, no systematic effort to take into account the religious dimension of other issues related to the Millennium Development Goals. Given that religion infuses all areas of a believer's life, development interventions, were they to deal effectively with religion, would need to engage with the religious precepts across all development sectors, such as health, environment, political involvement, economic activities and labour markets.

The donor community shows similar selectivity in terms of its engagement with religious actors as development partners. There has been a growing trend of active partnership between international donors and faith-based organizations. However, not all FBOs have received equal treatment. In a review of partnership between government donors and FBOs in the United Kingdom, Clarke (2007a) notes that the partnerships tend to occur with FBOs whose development practices show similarities with those of non-religious NGOs.

Even in its engagement with religious discourses, the development community is often seen to be biased in favour of so-called 'progressive' forces within a religious tradition who share common points with those holding a secular worldview. This often limits the credibility of development interventions in contexts where religious and secular worldviews are in greater opposition and tension. In many Muslim countries, for example, development interventions related to gender equity have heavily supported women's rights NGOs inspired by Western feminist thinking. They have engaged with the Westernized elite, and have consciously disengaged with Muslim women, in particular the Islamic female leadership. These development interventions have often marginalized women instead of empowering them – Chapter 6 will explore this further in the case of Pakistan.

All the above examples – the US strategy to curb Islamic militancy, the banning of religious political parties, the cherry-picking mode of engagement between donors and religious communities – highlight the limited effectiveness of current attempts at engaging with religion. They also bring to the fore the problems inherent in viewing religion only as a means to promote given ends, such as what donors conceive as valuable and desirable development outcomes.

We started this discussion by underlining a set of key questions that the reality of development work in developing countries confronts in relation to religion. The controversy surrounding the practice of Sharia law epitomized in an acute way the extent of the disagreement on how to answer these questions. It was also symptomatic of the gulf that exists between those holding a secular and those holding a religious worldview, a gulf which often taints relationships between developed and developing countries. But the controversy also made obvious the fact that these questions have to be asked, for religion cannot be sidelined as a taboo that cannot be addressed. While contestation remains the norm, there are some fundamental truths that development practitioners have to acknowledge when working in a developing-country context. Religion is what guides many people's lives. Considering it as irrelevant, or as ideological indoctrination which has to be counteracted, is a strategy which is likely to jeopardize development efforts, if not fuel conflict. Even if development workers do not see religion as relevant to their own lives, they still need to reckon with it, as it often lies at the foundations of the lives of those their interventions have targeted. Recognizing that religion matters involves another step. It involves acknowledging its public nature and giving up attempts to control it following the model of Western liberal democracies. Religion is a political force in developing countries; trying to confine it to a private sphere is likely to encounter opposition, if not to lead to a rejection of development models which do not recognize the inherent political nature of religion. It is therefore paramount for development practitioners to understand how a religion works and how the religious believer sees the world and establishes development priorities and outcomes. This entails that what development practitioners conceive as valuable actions or desirable social change might not always be in tune with the views of religious believers on these matters. Dialogue and openness is essential for fruitful development intervention. This means that disagreements have to be worked through, for religion constitutes a total way of life for religious believers and selective engagement is not an option. The forthcoming chapters spell this out.

Notes

1 'Civil and religious law in England: a religious perspective', lecture delivered at the Royal Courts of Justice on 7 February 2008. The text of the lecture is available at <http://www.archbishopofcanterbury.org/1575> (accessed November 2008).

2 This question is reminiscent of another controversy regarding Catholic adoption agencies losing their public funding if they refuse adoption to same-sex couples.

3 Quoted in an article published by *TimesOnLine*, 'Rowan Williams faces backlash over Sharia', 10 February 2008, <http://www.timesonline.co.uk> (accessed November 2008).

4 The Human Rights Commission of Pakistan has collected testimonies of forced disappearances affecting over 350 people.

5 'Pakistan: over 80 people victims of possible extrajudicial execution in Bajaur', public statement by Amnesty International, Asia Pacific, ASA 33/046/2006, 1 November 2006.

6 The English website of the Islamic Brotherhood can be found at <http://www.ikhwanweb.com> (accessed November 2008). For further information about political Islam and the Muslim Brotherhood, see Munson (2001) and Kepel (2006).

7 For a detailed account of Jama'at-i-Islami's political philosophy, see Nasr (1994).

8 'Short proceedings of the 2nd Annual Conference, Jamiat-i-Islami, East Pakistan, 14–16 March, 1958', p. 2.

9 Extracts from the letter can be found on the website of the UK-based Christian political thinktank Ekklesia at <http://www.ekklesia.co.uk/> (accessed November 2008).

10 For an analysis of relations between the Catholic Church and the dictatorship in Chile, see Cavanaugh (1998).

11 One could argue that the religious texts are themselves to some extent the product of historical conditions. However, religious believers contend that the ideas therein transcend time and space. In Christian theology, the method used to uncover the meaning of religious texts beyond their historical and social conditioning is known as biblical hermeneutics.

12 For the role of selected Muslim women in leadership positions in the early period of Islam, see Mernissi (1993a).

2 | Religion in Development Thought

How has development theory conceptualized the presence of religion in developing countries so far? By surveying the history of development thought, this chapter brings out five dominant modes of conceiving the role of religion in development processes: (1) religion is instrumental to development goals (such as economic growth and the Millennium Development Goals); (2) religion forms people's values and what counts as legitimate development; (3) religious freedom and worship is a fundamental human right that has to be respected; (4) religion is a constitutive part of people's wellbeing alongside health, knowledge and other dimensions; (5) religion is a political force that shapes a society's economic, social and political structures, either through civil society participation or direct involvement in political parties.

Doing a literature survey of development thought is not a light and unproblematic enterprise. First, there is the controversy surrounding what 'development' is and when it starts. In his *Development Dictionary*, Wolfgang Sachs (1992) situates the birth of 'development' in President Truman's inaugural discourse, which called for assistance to improve 'underdeveloped' areas so that they might equally benefit from the scientific and industrial progress that the countries of their previous colonizers enjoyed. In *Doctrines of Development*, Cowen and Shenton (1996) argue that development started with the industrial revolution in Europe and the concern to mitigate the negative social consequences of industrialization and economic progress. In an introductory book, *Development Theory*, Preston (1996) locates the start of development with the emergence of the social sciences in the eighteenth century, and more precisely with the writings of Adam Smith and the newly founded discipline of political economy. Thus, this overview chapter could include a discussion of both Adam Smith's *Theory of Moral Sentiments*, and the role of religion therein, and Karl Marx's famous view of religion as the opium of the people.

Another difficulty with this literature review is that the discipline of development studies is constituted by different social sciences: each of these not only has its own conception of development but also its own view of religion and its role in people's lives and in society. An economic textbook, like Michael Todaro's *Economic Development* (2006), offers a rather different understanding of development from the one advanced by cultural anthropologist Arturo Escobar in his *Encountering Development* (1995). Thus, this review could include an in-depth discussion of how economics has treated religion in its rational choice theory, or how the discipline of anthropology has treated religion as a sub-component of culture.[1]

Further, reviewing the treatment of religion in development implies setting boundaries to what exactly constitutes development thought. Does it encompass the countless documents written by international institutions, or what development practitioners say or do, or all the articles published in academic journals in development studies? In that case, this chapter should include an overview of how religion has been conceived in all these documents,[2] or even undertake biographical research on the extent to which religion has influenced key players in development thinking and policy.[3]

Given the limitless nature of the task at hand, we have chosen to focus on some key publications in the post-Second World War period. The reason for this focus is not an endorsement of the belief that the concept of development emerged with the decolonization era, or an assumption that development thought is contained in a handful of publications which have authority. These publications have been selected because they each present a different approach to conceiving the presence of religion in development, and they each characterize one dominant thought in the evolution of development ideas: modernization, basic human needs, human rights, multi-dimensional poverty and human development.

Arthur Lewis's *Theory of Economic Growth* is one of the founding texts of the modernization theories that dominated development thought in the period 1950–80. Surprisingly, it includes an extensive discussion of the role of religion in fostering capitalistic development and economic growth. In 1980, the academic journal *World Development* published a special issue on religion and development which summarized the state of affairs regarding the treatment of religion in development at the time. Our third selected text is the Universal Declaration of Human Rights of 1948, which included religious freedom as a core human right. It is only since the 1990s, however, that human rights have been integrated into development thought. Our fourth publication is the World Bank's study *Voices of the Poor*, which provoked a revolution in the conventional approach to poverty. In the newly established adoption of a multi-dimensional poverty agenda, religion figures prominently. Finally, Amartya Sen's *Development as Freedom* represents another turning point in development thought. Even if religion is not mentioned explicitly, this text has opened the door for considerable involvement of religion in development processes through civil society participation and through shaping people's values.

Modernization and economic growth

While development thought may have started well before President Truman's address to the nation and his appeal to share the benefits of the lifestyle of industrialized countries with the whole world (Sachs, 1992), only after the Second World War did the aim of raising the living standards of the world population become a political concern for Western nations. The newly established United Nations included in its constituting charter, in addition to the pursuit of peace and the provision of human rights, the promotion of 'higher standards of living, full employment, and conditions of economic and social progress and development' (Article 55).

In 1961, the UN General Assembly adopted a resolution stating that member states would 'intensify their efforts to mobilize and to sustain support for the measures required on the part of both developed and developing countries to accelerate progress towards self-sustaining growth of the economy of the individual nations and their social advancement' (quoted in Emmerij *et al.*, 2001, p. 44). That resolution set up what would be known as the 'UN First Development Decade'. Its main specific objective was 'to create conditions in which the national incomes of the developing countries would be increasing by 5 per cent yearly by 1970 and would continue to expand at this annual rate thereafter' (*ibid.*).

The first Development Decade was set against the belief that economic growth was central to achieving higher living standards. Without it, there would be no job creation, no income for families to pay for the education of their children, no tax revenues to pay for the provision of basic services, no savings to be invested in entrepreneurial activities. A key textbook behind that belief was *The Theory of Economic Growth* by Arthur Lewis, published in 1955. Judging from its title, the book may seem to have little to offer in so far as religion is concerned. However, Lewis makes frequent mention of the importance of religion in advancing or hindering economic growth.

He argues that economic growth depends on certain attitudes towards variables such as valuation of material goods, work, wealth creation, thrift, invention, population growth and the treatment of strangers. Countries have different levels of economic growth because they have different attitudes regarding these key variables, and religion may be accounting for these differences. Religion may be a hindrance to economic growth if it preaches asceticism and the virtuous benefits of consuming less rather than more. Although some religions do value asceticism, Lewis observes that it is mostly a concern for priests, monks and nuns and not lay people, who form the majority of the population. For them, religion is not incompatible with enjoying a higher standard of living earned without sin.

Religion becomes an obstacle to economic growth, Lewis argues, when it infuses in people certain negative attitudes towards wealth accumulation and economic opportunities. A religious society which fails to see wealth as a means to social status – because it accords social status to knowledge or military achievements – or which condemns seeking higher status as a sin, may not have favourable conditions for economic growth. Lewis sees the positive valuation of wealth creation by Christian theologians as a turning point in the economic development of Europe:

> It is true enough that mediaeval Christianity tended to condemn commercial activities as a way of life, and also regarded it as sinful for any man to want to become wealthy in order to raise his social status and that of his family. Nowadays, however, more importance is assigned to the growth of the opportunities for making money, which began to be evident in about the twelfth century. As wealth accumulated it became more respectable, and long before the Reformation the Christian theologians were engaged in adapting their precepts in order to show that trade and usury were not necessarily sinful activities. By the time the Reformation occurred in the fifteenth century, this adaptation was already advanced. This is an interesting illustration of the relationship between religious change and economic change. Since religion reflects economic change, economic attitudes cannot be explained exclusively in religious terms.

On the other hand, if only because of the time lag in religious change, the influence of religious beliefs upon economic behaviour is at any time of great significance. (Lewis, 1955, p. 27)

From the last sentence of this quote, one can observe that the relationship between change in the interpretation of religious teachings and change in economic attitudes such as the accumulation of wealth is not unidirectional. It is the changing social and economic circumstances of the late Middle Ages and the development of trade which made the Reformed theologians reinterpret the Christian teachings about sin in relation to usury, paving the way for the savings–investment virtuous cycle of economic growth.[4]

Attitudes to work and effort is another area in which religion plays a significant role. If work is positively valued as a way of disciplining the soul and using God's gifts for the service of fellow human beings, then religion is conducive to economic growth. In his summary of the relationship between economic growth and religion, Arthur Lewis emphasizes the crucial positive attitudes towards work and the production and consumption of goods as conditions favouring economic growth. In societies in which people profess a religion which holds the belief that one's salvation can be secured through hard, conscientious and efficient work, or which does not have a negative attitude towards wealth creation and accumulation, the rate of economic growth is higher than in societies in which the dominant religion does not have such attitudes to work and wealth.

In addition to the above factors, Lewis briefly mentions the impact of religion on other factors affecting economic growth. Technological innovation may sometimes be encouraged by religions which emphasize rational inquiry: 'Mediaeval theologians made much of the doctrine that God Himself is rational, and thus helped in laying the foundations for the revival of scientific inquiry in Western Europe' (Lewis, 1955, p. 102). Religions which encourage obedient attitudes rather than the rational pursuit of knowledge might prove detrimental to scientific discoveries. Population growth, something that theories of economic growth have traditionally considered as a significant hindrance to economic growth, can be negatively affected by religious attitudes towards contraception and family planning. Also, the religion's teachings regarding the treatment of strangers may negatively affect the growth in trade if they hold that people can only engage in economic activities with those professing the same religion: 'If the religion encourages people to treat strangers fairly it will facilitate trade and specialization. Whereas if [it] is exclusive, encourages hatred of unbelievers, and divides people instead of bringing them together, it diminishes economic opportunities' (Lewis, 1955, p. 103).

In sum, religion is helpful to economic growth if it positively affects attitudes towards key components of economic growth, and it is a hindrance if it negatively affects them. In that sense, the way religion has been taken into account in the *Theory of Economic Growth* follows the same logic as Max Weber's pioneering study on the role of religious ideas in economic development in his *Protestant Ethic and the Spirit of Capitalism*, a book which deeply influenced the treatment of religion in the social sciences in the twentieth century.[5]

Weber begins with the observation that Protestants are more involved in industrial, trade and business activities than other Christian denominations or religions. Out of that empirical observation, he puts forward the explanatory hypothesis that the beliefs of the puritan form of Protestantism as found in Calvinism explain why capitalistic expansion occurred in Western Europe and not in other parts of the world.

The Reformation challenged the view of medieval Christianity that the social, economic and political order was God-given and therefore not changeable through human efforts. The Calvinist doctrine of predestination laid the emphasis on attaining personal salvation through grace and faith. It held that God had predestined a few to be saved but that humans did not know who was chosen. Therefore, faith required the belief that one was among the saved. Calvinists expressed that belief through having an industrious lifestyle devoted to making good works in this world. In contrast to the Catholic medieval ideal of fulfilling God's calling through reclusive, celibate monastic life, the Reformation's ideal was that God called people to live in the ordinary sphere of daily life, through devotion to work and one's family. God could be glorified through mundane activities such as daily household tasks, craftsmanship and other forms of labour. Wealth creation was thus a God-blessed activity, though the wealth created by one's labour should not be used for a lavish and ostentatious lifestyle. It had to be reinvested in productive activities.

These features of religion were the precise ingredients required for capitalistic development: hard work and high labour productivity, high rates of saving (and investment), and production of goods beyond the satisfaction of material needs for biological survival. According to Weber, it is this 'this-worldly asceticism' of Protestantism which led to capitalist expansion. India and China were not able to follow such paths because the religions of Hinduism and Confucianism did not emphasize the form of asceticism necessary for capitalism to flourish.

Weber's study has been the object of widespread criticism. In his introduction to *The Protestant Ethic and the Spirit of Capitalism* (1992), Anthony Giddens argues that Weber mischaracterized Protestantism, for Calvinist ethics did not sanction the accumulation of wealth for its own sake but considered it as a sin. It saw wealth as a means of satisfying human needs and not an end in itself. Giddens also argues that Weber misinterpreted Catholicism, for Catholic theology was sympathetic to capitalism and Catholic theologians did not condemn trade activities. In Catholicism, as in Protestantism, life in the world could be as godly as life in a monastery. Another critique that Giddens highlights in relation to Weber's study is the lack of robustness of the empirical material. It is only in some regions of Europe that Protestants were prominent in business activities; other denominations were as present as Protestantism in the regions that Weber's study overlooked.

Notwithstanding these criticisms, the *Protestant Ethic and the Spirit of Capitalism* profoundly influenced the way in which development thought came to conceive of religion: there are some religious beliefs which are obstacles to development and others which are conducive to it. Today, even if development thought no longer considers that development is only a matter of economic growth and that a higher GDP *per capita* is the best indicator of development, this instrumental vision of religion is still widespread. Religion is often taken into account for the impact of its teachings on a set of development goals or indicators, such as the influence of Catholic teachings regarding contraception on HIV/AIDS prevalence rate in sub-Saharan Africa, and the impact of Islamic teachings regarding gender roles on the male/female ratio in primary and secondary enrolments.

It would not be fully accurate to conclude that Lewis's *Theory of Economic Growth* is a mere heir of Weber's study on how religious teachings affect key economic attitudes, seeing religion only from the perspective of its contribution to economic progress. Arthur Lewis makes two puzzling comments which foretell other aspects of religion in development that will be highlighted a few decades later: the political role of religion as a social mobilization force, and the interconnection between the religious, economic, political and social spheres. On the first, he notes that religion tends to favour the *status quo* when it comes to changing the social order and the nature of social relations. However, there are sometimes outstanding individuals who may denounce the current state of affairs if unjust:

> Nearly every religion has its prophets, who from time to time arise and denounce the *status quo*. Their influence tends to be restricted, in comparison with that of the hierarchy, who are usually well in league with the secular power and with the aristocracy of the day; but the existence of the prophetic tradition cannot be ignored. (Lewis, 1955, p. 103)

One can think here about the example of slavery. Some Christian voices, such as William Wilberforce, were denouncing the *status quo* but the religious authorities of the time took a long time to condemn slavery as a social institution. Another well-known prophetic voice in the wilderness is that of the Dominican friar Bartolomé de las Casas, who condemned the Spanish treatment of indigenous people in Latin America. He similarly confronted hostile religious authorities who were in line with the secular powers and aristocracy of the day (see Chapter 4 for more details).

Lewis's second point, that the relationship between religious and economic change goes in both directions, that the interpretation of religious teachings may change when economic and social conditions change, presents a seminal position at the time and a departure from Weber's causal link between religion and economic development. Lewis implicitly alludes to the fact that the central teachings of a religion may be subject to re-interpretation in the light of new situations in the world. The condoning of the charging of an interest rate in Christianity is an example of how a religion's teaching can change in the light of economic developments. The Second Vatican Council is probably one of the most striking examples of how the core teachings of one religion with regard to fundamental issues – such as its understanding of freedom, of authority and of participation in economic and political life – have been reinterpreted (see Chapter 6). But the fact that the economic and social worlds change does not always entail that the interpretation of religious teachings will change accordingly. Lewis cites in that respect the Hindu teaching regarding the treatment of cows which defies the logic of economic interests – the cow could be used for feeding the population in times of famine. One could also cite the Catholic teaching regarding contraception, which has not been reinterpreted since its first pronouncement in 1931 in Pope Pius XI's encyclical *Casti Connubii*, despite the reality of HIV/AIDS.[6]

After the publication of Lewis's book in 1955, religion becomes a forgotten subject in subsequent writings.[7] When William Rostow publishes his *Stages of Economic Growth: A Non-Communist Manifesto* in 1960, no mention of religion is made, except for the role of fatalist beliefs in maintaining the social and economic *status quo*. Rostow notes that a change of ideas is a precondition for social and economic change but rejects the Weberian thesis of religion's role in generating economic growth:

> [I]t is increasingly conventional for economists to pay their respects to the Protestant ethic. The historian should not be ungrateful for this light on the grey horizon of formal growth models. But the known cases of economic growth which theory must seek to explain take us beyond the orbit of Protestantism. In a world where Samurai, Parsees, Jews, North Italians, Turkish, Russian and Chinese civil servants (as well as Huguenots, Scotsmen and British north-countrymen) have played the role of a leading elite in economic growth, John Calvin should not be made to bear quite this weight. More fundamentally, allusion to a positive scale of religious or other values conducive to profit-maximizing activities is an insufficient sociological basis for this important phenomenon. What appears to be required for the emergence of such elites is not merely an appropriate value system but two further conditions: first, the new elite must feel itself denied the conventional routes to prestige and power by the traditional, less acquisitive society of which it is a part; second, the traditional society must be sufficiently flexible (or weak) to permit its members to seek material advance (or political power) as a route upwards alternative to conformity. (Rostow, 1960, p. 51)

The role of religion in fostering economic growth is thus played down. In one of the first critical writings on the conception of development as economic growth, the *Redistribution with Growth* study of the Institute of Development Studies at Sussex, religion disappeared (Chenery *et al.*, 1974). Despite its strong advocacy of redistributive policies in order to extend the fruits of economic growth equally and benefit the poor, religion was not mentioned as a factor influencing the capacity of a country to redistribute its wealth towards the marginalized. Although the study makes reference to the importance of changing poor people's awareness of the social structures which keep them in poverty, such as unequal land distribution, it does not attribute a significant role to religion in either perpetuating the unequal situation or being a catalyst for land redistribution, a policy that the study sees as the pre-condition for any effective redistributive policy. This seems an important omission, as many religious groups were actively involved in demanding land reforms in the 1970s at the time the study was made, especially in Latin America (see Chapter 6).

Basic human needs

Another major publication critical of the conception of development as economic growth at this time (1982) is the World Bank's *First Things First: Meeting Basic Human Needs in Developing Countries*. The book outlines the 'basic needs approach' as an alternative development paradigm to economic growth. The basic-needs approach does not mention religion explicitly but affirms that the aim of development should be the provision of basic human needs, even non-material ones, such as 'a sense of purpose in life and work' and 'self-determination':

> A basic needs approach to development attempts to provide the opportunities for the full physical, mental and social development of the human personality and then derives the ways of achieving this objective. . . . Nonmaterial needs are important not only because they are valued in their own right, but also because they are important conditions for meeting material needs. They include the needs for self-determination, self-reliance, and security, for the participation of workers and citizens in the decision making that affects them, for national and cultural identity, and for a sense of purpose in life and work. (Streeten *et al.*, 1982, pp. 33–4)

Within that understanding of basic human needs, one should respect the choice of a religious society to build a temple if it considers it more important than a road. Unfortunately, despite its original insightful inclusion of non-material human needs, the basic-needs approach was later associated with the provision of basic material needs such as health, food, infrastructure and education (Stewart, 1985).[8]

A special issue of *World Development* on the relationship between religion and development brought religion back into the basic needs approach. The special issue was edited by Charles

Wilber and Kenneth Jameson, and was the outcome of a seminar held at the University of Notre Dame in the late 1970s. In their opening article, they argue that the limits of development as economic growth and concerns for redistribution require revisiting the role of religion in development and the traditional Weberian 'Protestant ethic approach' to religion as instrumental in (economic) development. They summarize four widespread views regarding the relationship between religion and development in the literature of the time. The first is the instrumental view, which concentrates on the extent to which religious teachings and beliefs are fostering or hindering economic growth. The second is that religion is by definition a social institution which restrains development because it is basically incompatible with rational modernity. Third is the view that religion is not an issue in development as long as it remains a purely private matter. And, finally, there is the view that religion does not matter anyway because when societies develop and become more modern, religion disappears from people's lives.

Wilber and Jameson warn that these views ignore the essential nature of religion, which acts as the moral basis of society and provides the sets of norms under which to assess the legitimacy and validity of the development process. Viewing religious values only as means for achieving development goals derived from sources outside the moral base or value system of the society itself may put the whole enterprise in jeopardy:

> In most cases, the moral base of society has religious roots, and that moral base has been undermined during the process of capitalist development since 1945. But, unless this tension between moral base and development is resolved, the process of development will be self-limiting, and it is likely in many cases to engender major instability which can radically transform the entire experience. . . . This conclusion supports the claim that development must build on indigenous religious values because the preservation or growth of the moral base of the society is central to development. . . . Religion is more than a mere instrument for development. A broad definition as meeting basic human needs would include religious values as one of those needs that are ends in themselves. (Wilber and Jameson, 1980, p. 475)

Thus, ignoring religion as the moral basis of society may lead to a situation in which the development process, characterized by goals generated outside the country's value system, alienates people and makes them reject the whole development process. They cite the Iranian Revolution in 1979 as an example of this unresolved tension between the moral base of society and the development process. The modernization undertaken by the Shah had led to greater inequality and a growing feeling among the population that the process was increasingly out of tune with the Islamic values which underpinned the lives of most Iranians. Wilber and Jameson conclude that, if the development process fails to rest on indigenous (religious) values, it risks being alienating and becoming a source of conflict, distorting policy outcomes.

Given this new focus, Wilber and Jameson highlight four major links between religion and development that development theory ought to take into account: (1) the traditional linkage between religion and individual behaviour, such as the influence of religion on attitudes towards work, money, technology, health and education; (2) religion as the moral basis of society which can be either a source or a focus of resistance to development efforts, hence the necessity of synchronizing the moral basis of society with the development process; (3) religion as a positive impulse towards development through various religiously inspired initiatives, such as the role of Christian Base Communities in Latin America in calling for more redistributive policies or the Sarvodaya movement in Sri Lanka in combining development projects with religious performances; (4) religion as a transnational political force with the increasing importance of the voice of religious groups as transnational actors in global affairs, such as the World Council of Churches or the Catholic Church, which has a formal position as observer at the United Nations and other international bodies.

The articles in the special issue deal with various expressions of these four themes. They include (to name just a few): an econometric study of the relationship between religion and socioeconomic development; an analysis of whether Muslim men in Dakar, Senegal, tend to have different religious attitudes as they become more economically well off; a study of the effects of Buddhist values on attitudes to population growth, education and trade; an analysis of the role of Christian Base Communities in Latin America in demanding more political participation for the marginalized and greater social justice; a discussion of the historic role of religion and the Shia worldview in influencing social, political and economic change in Iran; and Denis Goulet's often-cited article, entitled 'Development experts: the one-eyed giants', which urges development practitioners not to treat people's values purely instrumentally but to base their development initiatives and policies upon these values (which still need to be critically examined in the light of human needs).

The original contribution of the 1980 *World Development* – its argument that religion ought to be considered as the moral basis infusing the very concept of development – has still to permeate today's development thinking and practice. For instance, international development agencies are keen to promote education for all, but when people in rural Pakistan value educating their children in madrasas rather than state schools, these agencies may be reluctant to respect people's values and sponsor the state education system instead. As will be explored in later chapters, the way the development community conceives of desirable social change, or in other words development, might not always be in tune with the way adherents of a religion conceive it.

Religious freedom

Although development thought was dominated by the 'Protestant ethic approach' in its treatment of religion until the 1980s, the Human Rights Declaration already signalled a non-instrumental approach to religion in 1948. It states in its Article 18 that 'everyone has the right to freedom of thought, conscience and religion; this right includes freedom to change his religion or belief, and freedom, either alone or in community with others and in public or private, to manifest his religion or belief in teaching, practice, worship and observance.'[9]

The adoption of the human rights agenda in development has been slow and it was not until the 1990s that the two merged, leading to a 'rights-based approach to development'.[10] In their intellectual history of the United Nations, Richard Jolly *et al.* (2004) attribute this neglect of human rights concern in development to the dominance of economics in development thinking and policy – this economic hegemony also thrust aside the disciplines of sociology, anthropology and politics in development policy making. Human rights fell under the discipline of law, and development under that of economics. When the Human Rights Declaration was signed in 1948, the branch of the United Nations that dealt with development issues was concerned with assembling the conditions for economic growth, such as appropriate rates of saving, investment and technological transfer. Setting development objectives and policies was a technical matter in which human rights was granted no room. The distance between development and human rights became even more pronounced with the Cold War and the ideological battles between civil and political rights, on the one hand, and economic and social rights on the other. Thus, guaranteeing the right to freedom of religion did not become the object of development concerns.

With a rights-based approach to development, one faces unavoidably the problems of compatibility with the guaranteeing of all rights set forth in the Declaration. Article 18 on the right to religious expression may clash with Article 16 that stipulates that 'marriage shall be entered into only with the free and full consent of the intending spouses', for a religion might include arranged marriages as part of its practices. The debate between religious freedom and other fundamental human rights is reminiscent of the relationship between another human right, that of the 'right freely to participate in the cultural life of the community' (Article 27) and development.

The 2004 *Human Development Report* on cultural diversity published by the United Nations Development Programme (UNDP) takes the position that, in case of conflict, human development concerns such as health and education should take precedence over cultural or religious rights. It states that, 'a girl's right to an education will always trump her father's claim to a cultural right to forbid her schooling for religious or other reasons' (p. v). In its introductory paragraph, the Report amalgamates various issues – such as the condemnation to death of adulterous women by Sharia law in Nigeria, the banning of religious symbols in French state schools, the political participation of indigenous people in Bolivia or the assimilation of Hispanics into American culture – into the wider question of managing cultural diversity in today's world.

Defining cultural identity as ethnic, religious, linguistic or racial and defining cultural liberty as 'the capability of people to live and be what they choose' (p. 4), the Report embraces religion as part of culture and deals with religion in the same way as it does with language, race or ethnicity. No one should suffer from economic, political or social marginalization because of religious affiliation. All countries should have maximum protection for religious minorities so that people can access the opportunities they value, whatever their religion. A development process which does not leave people free to choose the way they wish to live, according to the precepts of their religious or cultural communities, is not legitimate.

The Report does emphasize, however, that valuing cultural liberty is not done for its own sake and that cultural practices have to be examined critically in the light of other basic human rights. It highlights that cultures are not static and homogeneous but dynamic and heterogeneous. The reason for the dynamic structure of culture (read also religion, as the Report does not make distinctions between the two) is that cultural groups are not immune from domination by some leaders who may not reflect the views of other members of the group and who may impose their own will instead. Given these dangers of power and domination, the Report argues that accommodating cultural (or religious) freedom is to be done on the condition that cultural groups abide by democratic principles. This is why there need not be any trade-off between the right to religious freedom and other basic human rights, as long as active participation in decision-making processes within the religious community is guaranteed.

The Report concludes that democracy is the best way of ensuring harmony between different human rights within religious communities and providing an environment in which people can fully exercise their religious liberty.[11] It notes that, sometimes, movements arise which assert cultural (or religious) superiority and which seek to impose their visions of the world on others, disrespecting the freedom of others to live a life they value (as in the case of xenophobic political parties in Western democracies or political parties seeking to impose Islam or Hinduism as the only official religion). It argues that these movements often stem from real grievances and that, therefore, seeking to suppress them risks leading to their strengthening and radicalization, as happened for example in Algeria in 1991 when the military cancelled the elections and banned the winning political party, the Islamic Salvation Front, resulting in years of bloody civil war. The Report proposes instead to deal with these movements through democratic principles, such as prosecuting hate crimes, paying attention to school curricula, and helping communities come to terms with past hatred and violence (UNDP, 2004, p. 81).

Multi-dimensional poverty

It is not only the emergence of a rights-based approach that signals a change in development thought with regard to its recognition of the importance of religion in development processes. The gradual understanding of poverty as a multi-dimensional phenomenon also constitutes a shift. The World Bank study *Voices of the Poor*, published in 2000, is a landmark in the literature on poverty.

Dominated by economists, the analysis of poverty had long been confined to collecting data through household surveys about people's incomes and consumption patterns. Poverty was defined as not having sufficient money to buy a basket of basic commodities necessary for survival. In a break from the orthodoxy in poverty analysis, the World Bank study asked poor people themselves how they experienced poverty. This led to a different understanding of poverty. One of the study's most interesting findings is that religion permeates people's conception of wellbeing:

> For many a spiritual life and religious observance are woven in with other aspects of wellbeing. Poverty itself could get in the way. An old woman in Bower Bank, Jamaica says, 'I got up this morning and all I want to do is read my bible, but I share a room with my son and my grandchildren and all they do is make noise, I can't even get a little peace and quiet.' In Padamukti, Indonesia, being able to make the pilgrimage to Mecca means much, as does having *sholeh* (dutiful and respectful) children who will look after their parents in old age and pray for them after they are dead. In Chittagong, Bangladesh, part of wellbeing is 'always [being] able to perform religious activities properly'. For older women in Cassava Piece, Jamaica, their church gives them a spiritual uplift and physical support. The importance to poor people of their sacred place – holy tree, stone, lake, ground, church, mosque, temple or pagoda – is repeatedly evident from their comparisons of institutions in which these frequently ranked high, if not highest. (Narayan *et al.*, 2000, p. 38)

Another finding of the study's participatory exercises was that poor people trusted religious leaders more than politicians, because they listened to them, unlike the latter. Also, poor people rated faith-based organizations much higher than state institutions. In rural areas, religious institutions were often valued as the most important ones in people's lives. Given this prominence of religion, *Voices of the Poor* even includes a section entitled 'churches, mosques, temples, shrines, trees, stones and rivers':

> Spirituality, faith in God and connecting to the sacred in nature are an integral part of poor people's lives in many parts of the world. Religious organizations are also highly valued for the assistance they provide to poor people. However, the role that faith-based organizations play in poor people's lives varies from being a balm for the body and soul to being a divisive force in a community. In ratings of

effectiveness in both urban and rural areas, religious organizations feature more prominently than any single type of state institution. (Narayan *et al.*, 2000, p. 222)

The study argues that this finding about people's valuation of religion as a central part of their lives has considerable consequences for the way development has been conceived and practised so far:

> Reflecting on poor people's perception of poverty has driven us to revisit the meaning of development. What is significant change, and what is good? And which changes, for whom, matter most? Answers to these questions involve material, physical, social, psychological and spiritual dimensions. . . . The increments in wellbeing that would mean much to the poor widow in Bangladesh – a full stomach, time for prayer, and a bamboo platform to sleep on – challenge us to change how we measure development. (Narayan *et al.*, 2000, p. 234)

Voices of the Poor presents a challenging conclusion, which has dramatic consequences for development practice if implemented. Considering religion as an intrinsic component of people's wellbeing alongside health, education, shelter, material security and others, transforms conventional development practices which have so far ignored the religious dimensions. Vandeberg (1999) reports the story of resettlement practices following the building of a dam in Nigeria. The local community had to offer an animal sacrifice if their shrine, a rock, was to be relocated. The resettlement authorities did not offer compensation for the relocation costs on the ground that 'they were not compensating rocks'. With this new approach to development, the community should receive compensation for the costs incurred in moving a shrine as they do for the costs of moving house, given that people valued performing religious practices as much as their own shelter.[12]

Alkire (2002) describes a more positive case study of a development project in rural Pakistan which fully integrates people's values, including religious ones. A group of women had to decide between goat-rearing and rose cultivation projects. Although the goat project yielded more income, the women opted for the rose cultivation project because it enabled them to do more things they valued such as the ability to use the roses in their religious ceremonies, and the ability to walk in the rose fields and experience peace of mind and unity with their Maker. The spiritual dimension of wellbeing was rated as important as the material dimension by the women. Therefore the rose cultivation project was judged to be promoting their wellbeing more than the goat-raising one.

The human development approach

The multidimensional approach to poverty and wellbeing consti-tutes one of the cornerstones of the human development approach, the most recent paradigm in the evolution of development thought. But the approach adds to it the centrality of human freedom. The human development approach has its roots in the pioneering works of the Economics Nobel Prize winner Amartya Sen and his so-called 'capability approach'.[13]

In *Development as Freedom*, a book which summarizes his works and which was first delivered as a series of lectures to World Bank staff, Sen gives two reasons for viewing freedom as central to the process of development. First, there is an evaluative reason, for 'assessment of progress has to be done primarily in terms of whether the freedoms that people have are enhanced.' And second, there is the instrumental reason, for 'achievement of development is thor-oughly dependent on the free agency of people' (Sen, 1999, p. 4). In other words, development is about expanding the freedoms that people have reason to choose and value (such as the freedom to be healthy, to be educated, to participate in the life of the community, to live in a peaceful environment, and so on), and the way of doing this is through letting people be active agents of their own lives through democratic and participatory processes.

The human development and capability approach does not men-tion religion as such. Sen only makes explicit references to religion in *Identity and Violence* when he talks about the devastating effects (citing the communal riots in India after partition) of ascribing people to a single identity without giving them a chance to choose among their multiple identities. He also discusses the dangers of sending children to faith schools as it deprives them from being in contact with people who have different religious views (Sen, 2006).[14] Despite this negative account of religion, the human devel-opment and capability approach sets the foundations for taking reli-gion into account in a way that breaks new ground. Religion is more than a wellbeing dimension alongside others like education, health or political participation.

The greatest contribution of the human development and capa-bility approach is to bring values back to the centre stage. The process of development is a value-laden enterprise. What counts as 'development' is inevitably based on values. According to this approach, the only legitimate development process is one which is based on the underlying social concerns and values within a particular society. The message advocated twenty years before by Wilber and Jameson in the *World Development* special issue, that development is to be in tune with the moral basis of society, reappears and at last starts to penetrate mainstream development discourse – even if some may say that this insight still falls short of being applied in development practice. Insofar as religion is a framework that constitutes a society's moral basis, the human development and capability approach allows for the possibility of the development process to be guided entirely by people's religious values.

But there is a condition: development is not about promoting whatever people value but those they have *reason* to value. The values that guide the development process have to be examined critically through a thorough process of reasoning in the public space, allowing the views of all the members of the society to be heard. If a predominantly Christian society decides, after lengthy public debates within democratic decision making, that abortion cannot be made legal, even in the case of rape or danger to the mother's life, that decision should be respected. There is obviously the risk that democratic decision-making may be disrupted by some groups imposing their views on others or manipulating them. What is important, though, is that continuous public debate goes on and that the decision reached be always subject to revision.

There is another way in which religion comes into play, in addition to shaping a society's values and influencing what it considers valuable for policies to promote. After decades of a technical approach to development 'policy', the human development and capability approach brings politics back to the heart of the development policy process. Development is the outcome of how different political actors interact with each other in the public sphere. Examining this interaction and its effect on the policy process entails examining the influences, some of which may be religious, on political actors engaged in the policy process. Analysing the role of political parties in shaping the policy process may imply in some cases taking into account the influence of religion on that political party. For example, a study of the emergence of the welfare state in Europe would be intellectually impoverished if it did not include an analysis of how Christianity led to the emergence of social democratic parties and influenced their agenda. The empirical reality of political life in developing countries is not lacking in examples which illustrate the significant influence that religion exerts on political actors. As Chapter 4 will describe, it is difficult to comprehend politics in developing countries fully if one pushes religion under the carpet on the assumption that religion and politics should be clearly separated.

Political actors are not limited to political parties that citizens can vote for through elections, or to members of government, elected or not. Civil society is another prominent force shaping the policy process in democratic countries. Civil society is generally seen as the network of voluntary associations through which people are mobilized in order to shape the social order (Scholte, 2002). Voluntary associations include campaigning organizations, non-governmental organizations, non-profit organizations delivering social services, and environmental charities. Since the 1990s, with the weakening of the role of the state in the 1980s by the Reagan-Thatcher neo-liberal agenda and with the international pressure for democratization initiatives, the interest in civil society in development studies has surged. With the assertion of the important role of civil society has come the recognition of religious organizations as significant civil society actors throughout the world (Clarke and Jennings, 2007).

In an introductory summary to civil society in development studies, Ottaway (2005) highlights three functions of civil society: the generation of social capital, the representation of the interests and demands of the population, and the provision of goods and services. Religious organizations are increasingly seen in development studies as important generators of social capital through building networks between people and fostering trust relationships between their members.[15] Belonging to a church may be a way for poor people to enter into contact with others and seek help in times of trouble. Religious organizations also play a crucial role in development processes through mobilizing people to demand social reforms. The campaigning organization in Brazil to demand land rights for landless peasants, the Movimiento Sim Terra, was started by churches which mobilized the peasants to press the government on land reform issues. In Britain, the Citizens Organization Foundation is another example of how faith communities mobilize in social action. One of their successful campaigns was to demand that the London mayor secure a minimum wage adjusted to the London costs of living.[16] The third function of civil society is probably the one that has received most attention in the development studies literature, the recognition of the important role of faith-based organizations in delivering social services to the poor, in the absence of state-sponsored basic social services. It is in that particular area that international donors have shown an increased interest in faith-based organizations in recent years (see Chapter 4).

Summary

Given the vast enterprise of reviewing how the subject of religion has been treated in development studies, this chapter has focused on key publications that summarize the different ways in which religion has been conceived in the history of development thought. First is the instrumental vision or the 'Protestant ethic approach'. Religious teachings affect attitudes and behaviours that influence the development process. In the 1950s and 1960s, the dominant development paradigm was that of modernization, with economic growth and industrialization seen as key to the development process. Therefore, religions that taught attitudes regarding labour, saving, investment and technological innovation, all conducive to economic expansion, were seen as a strong asset in the development process. Those which did not teach these attitudes were considered an obstacle. The 'Protestant ethic approach' does not necessarily apply to the modernization era. It is still widespread to this day, with the difference that desirable development outcomes are no longer seen in terms of growth of economic output but in terms of other indicators such as the Millennium Development Goals. Religion is included in development analysis because of its positive or negative influences on behaviours affecting these outcomes. To name a few, religion-based attitudes to women might be detrimental to achieving gender equality in primary education, or religious attitudes towards care of the earth might be a springboard for catalysing social action against climate change.

The second treatment of religion in development is that of conceiving religion as the moral basis of a society, the source that infuses its values. This was first proposed in the early 1980s but was only taken fully on board in the late 1990s, with the recognition that development was not a technical process but entirely value-laden, and that religion was a crucial component of people's wellbeing. According to that perspective, taking religion into account amounts to basing development initiatives on the values that people have, including religious ones. If, for example, an earthquake-devastated community values raising a church, a temple or a mosque above building a school, this should be respected and not dismissed by aid donors, who might have other values regarding religion and the usefulness of building schools instead of sacred spaces.

The third treatment of religion in development is that of considering it as a human right. The right to religious liberty is inscribed in the Universal Declaration of Human Rights of 1948. Development policies ought to respect that fundamental human right, and people should not be discriminated against because of their religion. If a country has policies which, say, deny a religious group the same employment and educational opportunities as the majority religious group, this should be condemned in the same way as gender or ethnic discrimination. Sometimes the right to religious liberty might conflict with other fundamental human rights. When this happens, one should not dismiss religion but promote public debate within the religious group to spark a critical dialogue.

A fourth conceptualization of religion in development can be found in the literature on multi-dimensional poverty. Religion is often mentioned by people as an important component of their wellbeing. Development programmes aimed at promoting people's wellbeing or reducing poverty ought to incorporate this religious dimension, even if it may involve trade-offs with other important dimensions of wellbeing.

Fifth, religion is included in development analysis as a political force. This entails the need to bring under scrutiny all the actors influencing the policy process, including religious groups. Religious groups affect the political process through influencing the values of political actors, through being the explicit inspiration of political parties, or through being actively involved in civil society activities such as delivering social services or representing people's claims through advocacy and campaign work.

This chapter would remain incomplete if it did not mention another way in which religion has appeared in development thought, that of seeing 'development' as a religion itself, namely the secular religion of Western modernity. This point has been made forcefully by Gilbert Rist in his *History of Development* (1997). He argues that the idea of 'development' and progress towards better quality of life is rooted in a Western linear vision of history and Western rationality. In similar vein, Nederveen Pieterse (2001) draws parallels between development and religious discourses. He talks of development as the pursuit of a messianic course which follows the Christian perspective of history as a process of redemption and salvation, with faith replaced by reason and providence by progress – faith in God has been replaced by faith in progress. Even in writings which would not subscribe to these authors' postmodern conception of development, it is not uncommon to find development being referred to as a religion. For example, in their intellectual history of the United Nations, Emmerij *et al.* (2001) talk about the endorsement of development ideas generated within the UN system by the World Bank, IMF and OECD as their having 'got UN religion' (p. 119). The next chapter explores why a secular-based conception of development is sometimes close to being seen as a religion in itself.

Notes

1 See the working papers of the Religion and Development Research Programme of the University of Birmingham, which review the treatment of religion in economics, sociology, politics and anthropology. These are available at <www.rad.bham.ac.uk> (accessed November 2008).

2 Doing a search of all articles published in peer-reviewed journals in Development Studies between 1982 and 1998, Ver Beek (2000) finds that only five articles in *World Development* had religion as their subject, while 83 dealt with the environment and 85 with gender. He obtains similar proportions for other journals.

3 In a biography of development economist Hans Singer, Shaw (2002) writes that the religious instruction Singer received from the local rabbi profoundly shaped his moral outlook on the world and his later dedication to improving the lives of the marginalized. Another influential figure in shaping development thinking and policy who was inspired by her religion was Barbara Ward (Walsh, 2004). She was one of the first to advocate putting environmental concerns at the core of the United Nations and was a key figure in organizing the first International Conference on the Environment in Stockholm in 1972 (Jolly *et al.*, 2004).

4 The long-held consideration of usury as sinful in Christianity also enabled the thriving of Jewish banks, since Judaism did not forbid the charging of interest.

5 For an in-depth account of Weber's study, see Giddens (1987).

6 All papal encyclicals can be accessed on the Vatican website, <http://www.vatican.va> (accessed November 2008).

7 See Rakodi (2007) for a discussion of the absence of religion in development thinking until recently.

8 While not bearing directly on development theory, Maslow's famous hierarchy of human needs included reference to religion and the transcendent in relation to the basic human need for self-realization (Maslow, 1954).

9 The Declaration can be accessed in full at <http://www.un.org/Overview/rights.html> (accessed November 2008).

10 See Cornwall and Nyamu-Musembi (2004) for a discussion of rights-based approaches to development.

11 This of course assumes that religious traditions hold the view that the priority of the *vox populi* is not incompatible with the priority of the *vox dei* (this point will be discussed in Chapter 5).

12 Verbeek (2000) reports further examples of the disastrous effects of development practices which ignore the spiritual dimension of wellbeing in the lives of indigenous communities in Honduras.

13 For an introduction to the human development and capability approach, see Alkire (2005, 2008), Fukuda-Parr and Kumar (2003) and Robeyns (2005). See also the website of the Human Development and Capability Association, <www.hd-ca.org>.

14 Martha Nussbaum, another prominent 'capability theorist', deals more explicitly with religion than Sen's. Her account will be explored in Chapter 6.

15 Religion as social capital is becoming known as 'spiritual capital'. See the research programme on spiritual capital founded by the Templeton foundation at <http://www.metanexus.net/spiritual_capital/> (accessed November 2008). The programme is based on Robert Putnam's finding that religion is the largest generator of social capital in the United States.

16 For more information on their campaigns, see <http://www.cof. org.uk/> (accessed November 2008).

3 | Religion in Debate

Religion has been a highly contested field in development studies and in the social sciences more generally. This chapter explores three major areas of contestation which have had a deep influence on development thinking and practice. First, there is the widespread assumption in the social sciences that, as societies modernize, religion loses significance in the public space. This has been known as the secularization thesis. There is a wide dispute over whether this thesis is empirically verified, and whether religion will eventually disappear from the public sphere or not. A second area of debate and disagreement relates to the very definition of religion. Some conceive religion as a set of private beliefs. Others see it as a subset of culture or as an embodied doctrine about the afterlife which is historically and socially embedded. A third area of intense debate is that of the relationship between religion, fundamentalism and violence. For some, religion is the root of all evil and allowing it to enter into the public sphere is bound to make the world more insecure and violent. Others dispute the link between religion and violence and argue that many forms of fundamentalism are not of a religious nature.

In discussing these contested areas, we offer some conceptual clarifications regarding the role of religion in development processes and outcomes. This chapter deconstructs secularist interpretations of religion which see it as something that is best kept outside the public sphere. It also deconstructs conceptualizations of religion in terms of static private beliefs, and associations between religion and violence. It argues instead that religion is a significant public influence, that it is a dynamic set of social practices based on context-dependent interpretations of core beliefs and teachings, and that there is no intrinsic association between religion and violence.

The secularization thesis

We saw in Chapter 1 that the fathers of sociology, Emile Durkheim and Max Weber, both established an inverse relationship between modernity and religion. As societies become more modern,[1] the 'sacred' is assumed to lose significance and the 'secular' to become more prominent, what Weber famously called the disenchantment of the world. Religion no longer explains the world, rationality does. The rising of the sun is no longer explained in terms of the goodness of the gods conferring their favours on human beings, but is rationally accounted for by the movements of the planets. The death of cows in a rural village is no longer attributed to an old widow perceived by the community as a witch, but is explained through the presence of some micro-organisms causing animal diseases. Thus, when societies undergo a process of modernization and rationalization, it is believed that they also undergo a process of secularization, that is, 'a process in which religion diminishes in importance both in society and in the consciousness of individuals' (Berger, 2001, p. 443). Religion's loss of significance is generally expressed in falling attendance at religious ceremonies, such as Sunday worship for Christians and Friday prayers for Muslims.

The secularization thesis, which assumes that religion would disappear from people's lives as societies become more modern and wealthier, and which has underpinned the way Western societies conceived religion, has come under heavy fire in the social sciences. The American sociologist, Peter Berger, who was one of the strongest defenders of the secularization thesis in the 1960s, now proclaims the thesis false (Berger, 1999). Religions have not disappeared from the public space in either the developing or the developed worlds.[2] Protestantism is still of great influence in American politics. The Pope still draws interest and attention from world political leaders. The funeral of John Paul II in April 2005 attracted an impressive number of heads of states, including the presidents of Iran, Israel and the United States. Political parties based on the teachings of Islam, like Hamas in Palestine or the Muslim Brotherhood in Egypt, are being elected democratically in the Arab world. Thailand's political agenda, under the influence of its king, is explicitly based on Buddhist principles.

Thomas (2005), following Berger's revised view, argues that the increasing presence of religion in public life, which he calls the 'global resurgence of religion',[3] and which is empirically observed throughout the world, demonstrates that the secularization thesis is a myth. He cites the Iranian Revolution in 1979, the rise of the Solidarnosc movement in Poland and the role of the Catholic

Church in the demise of Communism, and September 11 as examples which bear evidence to the reality that religion has not lost its public significance in the contemporary world. Thomas goes further than setting out the case for the demise of the secularization thesis, however. He puts forward the argument that, when it becomes a model for export to developing countries, the secularization thesis entails serious risks of backlash. Indeed, the Arab countries which experienced a modernization process in the 1960s and attempted to establish a strong secular state (such as Algeria, Egypt and Iran) are now prey to vigorous religious movements laying claim to their place in the public space. Following Davie (2002), Thomas argues that using secularism as an analytical framework for analysing the reality of non-Western countries is comparable to using the map of the French Alps for analysing whatever may be called called mountains in the world. Such an approach is obviously problematic.

Norris and Inglehart (2004) also observe that the secularization thesis is not empirically verified in developing countries. Statistics show that religious observance is alive and well. However, instead of dismissing the thesis as irrelevant for studying the reality of developing countries, they propose a revised theory of secularization, what they call 'existential security', which they test against data from the World Values Survey in the period 1981–2001. Their argument is that people in developed countries experience existential security, that is, 'the feeling that survival is secure enough that it can be taken for granted' (p. 4). Therefore people in developed countries do not need religion as a safety boat to help them go through the insecurities of life. This is why affluent societies have undergone a process of secularization where religious practices, values and beliefs have progressively disappeared from people's lives and society. According to Norris and Inglehart, it is these 'feelings of vulnerability to physical, social and personal risks' (p. 4) which are the key factors explaining why people are religious. They do not argue that there is a law according to which an affluent society will automatically be less religious, but they observe that there is a tendency for the reality to be that way. The empirical evidence of the correlation between religious observance and affluence points to the fact that affluence and secularization go together. This does not preclude some wealthy individuals who have not grown up in insecure conditions being religious – such as Osama bin Laden – but these cases, they argue, are anecdotes and do not detract from the empirical reality that there is an inverse relationship between security (as measured by indicators of economic affluence and quality of life) and the significance of religion (as measured by indicators of regular worship).

Given the differential demographics between countries which experience existential security and those which do not, and given that insecure societies have higher fertility rates, Norris and Inglehart conclude that the secularization thesis is not going to be verified for decades to come. They do not declare the thesis false – they continue to hold that religion does lose significance as societies modernize – but they predict that it will not become an empirical fact as long as large parts of the world's population live in insecure conditions. If one does not know whether one will be able to find sufficient food to survive the week, have access to a treatment to cure a disease, or simply find water in the well, religion and the security of an afterlife, or divine intervention, becomes a way of coping with insecurity. There remain some anomalies in the affluent world, such as in Ireland and the United States, where religion persists. But, according to Norris and Inglehart, these cases do not falsify the secularization thesis. It is because these countries show high levels of social and economic inequality that a large segment of the population lives with existential insecurity, and hence one does not observe declining trends in religious participation.[4]

Another prominent sociologist of religion, José Casanova, has been cautious in dismissing the secularization thesis as false, but on premises radically different to those of Norris and Inglehart. In *Public Religions in the Modern World* (1994), he argues that seeing secularization as a myth which has not been empirically verified is a too-hasty conclusion. He begins by distinguishing three very distinctive propositions of the secularization thesis: secularization as religious decline, as privatization, and as differentiation. Of the first, he notes that religious decline in Europe had more to do with a rejection of a caesaro-papist church which united throne and altar than a decline of religion as such. In countries where there was no established church, like Poland, religion remained strong.[5] As for the second proposition, he points out that while the privatization of religion is an empirical fact derived from historical trends in Europe, the secularization thesis in this aspect is problematic when it becomes prescriptive and sets normative standards for the proper place of religious institutions in the modern world. It is the third proposition in the secularization thesis, Casanova concludes, which remains valid. As the world has modernized, it has passed through a process of differentiation between the economic, social, political and religious spheres, and the social and scientific spheres have progressively emancipated themselves from the prism of religious institutions and norms.

The development process thus goes hand in hand with secularization but what occurs is not a process in which religion becomes privatized and loses its influence in the public sphere. What does occur is a process of differentiation between the various spheres of society. According to Casanova, whether this differentiation process leads to the privatization of religion is only a historical option, which Western liberal democracies have chosen, but which is not an ineluctable consequence of differentiation. Even if there is a tendency for the Western liberal democratic model to impose itself ideologically on other countries, the privatization of religion remains an option.

If Casanova's argument is correct, the so-called global resurgence of religion in the modern world is nothing but the refusal of religion to be relegated to the private sphere. Religion reclaims its role in the public space in order to redefine the very boundaries of the differentiated spheres:

> Religious institutions and organizations refuse to restrict themselves to the pastoral care of individual souls and continue to raise questions about the interconnection of private and public morality and to challenge the claims of the subsystems, particularly states and markets, to be exempt from extraneous normative considerations. One of the results of this ongoing contestation is a dual, interrelated process of repoliticization of the private religious and moral spheres and renormativization of the public economic and political spheres. This is what I call, for lack of a better term, the 'deprivatization' of religion. (Casanova, 1994, pp. 5–6)

Behind the empirical reality of the presence of religion in the public sphere lies something more fundamental, the desire of religions to recapture the moral space which underpins all the spheres of society. The differentiation process of modernity has created the illusion that the economic, political, social, cultural, scientific, family, and religious spheres can all function independently of each other. The deprivatization of religion contests this. When the logic of markets leads to a situation in which people are paid below a living wage, religious bodies raise their voices in the public sphere to demand that the worker's dignity be respected, as in the case of faith communities in East London. When a political system becomes totalitarian, some religious authorities refuse to confine themselves to the care of souls and denounce the authoritarian tendencies of a head of state, as was the case in Latin America in the 1970s and 1980s. Even the apparently independent sphere of scientific inquiry does not escape the realm of religious discourse: genetic research, for example, remains largely codified by ethics committees whose norms and values are often religiously inspired.

It is beyond the scope of this book to make a critical assessment of the secularization thesis debate that takes place in the sociology of religion. What is to be retained from this discussion, as far as its implications for development thinking and practice are concerned, is that the very way religion exists and functions overflows into the public space. This is due to the quintessentially political nature of religion.

Saying that religion is inherently political does not mean only that the exercise of authority and power is intrinsic to religion (that is merely the reality of any human institution, and religion is not exempt from authority and power when it becomes institutionalized), but also that the deliberation about the good society, about how to live well together, forms a constitutive part of religion.[6] In some societies, religion expresses its vision of the good society through civil society. For example, in the face of world poverty and the social consequences of the debt burden that plagues many developing countries, religious groups formed a coalition of civil society organizations to launch a world campaign, the Jubilee Campaign for debt relief, to press political and economic leaders to take action. In other countries, religion expresses its concern about the good society directly by seeking political power through the formation of religious political parties, like the Islamic Salvation Front in Algeria.

As the next section demonstrates, religion is not a set of private beliefs which may or may not instrumentally affect people's attitudes; it contains its own norms and values, which define the boundaries of the different social spheres and determine the way they function. At the core of religion lies a certain understanding of what it means to live well, and this is not without political consequences. However, what religion is has been a contested matter.

Religion defined

The Oxford English Dictionary defines religion as 'the belief in and worship of a superhuman controlling power, especially a personal

God or gods'. In the chapter on religion in his sociology textbook, Giddens (2001) characterizes religion as involving a 'set of symbols, invoking feelings of reverence or awe, and is linked to rituals or ceremonials engaged in by a community of believers' (p. 531). The cultural and social anthropologist Clifford Geertz defines religion along similar lines, as

> (1) a system of symbols which act to (2) establish powerful, pervasive, and long-lasting moods and motivations in men by (3) formulating conceptions of a general order of existence and (4) clothing these conceptions with such an aura of factuality that (5) the moods and motivations seem uniquely realistic. (Geertz, 1973, p. 90)

The major point of debate in the sociology and anthropology literature is not so much about how to define religion as about the project of defining religion itself. The anthropologist Talal Asad has voiced strong criticism of such a project. He argues that offering what he calls a 'trans-historical definition of religion' is simply not 'viable' (Asad, 1993, p. 30). Finding a universal definition of religion is not possible because what one understands by religion is so intermingled with historical processes. He deconstructs Geertz's definition above to substantiate his argument.

First, he challenges Geertz's understanding of symbol as 'any object, act, event, quality, or relation which serves as a vehicle for a conception – the conception is the symbol's "meaning"' (Geertz, 1973, p. 91). According to Asad, a symbol does not have meaning outside the wider social and political world: 'A symbol is not an object or event that serves to carry a meaning but a set of relationships between objects or events uniquely brought together as complexes or as concepts, having at once an intellectual, instrumental, and emotional significance' (Asad, 1993, p. 31). For example, the cross was not a symbol of Christianity until the fourth century. It is the relationship between Emperor Constantine's vision of a cross in a dream and his victory in a battle the next day which caused his conversion to Christianity. The cross became thereafter the symbol of Christ's victory over the world, and a symbol of the Christian religion.

Second, symbols do not necessarily prompt certain motivations and dispositions. It is not because someone wears the symbol of the cross that s/he will be disposed to live out the Bible's teaching of loving one's enemy. But neither is it because someone shows reverence to the symbol of the cross in a religious ceremony and fails to act according to the precepts of the religion which the symbol represents, that the symbol of the cross loses its meaning. As Asad writes (1993, p. 33), 'religious symbols, even when failing to produce moods and motivations, are still religious (i.e. true) symbols – religious symbols possess a truth independent of their effectiveness'.

The reason why there is a lack of correspondence between religious symbols and religious motivations is that religion needs coercion, through law and power, to make individuals act according to religious precepts:

> It is not mere symbols that implant true Christian dispositions, but power – ranging all the way from laws (imperial and ecclesiastical) and other sanctions (hellfire, death, salvation, good repute, peace) to the disciplinary activities of social institutions (family, school, city, church) and of human bodies (fasting, prayer, obedience, penance). (Asad, 1993, p. 35)

Religious symbols cannot be separated from practices that are enforced and reproduced within a religious institution. Symbols play an important role in unifying believers within a religious community and in identifying their belonging to it, but they do not have religious power in themselves. The Christian symbol of the cross does not have meaning in itself. It only acquires meaning through the community of believers who strive to live according to the teachings of Christ, through the practices which embody those teachings in their lives, and through an apparatus of coercion and discipline to nurture, and sometimes enforce, these practices.

Thus, while Geertz insists on the primacy of meaning, he ignores the processes by which meanings are constructed. Religion is not a cultural system, a set of beliefs or symbols oriented towards the status of the individual believer. It requires embodied practices to express these beliefs or convey meanings to symbols. It also requires that discipline and power to enforce these practices, and an institutionalized community of believers in which this discipline is exercised – all of these conditions being subject to changes following events in the wider world. To give a few illustrations of the context-embeddedness of practices, symbols, beliefs and discipline: the Emperor Constantine's conversion and political victory marked the beginning of the use of the cross as Christian symbol; the religious practice of celebrating Christmas to commemorate annually the birth of Christ was a medieval political decision to Christianize a pagan feast; the discipline of daily meditation through Bible reading would not be possible without the technological invention of the printer.

The impossibility of understanding religious symbols, and the meanings they have, independently of social and historical processes is not the only reason why Asad rejects the project of defining religion. The idea of religion itself is a historical product which emerged in seventeenth century Europe. Until then, the word 'religion' was virtually unknown. If used, it was to refer to public and communal worship through which people linked themselves to God – the Latin *religere* means to bind back. In the Middle Ages, one spoke of 'religious' in reference to the 'religious life' and the life in monastic communities under the vows of poverty, chastity and obedience. At that time, in the West, Christianity was not thought of as one religion among many, but simply as the religion of the world (Griffiths, 2001). From the fifteenth century onwards, with the development of travel, new worlds were discovered. Christian missionaries were faced with practices that up to then they had not known. Attempting to label and identify them in comparison with Christian practices became essential.

It is the Reformation in the sixteenth century, and the disagreement about what constitutes proper Christian practices, which gave the final impetus for the need to define what religion is. In the midst of bloody conflicts about the proper way of living as a Christian, it became important that disagreements over the embodiment of Christian living should no longer threaten peace within and between European states. Here it is enough to name a few of the controversies of the Reformation: whether the Bible or the Pope was the only source of authority guiding the way of life of people; whether good works and deeds or professing faith in the resurrected Christ were sufficient to grant eternal life; whether sacraments or prayer and Bible study were essential to sustaining a Christian life.

Seeing Christian life as a set of beliefs which people subscribe to, and which would not influence one's loyalty to the state, came to be the solution for peace in Europe. So, the concept of 'religion' as a belief system separate from the wider political world was invented, along with the concept of the secular state. The state should remain neutral and should not enforce a particular religion with its characteristic practices.[7] Religion is no longer a matter of embodied practices, but is limited to the realm of the 'soul', leaving the state to care for the body (Cavanaugh, 2003).[8] Once religion was invented as sets of propositional truths that one could come to know, different beliefs could be compared with each other: Protestantism vs Catholicism, Hinduism vs Buddhism, or Islam vs Christianity.

That the definition of religion as belief systems emerged in the specific context of Christian history does not necessarily entail that religion escapes all attempts at definition or characterization. Lincoln (2003) criticizes Talal Asad's conclusion and argues that because languages are historical products in continuous evolution this does not mean that one cannot grasp what a language is and how it is constituted. He attributes four domains that a definition of religion must include. First, religion contains a discourse with transcendental concerns above the human, temporal and contingent world. Religion has a claim to truth based on transcendental authority. Second, it involves a set of practices which embody the religious discourse. Third, it requires a community whose members construct their identity with reference to the religious discourse and its practices. Even if there is disagreement, there is a common frame of reference allowing those who abide by the discourse and perform its practices to belong to a group which endows them with a specific identity. Christians and Muslims can therefore be clearly separated in different communities given their different defining discourse and practices – this does not mean, however, that there are no similarities between groups and mutual dynamics of change between them (as will be discussed in later chapters). The fourth and final defining domain of religion is the existence of an institution that regulates, reproduces or modifies religious discourse, practices, and community while always reaffirming their transcendental value. The structure of the institution varies, from the hierarchical structure of the papacy, bishops and priests in the Roman Catholic Church to the loose structure of Quaker meetings. No religion can function without a minimum level of institutional stability that guarantees its existence over time.

Such an understanding of religion, in terms of discourse, practices, community and institutions, has similar features to what Alasdair MacIntyre has called tradition of thought or inquiry:

> [A tradition of thought is an] argument extended through time in which certain fundamental agreements are defined and redefined in terms of two kinds of conflict: those with critics and enemies external to the tradition who reject all or at least key parts of those fundamental agreements, and those internal, interpretative debates through which the meaning and rationale of the fundamental

agreements come to be expressed and by whose progress a tradition is constituted. (MacIntyre, 1988, p. 12)

The tradition of liberal political thought, or liberalism, is an example of such tradition. It upholds the fundamental agreement that the good society is one arranged around the idea of individual freedom. These ideas about the best social order are then embedded into certain institutions and social practices such as the practices of freedom of expression and tolerance, which are enforced through laws and other institutions like courts. However, liberalism is continuously evolving and the idea of individual freedom is redefined, along with its corresponding practices and institutions, in response to critical voices within and outside that tradition. For example, freedom of speech is fundamental to a society ordered around the idea of individual freedom. But when it involves insulting others, should that freedom be limited? Is a cartoon with a caricature of the British prime minister the same as one of Jesus or the prophet Mohammad? There is a continuous argument about how to define and live the fundamental agreement that individual freedom is the central characteristic of a good society.

Secularism is another example of a tradition of thought. It is founded on the fundamental agreement that religion is best kept out of the public sphere. This is embedded in institutions and practices, such as those which guarantee a separation between 'church and state'. However, the precise nature and scope of the separation remains contested from within and outside the tradition. Should expressions of religious symbols be banned in secular institutions? Should a secular state ban religious holidays? If not, to what extent can it accommodate the demands of religious pluralism? These are a few of the numerous questions that are continuously debated within the secular tradition about how the agreement of the 'church–state' separation is expressed in concrete practices and institutions.

In the same sense, religions are traditions of thought which are founded on a fundamental agreement (that there is only one God and Jesus is his Son for Christians, or Mohammad is his Prophet for Muslims), and which experience a continuous argument over time about how to define and embody that agreement in concrete social practices. The difference, however, between the Christian and Muslim religious traditions on the one hand, and the secular and liberal traditions on the other, is that religious traditions are based on an agreement which includes a relation with the Transcendent. This gives them a more absolute, universal and time-resistant character than non-religious traditions of thought. The fundamental agreement that societies ought to be arranged around the idea of individual freedom is relatively recent and limited to Western societies. Whereas once the fundamental agreement that characterizes religious traditions is established (with the birth of Christ or Allah's Revelation to Mohammad), it is independent of time and space, even if the concrete embodiment of that agreement in practices and institutions is not.

Seeing religion as tradition entails the recognition that religions are constantly evolving and changing according to their understanding of what it means to live well according to their core teachings, and what social practices best express this. For example, before the Second Vatican Council, the Catholic Church thought that the right to freedom of conscience was incompatible with its interpretation of the revealed Truth. The publication of *Dignitatis Humanae*, the Declaration on Religious Freedom, in 1965 recognized the inviolable right of freedom of conscience. This radical change in the practices of the Catholic Church and the realization that the practice of freedom of conscience better expressed the sacredness of human dignity and what a good Christian life was about, was initiated by forces outside the Catholic tradition (namely the liberal tradition), and was then taken on board by influential theologians within the tradition itself (see Chapter 6).

The way religion is defined has important consequences for its treatment in development thinking and practice. Seeing religion as a set of static beliefs in the individual conscience means that the task for development research is to analyse the consequences of these beliefs for the functioning of the various social spheres: whether Christian beliefs influence one's attitudes to corruption, for example, or whether Muslim beliefs influence one's attitudes to entrepreneurship and financial risk. In contrast, seeing religion as tradition means that the task for development research is to understand how the religion's fundamental agreement and teachings are embodied in certain social practices, how certain social and historical processes have led to that particular embodiment, and how the religion itself redefines this embodiment in the light of the new social context. For example, the prohibition on charging interest in

Islam originated in seventh-century Arabia where people were forced to borrow money after natural disasters. It was seen as unjust to charge interest in these circumstances because it was an exploitation of people's misfortunes (Tripp, 2006, p. 128). Whether this practice in today's world still represents an exploitation of the poor, and hence a violation of the divine command of helping those in need, is subject to disagreement within the Islamic tradition. The Christian tradition underwent similar debates in the late Middle Ages when theologians declared it not sinful.

The domain in which a religion's fundamental agreement is embodied – how to live once one has confessed that Christ is the son of God or Mohammad is Allah's Prophet – encompasses the whole realm of social life as it bears on how to 'live well' according to their respective versions of revealed Truth. Adhering to a religion is therefore characterized by performing specific practices in all areas of life. But the religion's different adherents will often strongly disagree about how best to embody the religion's fundamental agreement in concrete social practices. A committed Christian woman might interpret how to live well according to Christ's revelation by being politically engaged with the Labour party and striving for a more just social order, and by choosing a profession as a lawyer specialized in immigration law for the sake of helping the immigrants. Another committed Christian woman might respond to the same fundamental agreement of Christianity with totally different practices, by having a large family and staying at home caring for her husband and children, showing no interest in political affairs, spending her free time cooking meals for the homeless and other charitable works. Both women respond equally to what they have interpreted as living well according to Christian teaching. Similar differences about how to live one's life as a committed Muslim woman exist.

Conceiving religion as tradition means analysing how its adherents interpret its fundamental tenets and embody them in relation to the specific contexts in which they live. This also means that special attention has to be paid to the dangers of a particular group within that tradition imposing their own interpretation on others. How a Christian or Muslim woman will interpret how to live well according to the religion's fundamentals is not immune from how men within these traditions interpret the same fundamentals and seek to influence how women should lead their lives.

Fundamentalism and violence

In addition to whether religion will disappear as people become better off, and the controversy surrounding the definition of religion, there is another highly contested issue with significant implications for the way religion is treated in development: the link between religion and violence. Western media have been prone to portray the increasing presence and influence of religion in public life as disruptive, if not a threat to peace and the social order: Christians killing doctors who perform abortions in the United States, Hindus destroying a mosque in India, Muslims killing Christians in Iraq, to name just a few religiously motivated violent acts which regularly fill the news in the Western world. The underlying message that the media risk conveying is that, if religion is allowed to express itself in the public sphere, it is bound to be violent and 'fundamentalist' in nature.

Fundamentalism is a term which has been widely used since September 11, but its use has often been disconnected from what fundamentalism really is. One talks, for example, of Jewish 'fundamentalists' who refuse to allow their children to be educated in the national curriculum and taught mathematics and science, or Muslim 'fundamentalists' who want to instate Sharia law all over the Arab world, or Muslim 'fundamentalists' who affirm their religious identity by wearing a religious symbol in whatever public place, or Christian 'fundamentalists' who stage protests at abortion clinics threatening to kill the staff, or Christian 'fundamentalists' who pray and worship in public places, or Hindu 'fundamentalists' who want to clear India of a Muslim presence: the list of religious expressions now called 'fundamentalism' could go on.

In a multi-volume series on the study of fundamentalism, Marty and Appleby (1991) discuss the difficulty of characterizing a category of religious expression commonly labelled as 'fundamentalism'.[9] They prefer to talk about 'family resemblances' (p. 816) rather than a defining category (see also Almond *et al.*, 2003). Fundamentalist movements are generally characterized by a high degree of religious idealism – that is, the movement has a certain idea of the divine and the proper social order that derives from it, and this idea provides the identity of the group and each of its members. Moreover, a fundamentalist movement rejects all forms of hermeneutics (reading the sacred texts within their historical and social context). It believes that it has the correct interpretation of the text. In other words, it only accepts its own hermeneutics, its own way of interpreting texts, and rejects submitting its interpretation to revision.

Once a clear identity is established on the basis of a selective interpretation of a text, fundamentalist movements set boundaries, classifying people who do not subscribe to their interpretation as 'other'. The task is hence to make the 'other' like 'us', and replace the existing (corrupt) social order with a purer one. The role of charismatic and authoritarian leaders will often be crucial in catalysing that drive to arrange the social order according to the divine command as interpreted by the group.

Marty and Appleby observe that fundamentalist movements often arise in times of crisis, when the identity of a group is threatened or *perceived* to be threatened, and that there is a close affinity between modernization and the rise of fundamentalism. As mentioned above, the secularization thesis was at the heart of modernization. As societies become more modern, the influence of religion was thought to disappear from the social and political order. In the case of developing countries, the perceived threat that the marketization of the economy and modernization of society would reduce the influence of Islam on society, and threaten the very identity of Islam, is at the source of many Muslim funda-mentalist movements.[10]

Thomas (2005) attributes the so-called resurgence of religion in developing countries to their rejection of the secularist assumption that relegates religion to the private sphere, and lies at the core of Western modernity. Hence, he argues, Islamic 'fundamentalist' move-ments often have an anti-West character. This does not entail that fun-damentalist movements reject modernity as a whole. They are fully modern in the sense that they use modern technology (like the Internet), modern finance (like international banking, if not money laundering financial facilities), and even consume modern consump-tion goods (like iPods and mobile phones), but they reject the per-ceived secularization aspect of modernity and its tendency to let the spheres of society develop themselves independently from God.[11]

Marty and Appleby summarize the family resemblances of fun-damentalist movements in these simple terms (1991, pp. ix–x): they fight back in response to a perceived threat to their identity; they fight for their conceptions of how society should be ordered and what proper conduct to adopt; they fight with a particular chosen repository of resources which they use as weapons (typically self-selected extracts from sacred texts which they regard as fundamentals); they fight against others; they fight under God.

In a little book on the subject, Bruce (2000) describes fundamentalism along similar lines. A fundamentalist movement is characterized by its desire to shape the world according to the way it sees it, and to use violent means if necessary to do so. Religious fundamentalism is further distinguished by the source of authority behind the vision of the world it seeks to impose: a religious text which the group sees as above error and complete – there is no need to subject the text to exegesis and further hermeneutics. Bruce, like Thomas, makes strong links between the secularization aspect of modernization and fundamentalism.[12] As he puts it, 'fundamentalism is a rational response of traditionally religious peoples to social, political and economic changes that downgrade and constrain the role of religion in the public world' (Bruce, 2000, p. 117). This is why he is reluctant to classify the so-called 'Hindu fundamentalism' of the Bharatiya Janata Party (BJP) in India as a religious fundamentalist movement, given that it is not as much a reaction against secularization and the decline of religious observance among Hindus as the rejection of a Muslim presence in India. The party is in that sense more like a xenophobic nationalist political party.

Bruce notes that the absence of a hierarchical body that sanctions what is proper and improper interpretation of scriptural texts in Protestantism and Islam (the interpretation of the Bible lies in the individual conscience of the believer; the correct interpretation of the Qur'an is the one given by the local imam) makes these religious groups particularly vulnerable to fundamentalist movements which seek to impose their interpretation on others. He argues that, in that sense, Catholicism is not likely to be subject to fundamentalism because of its international structure and the teaching authority of the Vatican. What Catholics worldwide believe depends on what the Church, in its gatherings of bishops, cardinals and expert theologians, under the authority of the Pope, agrees on as the correct interpretation of its fundamental texts.

One has therefore to be extremely cautious and sensitive in using the term fundamentalism. A 'fundamentalist' is not someone who takes her religion seriously and tries to apply the religion's fundamental teachings in all areas of her life, in what she does or thinks and how she lives – this is, after all, the essence of a religion, to give meaning to people's lives and guide their actions. A fundamentalist, as defined above, is someone who refuses to put his or her interpretation of the religion's fundamentals to the hermeneutical test, and who seeks not to propose but to impose his interpretation on others, including those who do not subscribe to the religion's fundamentals.

Religion, whether in its fundamentalist form or not, can sometimes express itself violently. While we argue in this monograph that the golden rule of putting oneself in the position of the other, and the love of one's neighbour that this implies, constitute the fundamental teaching of major world religions, and that Christianity and Islam are intriguingly similar in their approach to poverty and justice, it would be naïve to ignore the fact that religion is not always a force for good in the world but can be destructive. In the *Ambivalence of the Sacred*, Scott Appleby (2000) discusses why, in their sincere response to the sacred, some choose violence over non-violence, and sometimes subordinate human life to a higher good (like the suicide bomber who subordinates the killing of people to the higher good of obeying God's perceived command). According to Appleby, those who adhere to a religion and who live it radically may be tempted to resort to violence, especially as they face situations in which others do not hesitate to use violence against them, in whatever form this violence is expressed (direct physical abuse or indirect exploitation).

When a political regime excludes a large group of people from accessing basic services and resources, and prevents them from exercising basic economic, social and political rights, it is no surprise that religion becomes a source of resistance giving strength to a group to stand up to demand justice, using violent means if necessary. This is true of the Israeli/Palestinian conflict, but also of other conflicts, such as those in South Africa during apartheid or in many Latin American countries under dictatorship. Christianity was a force of resistance for black people suffering from the apartheid regime. The proper form of resistance against the violence of the state, especially following the Soweto uprising in 1976, was subject to debate within the Christian churches. Some Christians saw non-violent forms of resistance against the oppressive state through peaceful protests as useless.[13] In Latin America, Christianity was also a source of resistance against oppressive states. Some theologians saw armed struggles as a legitimate response, as part of 'just war theory', to the violence of the state. When the army killed innocent civilians who demonstrated peacefully to demand land reform, some Christians started to interpret the teachings of the Church on non-violence differently. The same debate went on within Christianity during the Second World War about the proper response to the violence of Nazism. While the Catholic authorities condemned the use of violence in resisting the oppression of Latin American dictatorships, their response to Nazism was more ambiguous and the authorities never condemned the priests and lay faithful engaged in the armed anti-Nazi struggle.

While external circumstances (such as the degree of violence used against a religious group or the degree of its marginalization) do play a role in how people will respond, violently or not, to the experience of the sacred, Appleby (2000) highlights the important role of those who have the skills and authority to interpret religious texts and frame a religiously inspired response: he calls this the 'critical interpreting role of leadership in forming and mobilizing the religious community' (p. 27).

As discussed above, religion contains an ongoing argument about how to live well, according to God's Word, in the concrete reality of human lives. Religious leaders, by their training and authority, have therefore the ability to interpret what 'living well' involves and transmit their interpretation to the faithful through their teachings. An imam may interpret the Qur'an in a way that leads him to teach that killing Israeli Jews is a sacred duty pleasing Allah; another may interpret it in a way that leads him to teach that seeking reconciliation, forgiveness and peace with Israeli Jews is what is most pleasing to Allah. A Christian theologian may interpret the 'Martha and Mary' passage in the Gospel (Luke 10: 38–42) as the proper place for women being at prayer in the church or at home serving the needs of the family. Another theologian may interpret the same passage as the affirmation by Christ himself of the full equality of men and women – when Jesus confirms the place of Mary listening to him, at a time when women were forbidden to listen to the teaching of rabbis, he is affirming the equality of women regarding religious teaching and ministry. Given the overwhelming importance of the way the sacred texts are interpreted for the behaviour and practices of the believing community, Appleby concludes that 'the ambivalence of the sacred gives religious leadership its decisive character' (2000, p. 55).

Summary

Religion has been a contested term in the history of the social sciences. This chapter has discussed three areas of contention which have particularly affected the way religion has been conceived and how its role in development processes and outcomes has been understood.

First, the secularization thesis has been a common feature of all social sciences in the twentieth century. According to the thesis, the significance of religion in society is assumed to disappear when societies modernize. There is a dispute whether the thesis is true or false. We have argued that there is, however, a consensus about the empirical reality that religion is not losing its public significance. We have advanced the claim that this is to be attributed to the very nature of religion. Religion refuses to be kept outside the moral space and continues to be a source of norms and values guiding the different spheres of society that the differentiation process of modernization has brought about. Religion is in that sense inherently political. If politics is the art of deliberating on the 'good society' and the social arrangements necessary for people to live well, and if religion is about how to live well according to God's commands, religion cannot avoid, by virtue of its very essence, overflowing into the political sphere.

A second area of intense debate relates to the definition of religion. We have argued that religion is best defined as a tradition, that is, it rests on the fundamental agreement that a good life is one which abides by God's commands, but that agreement never ceases to be redefined and reinterpreted in the light of the specific social and historical context in which humans live. How to embody in concrete social practices God's revelation as contained in sacred texts is a continuous source of argument among the community of believers. Religion always transforms itself. This continuous argument about a religion's fundamental agreement gives religion a non-homogeneous character and leaves it vulnerable to abuses of power – one group imposing on the whole community its own interpretation of God's commands and their embodiment in local realities.

Finally, there is the contention that religions are prone to fundamentalist and violent expressions, and that, therefore, peace is best secured by keeping religion out of the public sphere. There is indeed a risk that religion may take a fundamentalist form, that is, for its adherents to select some religious teachings without submitting them to critical interpretation and to impose their own interpretation on others, sometimes through force. There is also a risk that religion may adopt violent expressions, especially if religious adherents suffer from violence and try to articulate a religion-based response to it. We have particularly emphasized the crucial role of the religious leadership in framing a possible violent response to harms inflicted on them. Therefore, an internal change, within the religious tradition itself, of the leadership's interpretation of a religion's fundamentals is often the legitimate way of curtailing religious-inspired violence (see Chapter 6).

Notes

1 Thomas (2005) attributes the following characteristics to modernization: (1) a clear distinction between 'traditional' and 'modern' society; (2) modernization is seen as a linear, progressive process of social change which could be universal and applicable to all countries; and (3) secularization. For a historical treatment of modernity, see Gray (2003).

2 For a critical discussion of the secularization thesis in developed countries, see Davie *et al.* (2003). Davie (2002) has argued, in particular, that the decline of religious attendance in Europe does not mean that religion ceases to be important in people's lives. It remains so in a non-institutionalized form. People believe without belonging (Davie 1994).

3 See Kepel (1994) for a discussion of the 'resurgence' of religion observed in the world in the late twentieth century. See also Westerlund (1996) for case studies of the resurgence of religion in politics in the 1980s and early 1990s.

4 For a critical discussion of Norris and Inglehart's existential security thesis, see Thomas (2007).

5 Casanova (1993) attributes the strong presence of the Catholic Church in Poland to the long inexistence of a Polish nation. The Church served as a substitute for Polish identity when Poland ceased to exist as a nation state.

6 We follow here the Aristotelian understanding of 'political'. Humans are 'political animals' because they have the ability to communicate and deliberate about what is good and to act accordingly (*Politics*, 1253a1–17). See Miller (2003) for a short introduction to political philosophy and a discussion of politics as the art of deliberating together about the good society and which laws and policies should ensue from it.

7 European states are secular in the sense that 'they share the assumption, enshrined in their legal systems, that religion is a matter of personal, private choice not to be dictated by the state, and that the state, while ensuring religious freedom, does not enforce a particular set of religious practices or beliefs' (Lehmann, 2006, p. 281). Lehmann discusses, in particular, how the boundaries of the public/private and the very nature of the secular state are being questioned today in Europe.

8 See also Thomas (2005) for a discussion of this transformation of religion as a 'community of believers' with embodied practices into a 'body of beliefs' in people's minds.

9 The term 'fundamentalism' originates in the publication of a series of pamphlets called 'The Fundamentals of the Faith' by a Protestant group in the United States in the 1920s (Bruce, 2000, p. 10).

10 One should, however, make a careful distinction between 'fundamentalist'

movements and movements which only seek to reassert a religious identity in the face of the secularist threat. Fundamentalist movements are characterized, following Marty and Appleby's analysis, by a literal interpretation of text and a desire to impose it on others, through violent means if need be.

11 Eisenstadt (2000) speaks about 'multiple modernities' and the danger of equating modern with anti-West.

12 For an in-depth study of the link between religious fundamentalism and secularization in Judaism, Christianity and Islam, see Armstrong (2000).

13 For a detailed description of the internal debate about the use of violence among Christians in South Africa, see Appleby (2000, pp. 34–40).

4 | Religion in Development Practice

The second chapter reviewed the treatment of religion in the history of development thought and described various modes of engagement found in the literature. This chapter assesses the practical effect of religion on processes of social change in developing countries and development outcomes. In discussing how different religious traditions have engaged in development work, the chapter demonstrates that the relationship between religion and development is not of an instrumental nature. The empirical material reviewed here reveals that development is inherent in what members of religious traditions have been doing for a long time, and continue to do. The development activities of religious communities (such as advocacy, participation in political debate, or the delivery of social services) are not 'add ons' that came with the development age; they are part of what a religious community understands itself to be. There are profound links between worship and development activities.[1]

From the review of the role of religion in development practice, a mode of engagement comes to light which is quite distinct from the different modes of engagement that have been analysed, and sometimes advocated, in development thought: religion is not a variable that is instrumental to development, as if the latter was external to it. Because development is intrinsic to what religious traditions are and do, one has to understand what religions are and how they function in order to conceptualize the role of religion in development processes and outcomes. This implies examining the social, political and economic dimensions of religious traditions.

This chapter analyses how the development activities of the Christian and Muslim religious traditions are understood as part of their fundamental beliefs and teachings. However, the way each religious tradition interprets these teachings, and embodies them in social practices, varies over time and responds to different social, economic and political contexts. In other words, the development activities arise out of attempts by religious communities to live a 'good life' in accordance with the fundamentals of the religion in the context in which its adherents live.

We have gathered the development activities of religious traditions into three main categories. First, the development work of religious traditions emerges from their relationship with the transcendent and their worship activities. This has taken the form of missionary work in the Christian tradition, and Da'wa groups in the Muslim tradition. The activities that arise from God's call to proclaim His message and revelation to the world can be further split into two categories: charity and political engagement. The chapter reviews many instances of how the Christian and Muslim traditions have conducted charity work and been politically engaged as a response to their relationship with God. What all the empirical case studies reveal is that development work is an expression of how these traditions attempt to live their fundamentals in response to the social, economic and political context in which Islam or Christianity is practised.

The Christian mission

Mission lies at the heart of Christianity. The message of salvation that God has revealed through the life, death and resurrection of His Son, has to be proclaimed to the whole world. When Jesus first appeared after his death to Mary Magdalene, he told her to go and tell his disciples what she had seen (John 20: 17–20). When he appeared afterwards to his disciples, he urged them to go and make disciples of all nations (Matthew 28: 19). The last command he left, at the Last Supper, was for his disciples to love one another as he had loved them (John 13: 34).

However, how to live God's commandment of 'loving God with all one's mind, heart and soul and one's neighbour as oneself' (Luke 10: 26), and how to communicate it to others has been subject to wide disagreement ever since the beginnings of Christianity. Chapter 6 of *Acts of the Apostles* describes a disagreement in the community about caring for the welfare of widows and the preaching of the Word of God. Some saw the care of the poor, the sick and the marginalized as an integral component of the proclamation of the Word of God. Others complained that the direct preaching of the Gospel was being neglected. It was decided that the community should be divided between those who devoted themselves entirely to the ministry of the Word and others who concentrated entirely on ministering to the sick and vulnerable.

In *Transforming Mission*, a classic textbook in missiology, the South African theologian David Bosch (2004) argues that 'the relationship between the evangelistic and the societal dimensions of the Christian mission constitutes one of the thorniest areas in the theology and practice of mission' (p. 401). He defines evangelism as 'the proclamation of salvation in Christ to those who do not believe in him, inviting them to become living members of Christ's earthly community to begin a life of service to others' (p. 10). However, salvation in Christ is not only concerned with other-worldly matters, but has also to do with human flourishing on earth. According to Bosch, because evangelism is 'always contextual' (p. 417), that is, the preaching of the Gospel is always rooted in a historical and social reality, it can never be separated from struggles for justice.

An encyclical written by Pope Paul VI in 1975 on 'Proclaiming the Gospel' (*Evangelii Nuntiandi*) describes very well the close connection between evangelism and social justice. While the encyclical affirms that evangelizing has to bear on the final destination of all men and women, in the new Creation when each will meet their Maker face to face, it also insists that the preaching of the promise of eternal life has to start with life here and now:

> [E]vangelization would not be complete if it did not take account of the unceasing interplay of the gospel of man's concrete life, both personal and social. This is why evangelization involves an explicit message, adapted to the different situations constantly being realized, about the rights and duties of every human being, about life in society, about international life, peace, justice and development. . . . The Church, as the bishops repeated, has the duty to proclaim the liberation of millions of human beings, many of whom are her own children – the duty of assisting the birth of this liberation, of giving witness to it, of ensuring that it is complete. This is not foreign to evangelization. Between evangelization and human advancement there are in fact profound links. These include links of an anthropological order, because the person who is to be evangelized is not an abstract being but is subject to social and economic questions (paragraphs 29–31).[2]

The encyclical incorporates in these paragraphs material from a letter entitled 'Justice in the World' that the world's bishops (gathered in a synod) wrote in 1971. In that letter, the bishops made an explicit statement about the links between evangelization and development, affirming that 'action on behalf of justice and participation in the transformation of the world' is 'a constitutive dimension of the preaching of the gospel' (paragraph 6).[3]

Although mission is constitutive of Christianity, the word came to be particularly associated with colonial expansion. Given that the first colonial powers were Catholic (Spain and Portugal) and that the political jurisdiction of the newly discovered territories was also ecclesiastical, colonialism and Christianization went hand in hand, as if 'the right to colonize entailed the duty to evangelize the colonized' (Bosch, 2004, p. 277). Paradoxically, the subjugation of Indians to the authority of European political and religious leaders led to one of the most striking articulations between religion and resistance to oppression under the charisma and leadership of Bartolomé de las Casas.[4]

Of colonizer parents, Las Casas became a diocesan priest, the first one to be ordained in the Americas. He witnessed and accepted without critical questioning the atrocities that the Spanish conquistadors were inflicting on the Indian population under the pretext of bringing them the Christian religion. One day in 1511, he attended a Mass in which a Dominican, Montesinos, preached. The Dominican order had started a critical reflection of the treatment of the Indians in the light of the Gospel. In his sermon, Montesinos questioned the right of colonizers to conquer and enslave the Indian population. 'Are they not human beings?', he asked. The colonizers reacted angrily, including Las Casas (who himself possessed land on which enslaved Indians worked). It was only three years later that Las Casas, when preparing a sermon, realized that the enslavement of Indians was against the Gospel. He gave up his land, freed his slaves, became a Dominican friar, and devoted himself entirely to speaking and writing about the right of Indians, including their religion, to be respected. Made Bishop of Chiapas in Mexico, he was forced to resign under pressure from the colonizing authorities, and came back to Europe. Las Casas was the first person in history to speak about human rights and the freedom of religion.

This integration of evangelism with social justice can also be seen very clearly in India at the time of its colonization. In a doctoral dissertation which examines the evolution of missionary activities in the tribal areas of the state of Jharkhand, Ed Violett (2003) relates the following narrative. When the first Christian (Lutheran) missionaries arrived in the area in the middle of the nineteenth century, they learned the language, translated the Bible and preached the Gospel, but to no avail. After some time, as the missionaries listened to the lives of tribal people and their oppression by abusive landlords who denied them the right to land, they found themselves advising them on their rights, and indirectly helping them to resist the oppression. Tribal people started to flock to the school the missionaries had established. Although the teaching imparted was primarily of a religious nature, this nonetheless gave them basic literacy skills that enabled them to stand up against their landlords and defend their property rights. Soon, the missionaries were accused by the British and Indian authorities of fomenting troubles and were asked to stop their political empowerment activities among the tribal people. The missionaries complied and reverted to the purely evangelistic dimension of mission. The tribal people felt betrayed and left Christianity.

When Catholic missionaries came to the area after the Lutherans had left, a similar narrative unfolded. They started a purely Catholic village (with some welfare provision) away from the power of landlords to avoid the risk of social and political involvement. As a strategy to expand the Catholic population, new missionary arrivals decided to have mission posts spread across the tribal territory. By travelling around for their pastoral visits, the missionaries again became first-hand witnesses to the sufferings inflicted by the landlords. They started to help with court cases and even provided a legal aid service. Some Catholic missionaries opposed this political involvement but the promulgation of the encyclical *Rerum Novarum* in Rome by Pope Leon XIII in 1891 sanctioned it.[5] Their Rome-blessed activities did not spare them, however, from accusations by the British and Indian authorities that they were making trouble in the region. The landlords fought back forcefully, alarmed by their sudden loss of privileges. To avoid conflict, the missionaries limited themselves to conducting purely religious duties such as the administration of sacraments. And, again, the tribal people left the church after their betrayal by those who had supported them.

Such a narrative was not to be repeated for a third time, however. Violett singles out the arrival of a Jesuit missionary at the beginning of the twentieth century as the pivotal element of change. The Jesuit studied Indian civil and criminal law and successfully lobbied the Indian government to reform the law so that the customs and property rights of the tribal people could be respected, the only guarantee of lasting peace in the region. Along with the law reform came the creation of employment opportunities. The missionaries established economic projects, such as carpentry and lace-making activities, to ensure the economic sustainability of the region. In addition to schools and hospitals, they created a cooperative bank and credit union.[6]

The above narratives from Latin America and tribal areas in India are clear illustrations that missionary work is always an attempt to express the fundamentals of the Christian faith in the concrete historical, social, economic and political reality of human living, for better or worse. Mission therefore always reinvents itself in response to particular historical circumstances and finds different ways of living its evangelistic nature. Mission is politically, socially, culturally and historically embedded. Many priests who were sent to evangelize the pagans in Latin America undoubtedly had a sincere faith and were convinced that what they were doing was for the greatest glory of God. Bartolomé de las Casas himself was one of them, until the day he realized that what he had believed to be God's mission turned out to be the mere political mission of human mortals thirsty for power and wealth. His faith-based reaction to defend the right to freedom of religion of indigenous people had far-reaching political consequences. Nearly two centuries later, a group of Quakers and Anglicans, William Wilberforce the most illustrious of them, similarly confronted the colonial powers on their abuses and signally advanced human rights through campaigning for the abolition of the slave trade.[7]

The story of the Indian mission among tribal people illustrates particularly well the intrinsic political dimension of religion and the necessary contextual interpretation of the command of 'proclaiming the good news to the end of earth'. The missionaries could not preach the Gospel in a credible way without attending to the temporal needs of the people they were sent to evangelize. In the context in which they were working, this meant political engagement, at the risk of conflict with the political authorities. It was these authorities who forced them to retreat into purely religious duties and who delineated what missionary religious practice should be about.

The evangelization of the African continent is another example of the intertwining of politics and religion. In his historical study of Christianity in Africa, Adrian Hastings (1994) notes that the missionary movement in Africa became closely connected to the expansion of the British Empire. At first, Africans were very unresponsive to the biblical message of salvation preached by the Protestant missionaries. It was their medical skills, their technology, the employment opportunities they offered and the education they provided that led their converts to embrace Christianity. Basically, Hastings concludes, the 'power of Britain was appealed to as demonstration of the truth of the Bible' (p. 274).

Another political legacy that the missionaries left in Africa is that of a fragmented sense of nationhood. Hastings (1997) argues that the translation of the Bible into as many local African languages as possible did not help to create a common bond between people who would later share a nation-state. It forced them instead to rely on the colonial language as a source of unity. This strategy contrasts with that of seventeenth-century Europe, where the translation of the Bible into a single, unifying vernacular language was key to the formation of national consciousness and the nation-state. Religion, politics, society and history are never fully disentangled. Evangelism, 'the proclamation of salvation in Christ to those who do not believe in him', one of the fundamentals of the Christian religion, is thus always context-dependent. What it means to proclaim Christ's message of salvation is never free from political interferences. The so-called 'evangelical wave' that is currently sweeping the global South is another illustration of this.

Evangelism and evangelicalism

Evangelicals are defined by their identification with the gospel (*evangelion* in Greek) which they believe should be proclaimed to all in both word and deed. In his study of the history of evangelicalism in Britain, Bebbington (1989) attributes four defining characteristics to the evangelical: (1) emphasis on changing one's life; (2) special importance of the Bible, although not in its purely literal interpretation; (3) emphasis on mission; (4) centrality of Christ's death and resurrection. As a Christian denomination, evangelicalism generally refers to Christians who live according to the above attributes outside papal authority, that is, within Anglicanism and Protestantism.

The spectrum of evangelicalism is as wide as that of Christianity, according to the different interpretations of the Bible. It ranges from those who take the Bible at its face value, interpreting it as they see fit for themselves, to those who situate Bible reading within the wider Christian community, relying on scholarly biblical exegesis. The much-publicized debate about creationism probably differentiates the two ends of the spectrum most vividly: those who take the story of Genesis literally, and those who read it within the context of Hebraic mythology and symbolism.

Evangelicals are commonly associated in popular opinion only with one end, those who interpret the Bible literally out of its historical, social and political context, and, more specifically, with those who interpret the Bible to fit the interests of American conservatism. This confusion between evangelicalism and conservatism is very unfortunate as it hides a large diversity of opinions and ways of conceiving the world. In a survey among evangelical leaders in the United States, the National Association for Evangelicals emphasized that the misunderstanding and misinterpretation of evangelicalism was one of their greatest concerns.[8] Evangelicalism, like any other Christian denomination, houses both the right and the left in political terms.[9]

In its charismatic manifestation within Protestantism, evangelicalism is known as Pentecostalism. It has the same four characteristics of evangelicalism, with the addition of the focus on the gifts of the Holy Spirit (speaking in tongues, peace of mind, casting off devils, etcetera).[10] Jenkins (2007) predicts that this form of Christianity will soon be predominant in developing countries and that Christianity will displace itself from its current Western centre.

The reasons why people in developing countries are attracted to evangelical forms of Christianity are manifold. In some contexts in Latin America, the growth of evangelicalism has been a safety mechanism. In countries like Guatemala and El Salvador, where many Catholics were struggling for social justice, demanding land redistribution on the basis of biblical teachings about justice, and siding with the oppressed, being a Catholic meant being 'subversive' and was often life-threatening. Shifting to Protestantism was a way of escaping persecution.[11]

Pentecostalism can also be seen as a way of solving one's problems with immediate results. The pastors tell people that their poverty and misery is due to demons. Casting them out will restore again their fullness of life. After services, people 'feel good' and relieved of their burden. In his study of Pentecostalism in Latin America, Lehmann (1996) notes that Pentecostalism is very much a 'personal service church' (p. 145) where people come to feel better, to solve their problems, and to get richer – this stems from an interpretation of the Biblical promise that it is only in giving that one receives; therefore, if one gives money to the church, òne can hope to receive much more through God's providence. In the African context, the evangelical wave has sometimes been explained in terms of its similarities with Africa's traditional religions: features such as the casting out of demons and a highly charismatic form of worship are cited (Brouwer *et al.*, 1996; Ellis and ter Haar, 2003; Gifford, 1998, 2004). This new form of Christianity is not without consequences for development.

Like the older, long-established institutional churches, these new churches have development projects attached to their ministry. Like the former, they have come to understand that the Gospel could not be preached credibly without caring for the sick, providing for the orphans and giving food to the hungry. HIV/AIDS is not to be tackled by miraculous healing. The hungry will not be fed by having stones miraculously transformed into bread. For example, the Zambian Pentecostal Church has numerous development initiatives such as schools, HIV/AIDS programmes, projects with orphans and street children, and rehabilitation schemes for sex workers.[12] In Ghana, the Assembly of God Church has a series of programmes offering health care, emergency and rehabilitation response, poverty reduction, HIV/AIDS awareness education and other services.[13]

In a study of the new Pentecostal churches in West Africa, Gifford (2004) argues that they tend to shun direct political involvement and spiritualize politics. They believe that only the Word of God, not governments, can change societies, through the transformative power of the Gospel in the (moral) life of each individual. While personal and structural change are indeed deeply linked – a born-again Finance Minister can refuse corruption and launch an initiative to eradicate corruption structurally, just as the personal conversions of Las Casas and Wilberforce had ground-shaking structural implications – these churches tend to privilege the former and ignore the latter. As Gifford puts it with reference to Ghana, 'Nobody denies that Ghana would change if all citizens became paragons of love, truth and justice and every other Christian virtue. But Ghanaian society would also change if it had an Auditor General, Controller and Accountant General, Electoral Commission, etc.' (p. 167).

In contrast to Gifford's analysis, Freston (2001) concludes, from a survey of Pentecostal political engagement in 27 countries, that no general pattern of political engagement emerges, and that one cannot assume that evangelicalism shuns political action and structural transformation *per se*. He argues that the degree and mode of political engagement is context-dependent, and that Pentecostalism tends to follow the mode of the dominant institutional religion in the country in terms of its relationship with politics.

The emergence of these new churches in developing countries is not totally unconnected to political motivations elsewhere in the world. In *Exporting the American Gospel*, Brouwer, Gifford and Rose (1996) find close links between the evangelical wave and American imperialism. They trace this back to the Cold War period. Communism was seen as the greatest enemy of free America. Being a good Christian came to be equated with being anti-communist and a good American. The risk of humanity disappearing in a nuclear holocaust was real. The restoration of Israel was also perceived as a sign that the end of the world was near. The end of the world would see the second coming of Christ, so it became of paramount importance that Christ's injunction to proclaim his good news of salvation to the world's remotest end was fulfilled. American Protestant missionaries therefore set out to evangelize the world with this American interpretation of the Gospel, with the help of all the communication means that the modern age had to offer (TV broadcasts, videos, free cassettes, free books). With the collapse of communism, the conflict between Israel and its Arab neighbours replaced the US/USSR confrontation, and Islam replaced communism as the Great Satan.[14]

In addition to this Manichean vision of the world divided between Good and Evil, Brouwer *et al.* discuss another specifically American interpretation of the Bible that was exported to developing countries, the so-called 'prosperity gospel'. America was the land of the promise of wealth. Migrants who came with nothing soon were blessed with their work and became economically prosperous. While the Protestant pioneers applied their Christian faith to diligence to work, blessing God later for material rewards, the medium of work disappeared. Christian faith became sufficient to guarantee material rewards if one truly believed in the miraculous wonders of God's Providence in one's life. Believing in God and His Word as a way of getting material benefits became a core characteristic of this particular brand of exported American evangelical Christianity.

How the evangelical branch of the Christian tradition interprets the fundamentals of Christianity may be conditioned by American history and politics and there may be close connections between US foreign policy and the rise of evangelicalism in developing countries, as Brouwer *et al.* have suggested. But one should be cautious about drawing the conclusion, as Brouwer *et al.* would seem to, that *all* evangelical churches are mere channels of American imperialism and capitalist expansion. Evangelicalism in developing countries equally responds to the local context in which adherents of the evangelical tradition live.

In his study of Pentecostalism globally, Freston (2001) concludes that one should not neglect the influence of the American political right in using evangelicalism for its own interests, as indeed it uses other Christian denominations too.[15] But, he warns, 'such activity cannot be assumed *a priori* to account for a great deal of what Third World actors do. The autonomy of Third World evangelicalism, or at least the autonomous appropriation of messages, should be assumed unless proved otherwise, and not vice-versa' (p. 283).

Moreover, the portrayal of Pentecostals as having a tendency to see the world's poverty and injustices in terms of personal moral failure, and to show no concern for social, political and economic issues, should not be assumed unless empirically observed. Many evangelical churches in Africa are responding to poverty through delivering welfare and social services to people in need, as noted earlier. As time goes on and these churches mature, they may come to interpret the evangelistic injunction to go and proclaim the good news to the ends of the earth through changing the social structures that keep people in poverty, as the older institutional churches have done. Within the history of the evangelical tradition itself, they might find rich material for political engagement in the structural transformation of society towards a more just social order.[16] Major evangelical organizations and churches have already come together under the 'Micah Challenge' to call for greater political advocacy among evangelicals to meet the Millennium Development Goals.[17] The lack of institutionalization of Pentecostal churches might be an obstacle for the moment in generating a theological reflection on economic, political and social engagement, but their increasingly greater involvement in delivering social services for the poor, as well as the influence of other Christian churches, will most probably make such a reflection and political engagement unavoidable in the future.

Charity and political engagement

No inventory exists to date of the global percentage of health and education services run by organizations with a religious foundation, but the proportion is not likely to be insignificant. We have noted already that about half of health and education services in sub-

Saharan Africa are provided by FBOs. In India, the Catholic Church (less than 2 per cent of the population) is the second-largest provider of health and educational services, after the government (UNGASS, 2005). The charitable heritage of Christianity is very large, and existed well before the age of 'development'. Before the state took them over in Europe, most hospitals, schools and poverty relief services were run by religious orders or were parish-dependent.[18] The missionary enterprise was also central to providing social services in developing countries. Donovan (2004, p. 7) notes that, at the time of Tanzanian independence in 1961, before the government took over the education system, 70 per cent of all the schools were run by the missions.

As the discussion on missionary work showed, the Christian religious tradition has not always only devoted itself to offering health and educational services. It has been *politically* engaged too. The Universal Declaration of Human Rights, and even the United Nations, would never have seen the light without the political involvement of Christian churches (Linden, 2007; Nurser, 2005; Warren, 1998). In contrast to what the secular tradition holds, the Christian religious tradition has had significant political dimensions and an overwhelming influence on political processes in developing countries. Churches have had a significant role in pro-democracy movements worldwide (De Gruchy, 1995; Haynes, 1998; Moreno, 2007; Woodberry and Shah, 2004).[19] The story of the vindication of the apartheid regime in South Africa has been one of the most acclaimed illustrations of the inherently political nature of religion.

While Christianity was appealed to by white Afrikaners attempting to justify the apartheid regime (one had to accept one's lot in life, one's place in the given social order, and one would get rewards in the afterlife), the same religion was a tremendous force for change. When the African National Congress was banned, together with other political movements opposed to apartheid, the Christian churches became one of the few spaces left for people to voice their concerns and oppose the injustices and atrocities committed by the apartheid regime of the South African government.[20]

In 1985, a group of South African and international theologians came together to assess how the churches could be engaged in the crisis and end human rights abuses. The document, entitled *Kairos*, called the South African state a tyranny, and urged the churches and religious institutions to take political action against the inhumanity of apartheid. The document created a direct confrontation between 'church and state'. The apartheid state was already cracking down on whoever was opposing the South African regime, irrespective of religion – even the then Catholic Archbishop, Denis Hurley, was put on trial for denouncing South African atrocities in Namibia – but the document did not ease the relationship between the government and church authorities.

Christian churches remained divided, however, as to what attitude to take to the oppressive state. The Dutch Reformed Church was split between those supporting apartheid as God-given and those resisting it as a violation of God's love for humankind. The Catholic Church was also divided and not all agreed with the political involvement of its clergy. The apostolic delegate in South Africa told Archbishop Denis Hurley that the Pope had made strictures on the political role of the South African Bishops' Conference. The Archbishop wrote to Pope John Paul II and argued for the inappropriate nature of these accusations. Life in South Africa was governed by politics, and as a religious leader, he could not withdraw from the life of his people. The apostolic delegate was later sacked by the Pope.[21] The Vatican remained extremely cautious, however, in backing political action against apartheid, and limited itself to condemning the apartheid regime in statements.

The final push against apartheid came in 1988 with a march organized by the Christian churches from the Anglican cathedral to the Parliament. They were planning to bring a petition to the President calling for the unbanning of all anti-apartheid organizations and the release of political prisoners. The marchers, including church leaders such as the Anglican Archbishop Desmond Tutu, were arrested. The South African government response to the non-violent church action shocked the international community. The church–state confrontation intensified (the headquarters of the South African Council of Churches was even bombed). The President, P. W. Botha, reiterated that South Africa was a Christian state and accused the South African churches of being infiltrated by communists. The state subsequently tried to ban all church services on the pretext that they were used for illegal political goals. But the churches continued their non-violent resistance, finally helping to defeat, in association with popular forces and international pressure, the apartheid regime.

Similar confrontations between church and state occurred in other parts of the world, too. We have already mentioned the case of

Archbishop Romero in El Salvador in the first chapter. Archbishop Helder Camara in Brazil confronted the dictatorship and defended the rights of the oppressed in a similar way. Both of them were accused by the political authorities of their country, and the Vatican, of overstepping their pastoral and religious duties and mixing themselves improperly with politics. Helder Camara famously replied, when accused of improper political engagement by the Vatican: 'If I give food to the hungry, I'm called a saint. If I ask why that person is hungry, I'm called a communist.'[22]

What the church's public role should be about is thus not immune from political interference by the state. Less dramatically, in the United Kingdom, the Catholic and Anglican churches directly confronted Thatcher's government in the 1980s over the social damage its policies were causing. Their report, *Faith in the City*, published in 1985, was critically received by those segments in the church which saw the document as a step too far in the church's political engagement. Another important historical example of the church's resistance was the stance of part of the Lutheran and Protestant Church, which came to be called the 'Confessing church', against Nazism in the 1930s. In the Barmen Declaration of 1934, theologians Karl Barth and Dietrich Bonhoeffer confronted the German state and opposed the national socialist party's attempt to Nazify the church. Both Barth and Bonhoeffer suffered persecution – Barth fled to Switzerland and Bonhoeffer was imprisoned and killed by the Nazis. The German Confessing Church's opposition to Nazism was a significant source of inspiration for the South African churches' resistance to apartheid.[23]

The mode of engagement of the Christian religious tradition in politics is extremely varied. It ranges from the direct involvement of Christians in political parties to civil society participation in political advocacy, to diplomacy, to moral leadership, and many other forms. Let us say a few words for each.

At the end of the nineteenth century, with the promulgation of Pope Leon XIII's encyclical *Rerum Novarum*, Christians were strongly encouraged to get involved in trade unions and politics to advance the rights of workers. In some countries, such as Belgium, the Netherlands, Germany and Norway, political parties directly inspired by the Christian social doctrine emerged. The Christian social democratic movement shared with the social democratic movement the values of justice and solidarity, but emphasized in addition the principles of subsidiarity and personal responsibility for guiding public policies (Stjernø, 2005, pp. 248–9). In countries where there were no such political parties, Christians still played a significant role in politics by contributing to existing political parties. In Britain, Christians made a major contribution to shaping the Labour Party (Dale, 2000). Costa Rica, one of the few developing countries that could be called a social democracy, was also deeply influenced by the Christian social doctrine (Deneulin, 2005).

In terms of civil society engagement, a large number of churches and religion-based organizations have participated in advocacy campaigns, such as Make Poverty History and the Jubilee Campaign for debt relief. The role of the churches in apartheid South Africa, against the dictatorship in El Salvador, Brazil, Zimbabwe, the Philippines and Chile,[24] or against the injustices of the neo-liberal governments of Britain and the United States, is also an illustration of the powerful counteracting power of churches as civil society actors – forces independent of government that are able to challenge it when it violates human rights and deepens inequalities and injustices.

Faith-based diplomacy is another area where the Christian tradition has been influential (Johnston, 2003). The case of the end of the civil war in Mozambique and the peace agreements concluded through the mediation of the Catholic lay community San Egidio has been one of the most documented cases. Christianity may have brought an end to some conflict in Africa but, some may object, it has also been a source of conflict. The Catholic Church was powerless in the face of the Rwandan genocide. Some may even argue that the division between Hutus and Tutsis had been created by the colonizer and accentuated by the Church (van Hoyweghen, 1996). In Sudan, the conflict over resources in the South has turned into a religious conflict between the Muslim North and the Christian South (Mansour, 2002).

Two responses can be made to this objection. The first is that one should not draw too hasty a conclusion that what appears on the surface to be a religious conflict has religious roots in reality. Often the conflict is generated not by religion *per se* but by inequalities between groups of people. If a group has been marginalized because of its religion and rebels against its marginalization, it is not so much the religion that causes conflict as the discriminatory penalty that holding a certain religion carries (Stewart, 2007). Religion then becomes a source of resistance, sometimes violent, against an oppressor or oppressive system. This leads us to our second response to the objection that religion is a source of conflict. While some interpret the fundamental agreement of the Christian tradition in terms of peace, others may use it to justify conflict. In Chapter 2, following Appleby (2000), we called this the 'ambivalence of the sacred'. We have argued that this ambivalence, and the risk that religious expression may sometimes take a violent form, does not constitute a sound basis for dismissing religion and its potential to broker peace.[25] What is needed instead is a critical dialogue and engagement with the tradition itself and how it interprets its fundamentals.

Finally, another important political engagement of the Christian tradition takes the form of moral leadership. Christian social thought, that is, the body of social thought and action that has been developed in the Christian tradition over centuries, has helped to form the moral basis of individual and institutional action throughout the world. It is this moral formative role of the churches that inspired many black (and some white) South Africans in the resistance against apartheid. The role of Christian churches in forming the moral character of people and giving them the courage to stand up against discrimination was also highly significant in the case of the civil rights movement in the United States.[26] It is not only the personal faith of the individual believer that matters but her being part of a wider community of believers, through the local church or wider religious institutions, where this contribution to the formation of moral character takes place.

Da'wa ('God's call')

In Islam as in Christianity, caring for others in need is not a requirement that the development age has laid on religious communities; it is part of how Islam understands itself. There is a close connection between worship and development-related activities because ensuring social justice is a critical part of being a good Muslim. Islam places strong emphasis on social justice and brotherly (or sisterly) care. In his famous treatise on *Social Justice in Islam*, Sayyid Qutb (2000), an Egyptian Islamic scholar and one of the most influential Islamic ideologues of the twentieth century,[27] highlights three basic elements: absolute freedom of conscience; complete equality of all men and women; and social interdependence among members of society. He argues that central to an Islamic conception of social justice is the prerequisite to view human life in its entirety and not as divided into a number of unrelated parts. For him the mutual responsibility of individuals and societies is integral to the notion of social justice.

Considering the first basic element, Qutb maintains that social justice can only be attained with a totally free human conscience that recognizes no superior authority over any individual except God. Power is only in the hand of God, and nobody can work as a mediator between Him and His creatures, even if the believer is a prophet. The Qur'an maintains:

> O people of the Scripture! Come to an agreement between us and you: that we shall worship none but Allah, and that we shall ascribe no partner unto Him, and that none of us shall take others for lords beside Allah. And if they return away, then say: Bear witness that we are they who have surrendered (unto Him). (3: 64)

The idea is that when the conscience is free from the instinct of servitude and worship of anyone other than Allah, and when it knows that it has direct access to Allah and does not need to rely on a mediator, it rids itself of all human fears – be they linked to life, livelihood or anything else. Qutb argues that this fear is an ignoble instinct, which lowers the individual's estimation of himself, and often makes him accept humiliation or abdicate his honour or many of his rights.

Second, closely related to the above idea in Qutb's notion of social justice is the concept of equality among people. No one is superior to others on the basis of their lineage, education or any other economic, social or political dimension. What makes someone superior to another is performing good practices: 'Lo! The noblest of you, in the sight of Allah, is the best in conduct. Lo! Allah is Knower, Aware' (49: 13). This provides the incentive for believers to engage in caring for others if they want to be considered superior in the eyes of God. Even in terms of relations between sexes, Islam has guaranteed complete equality between women and men. The difference is in terms of the roles and responsibilities but not status; they are equal in the spiritual and religious sphere: 'Whoever does good work, man or woman, and is a Believer – such shall enter into Paradise and shall not be wronged one jot' (4: 123).

This leads us to the third central element of social justice in Islam that Qutb singled out, social interdependence. While it emphasizes individual freedom, Islam also places high emphasis on both individual and social responsibility. Islam presents a very clear conception of mutual responsibility, with roles assigned for all: towards the immediate family, between the individual and society, between communities, between generations, and even towards oneself. The latter requires exercising discipline in pursuit of pleasures and following the path of righteousness and salvation: 'Do not hand yourselves over to destruction' (2: 191).

In terms of responsibility towards society, every individual is required to work conscientiously because his work contributes to producing a collective good. Society as a whole is in turn responsible for the care of its weak members. Therefore, society must develop mechanisms to dispense *zakat* effectively (see below). If any individual spends a night hungry, the blame is to rest with the whole community. One of the *Hadiths* maintains: 'Whatever people allow knowingly that a man remain hungry among them, the protection of Allah is taken from them.'

Other Islamic thinkers, especially those involved in Islamic movements, have placed similar emphasis on the idea of social justice. As briefly discussed in Chapter 1, Mawlana Sayyid Abu'l-A`la Maududi, a leading Islamic scholar from South Asia and founder of Jama'at-i-Islami, also argued that establishing social justice was the primary motive for attaining political power. This contribution of Islam to social justice is visible in the debate around two Islamic central principles that relate to the responsibilities of the believer: *Haqooq-ul-Allah* ('rights of God') and *Haqooq-ul-Abad* ('rights of people'). Islam prioritizes the latter over the former, that is, if responsibility towards God through prayer and worship was missed, this could be forgiven, but failing to meet one's responsibilities towards others could not be forgiven. As will be discussed in the section on *zakat*, Islam clearly specifies duties to the poor, the neighbours, the elders, and others.

Da'wa, which is interpreted as responding to God's call and to the invitation to preach the way of the Lord,[28] has increasingly incorporated the social justice component in its core function of propagating Islam, just as the Christian tradition increasingly included a social justice dimension to its evangelism and missionary work. From the very beginning, the Da'wa teachings have placed heavy emphasis on the notion of a just society. Through these teachings, the Da'wa groups have focused on inculcating a sense of social responsibility among believers. The explicit linkage with the early interpretation of Da'wa is the assertion that Muslims, obliged to follow God's call, must respond to the Qur'anic duty to create balance and justice in human affairs.

Some Islamic interpretations view Da'wa as the responsibility of the entire community of believers to promote what is right and to forbid what is wrong, as this will automatically lead to establishing a just society (Schulze, 1995). The Qur'an maintains: 'Let there be one nation (ummah) of you, calling to the good, enjoining what is right, forbidding what is wrong; those are the ones to prosper' (3: 104). Over time, Da'wa has been institutionalized through different forms of organizations, some aspiring to transnational influence while others remaining focused on their own regions. An example of the former is the Muslim World League, established in 1962 by the Saudi government to unify and spread the call of Islam. The success of such efforts was limited, however, by cultural and political differences regarding the true content of Islamic teaching in various contexts. Organizations with a more focused agenda in a specific region, like the Muslim Brotherhood, have been more effective (Schulze, 1995).

Central to Da'wa is the propagation of Islamic precepts and spread of Islamic education. Whether formally at court, as with the Fatamids (the Isma'ili Shi'ite dynasty of North Africa and the Middle East, 909–1171), or in informal circles of scholars, the Da'wa groups spread the Islamic knowledge of how to recite the Qur'an, apply the Sharia, and conduct the affairs of everyday life in an Islamic spirit. But for most of Islamic history, Da'wa work remained an individual effort. Evidence suggests that institutionalized and organized Da'wa began only after 1915. The modern Da'wa networks are mainly active among Muslims rather than among members of other faiths.[29] Hasan al-Banna, founder of the Muslim Brotherhood, defined the priorities of Da'wa in the following way: self, home, society, country, government, Muslim ummah, and world (Schulze, 1995). A good example of the actual working of Da'wa groups is Tablighi Jama'at, a Da'wa group established by Maulana Muhammad Ilyas in 1920 in India, which today maintains an influential international network.

The Jama'at maintains that it is the fundamental responsibility of every Muslim to spread Islamic teaching and that this duty is not just confined to the ulama or Sufi saints (Sikand, 1999). It primarily targets all Muslims, with the aim to make them 'better Muslims', so that they follow the injunctions of Sharia in every aspect of life.[30] The Jama'at's actual working includes formation of *Tablighi* groups, composed of trained ulama as well as ordinary Muslims, who are then assigned to spread the Islamic messages in a selected area over a certain period of time. During this period, group members are required to contact local Muslims and impart to them knowledge of the basic Islamic teachings and rituals. Unlike other Islamic groups engaged in Da'wa, which have political aspirations, the Jama'at discourages direct involvement in political activity, placing its emphasis on personal reform.

Like Christian missionary work, Da'wa has not been free of political associations and influences (see also Kroessin and Mohamed, 2007). We observe here yet again that a religious tradition, and the way it interprets its fundamentals, can never be separated from the wider context in which the members of the tradition live. Historically, Da'wa has been used to propagate the specific claims of the dynasties such as the Abbasids and sects such as the Ismailis. This trend consolidated in the twentieth century, when Da'wa work engaged with politics in three dominant ways: to resist the colonial rulers; to develop resistance against the state; and in its use by the state itself to counter the influence of Islamist political parties.

The struggle against colonial rule was defined as Da'wa to seek independence from non-Muslim rule and to establish or restore *dar al-Islam* (homeland of Islam). These ideas called for local self-government and expulsion of colonial rulers. This also helped popularize the political movement in otherwise ethnically or linguistically polarized communities (Masud, 1995).

Da'wa work as a means to resist the state has been visible in the working of groups like Hiz al-Dawa al Islamiyya (Islamic Call Party), a Shia group in Iraq that opposed the rule of Saddam Hussein (Eickelman and Piscatori, 1996). All Islamic political parties have a Da'wa arm. Hizbullah (the 'party of God') has also developed an extensive social welfare system in Lebanon that involves educational, agricultural, medical, and housing assistance.[31] Similarly, Jama'at-i-Islami in Pakistan and Bangladesh upholds the establishment of social justice as its primary aim. Its political activities and welfare work share a common purpose: both are means to establish God's order in this world, central to which is the idea of social justice.

Da'wa as a state ideology emerged more clearly in the 1960s under Gamel Abdel Nasser who established a Da'wa network in the Middle East and Africa with the help of Al-Azhar University in order to promote Islam, the Arabic language, and Arab nationalism (Masud, 1995). Two other Muslim states, Saudi Arabia and Libya, sensing that Da'wa by Islamic religious parties and independent groups was a threat to their rule, organized their own Da'wa supporting their particular interests (Masud, 1995).

Over time, the tradition of Da'wa has increasingly engaged with social welfare activities – free medical clinics, soup kitchens for the poor, subsidized housing, and other forms of mutual assistance, often substituting for ineffective government services (Eickelman and Piscatori, 1996). It is argued that since Islam, like any other religion, involves a total way of life, Muslims would be abdicating their basic responsibility if they did not strive to redress social injustices and economic inequalities in any society. The Muslim World League adopted social welfare in its Da'wa programme in 1974. In addition, with the rise of an NGO culture, some international Muslim NGOs are combining the Da'wa and relief work. More than 250 Saudi NGOs are estimated to be involved in domestic and international relief and development activity. In their study of the activities of three such NGOs in Somalia, Kroessin and Mohamed (2007) show that these organizations carry out missionary-type activities to varying extents, alongside their humanitarian work. Like other Da'wa groups, they remain focused, however, on Muslim populations. Ashfaq Ahmad, a member of the Islamic society of Papua New Guinea, defends the need to combine social work with Da'wa in the following terms:

> Da'wa work must be supplemented with the social, cultural, and economic development of the country. A substantial amount of funds should be allocated to be spent in these countries for health, education, and better living conditions for the people living there in the form of grants, aids or loans. . . . The Spirit of service and brotherhood should inculcate and permeate all the activities of development, so that people may appreciate the difference between this work and colonialism.[32]

Zakat and waqf

While the previous section highlighted the overall emphasis on social justice and mutual care as intrinsic to the Islamic tradition, this section analyses the institutionalized mechanisms within Islam to ensure the financial means to meet the demands of justice and care. Religious giving, or *zakat*, is the cornerstone for undertaking welfare and development work within Islam. The importance of *zakat* is repeatedly emphasized within the Qur'an: 'Observe the prayers, pay the *zakat*, and obey the Messenger; it may be that you will receive mercy.' (24: 55). 'Allah will surely help the man who helps Him; verily Allah is Powerful, Mighty. Such, if We establish them in the earth, will observe the prayers, will pay the zakat, will urge to good and will restrain from evil' (22: 41–42). 'Who is he who will make a fair loan to Allah, and He will double it for him. For such a one there is a noble reward.' (57: 11).

Zakat is one of the five pillars of Islam that every believer must respect. These are: (1) the belief that there is only one God and that the Prophet Mohammad is his Messenger (tawheed); (2) praying five times a day (namaz); (3) zakat; (4) pilgrimage to Mecca (haj); (5) fasting from sunrise to sunset during thirty days (Ramadan). The denial of any one of these obligations is considered tantamount to disbelief. Therefore failing to practise zakat amounts to dishonouring God.

Zakat is a compulsory tax on all affluent Muslims. A specified amount (2.5 per cent) is to be deducted from their wealth each year. Occurring thirty-two times in the Qur'an, the word zakat is often joined with the command to offer prayer, the second pillar of Islam, thus highlighting its importance to believers. Islamic jurisprudence maintains that zakat is the right of the poor in the wealth of the rich that has been determined by God. It has two purposes: to refine the conscience, and to foster a belief in the inherent solidarity of mankind (Qutb, 2000). Zakat aims to eliminate poverty and destitution from society.

The Qur'an clearly defines the proper beneficiaries of zakat: 'Zakat expenditures are only for the poor and the needy, and for those employed to collect (zakat) and for bringing hearts together and for freeing captives and for those in debt and in the way of Allah and for the travellers' (9: 60). Kroessin and Mohamed (2007) find these translatable to the following present-day sectors: poverty reduction; administrative overheads for civil servants dealing with public welfare; peace building and community cohesion; promotion of freedom, basic human rights and civil liberties; personal insolvency settlements; public work, particularly security and defence; and provision for the homeless, refugees and migrants.

A Muslim believer is supposed to dispense zakat personally if the state does not have a central system to collect it. Islamic sources maintain that an extensive system for collection of zakat existed during the lifetime of the Prophet Mohammad, whereby some of his closest companions were among its innumerable collectors. This practice, however, did not survive the course of time. By the twelfth century, the practice of collection of zakat by the state had come to a halt across the Muslim world. The exception is Yemen, where collection of *zakat* by the state is said to have remained uninterrupted, while five other countries have reintroduced the system: Saudi Arabia in 1951, Libya in 1971, Pakistan in 1979, Sudan in 1984 and Malaysia (Gilani, 2006).

In Pakistan, *zakat* is collected from saving accounts by banks and financial institutions at the rate of 2.5 per cent on the first day of Ramadan and is utilized for educational scholarships for children in need, supporting madrasas, and providing monthly stipends to widows and the destitute. The *zakat* disbursement system has a complex hierarchy. The Central Zakat Council is followed by the Provincial Zakat Councils headed by serving or retired judges of the High Courts. The 39,915 local Zakat Committees are the most important grassroots tier of the *zakat* system, responsible for the crucial task of identifying *mustahiqeen* ('deserving candidates') from among the numerous applicants. They are also responsible for maintenance of the records of the local Zakat Fund. Interestingly, while in Islam *zakat* acts as the wealth tax, in practice in Pakistan *zakat* deductions are not really viewed as a tax and are collected in parallel with regular income and wealth tax. Thus the current structure of *zakat* collection and its disbursement in Pakistan operates in an *ad hoc* arrangement, which utilizes *zakat* funds for meeting short-term relief programmes rather than undertaking long-term development projects.

In addition to *zakat,* Islam lays down two other principles for religious giving: *sadaka* and *khayraat*. Each has its own significance, its own guidelines around how to administer it, its own criteria for selecting the recipients, and its own rewards. In opposition to the structural and obligatory nature of *zakat, sadaka* contains the meaning of voluntary alms giving. In Islamic scholarship *sadaka* is often referred to as *sadakat al tatawwu* ('alms of spontaneity'), or *sadakat al-nafl* ('alms of supererogation'). Albeit non-obligatory, *sadaka* and its related verbal forms are used twenty-four times in the Qur'an and form the subject of many *Hadith. Sadaka* involves giving to people close by, even non-Muslim, such as one's neighbours and relatives rather than distant people. Unlike *zakat*, where Islamic law fixes the nature and value of the amount due, the giver of *sadaka* is free to determine what and how much to give, so that there is no minimum or maximum amount prescribed. In actual practice it normally translates into giving money to the destitute, orphans and the sick to help them meet their basic needs. It is interesting to note that the distinction between *zakat* and *sadaka* parallels two mainstream types of development interventions: recognizing the need for long-term development programmes while ensuring provision for immediate relief and safety nets for the poorest.

Whereas *zakat* is explicitly based on the notion of social justice and redistribution of wealth in society, *sadaka,* though socially also serving the same role, is explained mainly in terms of inner cleansing (expiation of sins) through self-denial. Closely related to the expiatory function of *sadaka* is its special role in affording protection against evil. The giver is promised a reward in the afterworld if the gift serves others. *Sadaka* is also encouraged as a means of increasing wealth in this world. The giver of *sadaka* is promised a reward many times the amount he gives in terms of enhanced wealth in this world and promise of salvation in the other. There is also a concept of *sadaka jariya* ('permanent alms'), which basically refers to a gift or deed that will benefit others over a period of time. *Sadaka jariya* can thus often result in the establishment of *waqfs,* wherein property is given for public use in the name of God. This builds into the notion of *sadaka* a provision for undertaking long-term development work.

Waqf is an endowment of movable or immovable property for religious purposes. When a property has been made *waqf* it becomes inalienable, meaning it cannot be given away or sold, while its resources must be used for the purpose originally declared (Mann 1989). The notion of *waqf* has been critical in Islamic history in supporting much welfare and development work. Examples of *waqfs* include hospitals, lodges for the elderly, widows and the poor, and Qur'anic schools for orphans. For example, in mid-sixteenth-century Jerusalem, Haseki Hurrem Sultan, the wife of the Ottoman sultan Suleyman (1520–66), established a complex of three *waqfs*: a soup kitchen, a lodge for devotees living in the city, and a lodge for travellers. *Waqfs* were also critical in supporting the educational and intellectual demands as well as the economic and social development of Muslim societies. *Waqf* endowments facilitated the establishment of madrasas, the centres of Islamic learning through Muslim history. A prominent example of the role of *waqf* in present-day Muslim societies is the Hamdard Foundation in Pakistan.

Established in 1964 by the founder of the largest manufacturer of *Unani* medicine in the world, the Foundation today makes a significant contribution in the field of higher learning.[33] A chain of

Hamdard universities and educational institutions runs across the country. The Foundation also runs schools for disadvantaged communities and provides scholarships to children in need. Also operational in India, the Hamdard group, in addition to supporting other social service activities, bears the major costs of the running expenses of Jamia Hamdard, a university in New Delhi which offer courses in subjects ranging from pharmaceutical and computer sciences to management studies and the *Unani* system of medicine.

The third main form of giving in Islam is *khayraat*. Like *sadaka*, it is highly encouraged but is non-obligatory. *Khayraat* is basically the extension of the notion of social responsibility established through *zakat* and *sadaka*. It entails giving away as much of one's wealth as one can for public welfare or to the poor and needy. In turn God promises to reward the giver in this life, where his wealth gets multiplied many times the amount he gives, in addition to the reward promised in the thereafter, as written in the Qur'an: 'Who is it that will make God a goodly loan so that He will increase it many times' (2: 245).

The practice of *zakat*, and the distribution of other forms of charity, is not only an individual duty which the believer undertakes as a way to communicate with God, implore Him for deliverance at times of personal distress, thank Him for success or expiate one's sins. It also has important collective implications. Through its obligatory nature, and the great emphasis placed on *sadaka* and *khayraat*, it mobilizes large financial resources within Muslim societies. If strategically used by the state, these can help undertake major development projects and, if distributed individually, can act as safety nets for the poor. The major difference, though, between these *zakat*-based development activities and those of secular NGOs is that they cannot be compartmentalized into 'development activities' dissociated from religious worship and from the 'total way of life' that Islam involves.

In addition to further pointing towards the non-separation between development and religion, and the need to understand a religion's functioning in order to understand its development work, this discussion of forms of Islamic practices of charity also underlines the two-way relationship between a religious tradition and the context in which it is practised. While the political context influences a religion's interpretation and embodiment of its fundamentals – the modalities of how *zakat i*s practised in Islamic countries depend on their political systems – religious practices deeply shape the social and political world of the societies in which they have been performed. These two points are further illustrated by Islam's political engagement. Another point that the next section illustrates is the non-homogeneous character of a religious tradition and the diversity of interpretations of its fundamentals.

Islam and political engagement

The relationship between religion and politics constitutes a complex debate in Islam. Most discussion assumes that the religious and political realms are inseparable in Islam. Western scholarship – and, to a significant extent, Muslim scholarship – contrasts this with Christian political thought, which conceives the relationship between religion and politics as one of mutual influence between separable variables. This inseparability between the two, it is argued, finds support in more than forty Qur'anic references, which call for the needy to obey 'God, His Prophet and those of authority among you' (4: 59). It also builds on the example of the Prophet Mohammad, who was at once a spiritual leader and the head of a political community: as the leader of the Muslims he also led many wars.

The institution of the caliphate in Islam draws upon the same principle: that religious and political power need to be combined so that Islamic precepts can shape the functioning of the whole society (Esposito and Voll, 1996). The notion of the caliphate entails that man is God's agent and is required to exercise the divine authority on earth within the limits prescribed by God. In practice, the rule by a *khalifa*, literally 'successor of the Prophet', lasted mainly in the two Muslim dynasties, the Umayyads (661–750) and Abbasids (750–1258). The system of the caliphate came to an end with the Mongol conquest of Baghdad in 1258, though again gaining ascendancy in the Ottoman Empire. The fall of the Empire marked the end of the practice of the caliphate (*ibid.*). Among Islamic political groups today, the call for establishing the caliphate remains an exception given that the notion entails acceptance of one Muslim figure as a leader of all Muslims, irrespective of their national identities, a highly implausible scenario given the political rivalry between Muslim states. These groups do argue, however, for establishing the law of the Sharia within the boundaries of a given nation state. As Khomeini wrote in his will: 'As for (those) who consider Islam separate from government and politics, it must be said to these ignoramuses that the Holy Qur'an and the Sunnah of Prophet contain more rules regarding government and politics than in other matters' (Rahman, 1982, p. 22).

Opposed to this dominant view is another school of thought within Islam that argues against the indivisibility of religion and politics. It maintains that too great an involvement with politics may mislead or corrupt believers. For example, Tablighi Jama'at, a significant movement of reform that originated in South Asia but now operates worldwide, believes that the separation of religion and politics is necessary in the short term. It implicitly criticizes the quest for political power, such as the one in which groups like Jama'at-i-Islami and the Muslim Brotherhood are engaged. As God's viceregents, men are given the earth to govern but are not worthy to do so until they can govern themselves. In effect, therefore, they must eschew politics until they have proved themselves possessed of such Islamic virtue. Only when their lives are shaped entirely by Sharia principles can they become worthy of entering politics.

A prominent Islamic scholar, Fazlur Rahman, is equally critical of this unity of state and religion. He argues that while Islamic precepts should govern politics, the reality is that, in places where this has happened, political groups and elites have exploited Islamic concepts and organizations. The result has been 'sheer demagoguery' rather than morally inspired politics. In his view, 'The slogan "in Islam religion and politics are inseparable" is employed to dupe the common man into accepting that instead of politics or the state serving the long-range objectives of Islam, Islam should come to serve the immediate and myopic objectives of party politics' (Rahman, 1982, p. 140). Authors with these views normally refer to the authoritarian regimes in the Arab world, which continue to exercise the right to rule without ever exposing themselves to public ballot and lead states with a history of curbing any civil or political dissent through brute force (Diamond *et al.*, 2003). It is argued that the state in these societies co-opts the religious elite to defend exploitative structures rather than challenge them. A dominant stream of scholarship on Pakistan holds the religious elite responsible for providing legitimacy to a succession of military rulers (Hussein, 2005).

Between these two positions there is a wide range of Islamic groups that have become involved in politics as a response to changing socio-economic and political contexts. This parallels the similar involvement of Christian churches in politics highlighted earlier – in resistance against apartheid, Nazism, or neo-liberal political regimes.

Islamic Sufi orders played a prominent political role in resisting colonial invaders in the late nineteenth and early twentieth centuries in parts of West Africa and Central Asia. Shaykh Uways bin Muhammad al-Barawi al-Qadiri, born in southern Somaliland in 1847, led the Qadiriya Sufi order, one of the most widespread Sufi brotherhoods in Somaliland, to play a leading part in opposing German rule. The order's missionary activities were focused on the Rahanwayn tribes of the upper Juba and on Zanzibar in East Africa.

In the late 1880s, when the European powers exerted pressure to displace Sayyid Bargshah, the Muslim ruler of Zanzibar, Shaykh Uways, who had close relations with Bargshah and his successors, mobilized Qadiriya members and the general community to resist the foreign invaders by circulating letters inciting resistance and developing schemes for cross-country alliances to resist the foreign occupiers (Martin, 1969).

The Sanusiya order of Cyrenaica,[34] an important movement in the history of Sufism in North Africa and the Sahara during the nineteenth century, similarly played a pivotal role in resisting French and Italian colonialism, which threatened local support networks and local structures (Vikor, 1995). This Sufi order had a strong tradition of working within the Bedouin community, with a focus on both religious piety and integration in modern trade and economic development.

These different positions within the scholarship and practice on religion and politics in Islam illuminate the multiplicity of interpretations within each religious tradition. It is thus problematic to treat religions as based on a single hegemonic interpretation of their fundamental teachings, and more helpful to understand religious traditions in their own terms, in all their complexities. But despite these variations of interpretation, the central role of political power in Islam for establishing God's order in this world is clear. Even the Tablighi Jama'at, which otherwise condemns political engagement, is not entirely devoid of a political dimension. By exhorting Muslims to follow Islamic teachings in their everyday lives and actions, it encourages the notion of social justice and mutual responsibility. This automatically entails intervention in the public space, as Islam with its emphasis on striving for social justice requires the believer to move his focus from himself to the collective. Thus despite conflicting positions on the specific nature of political engagement, all Islamic groups highlight the inherently political nature of Islam, and its development overtones.

Summary

In reviewing some examples of the involvement of the Christian and Muslim traditions in development work, this chapter has shown that the so-called development activities of religious communities are part of how the Christian and Muslim traditions understand their fundamental agreement. These activities seek to embody in the best practices available the fundamentals of their religion in specific social, economic and political contexts. In order to illustrate these points the chapter examined the missionary activities of the Christian Church, the working of Da'wa groups in Islam and the charity activities and political engagement which issue from God's call to proclaim His message in both the Christian and Muslim traditions.

Within the Christian tradition, the chapter has discussed the relationship between the evangelistic and the societal dimensions of the Christian mission. For many Christian thinkers salvation in Christ is not only concerned with other-worldly matters, but also has to do with human flourishing on earth. The chapter has documented that although mission is constitutive of Christianity, it came to be particularly associated with colonial expansion. Mission is a response to living the fundamentals of the Christian faith in the concrete historical, social, economic and political reality of human life, for better or for worse. What it means to proclaim Christ's message of salvation (evangelism) is never free from practical political consequences. The chapter has also discussed some confusion between evangelism and evangelicalism, and some misinterpretation regarding the latter.

The chapter has shown a similar emphasis on social justice within Islam, and a similar context-dependence in the response of believers to the fundamentals of their religion. Islam places strong emphasis on social justice, brotherly/sisterly care and social responsibility. In a similar fashion to Christian mission, in addition to promoting social justice through the propagation of Islamic teaching, Da'wa groups have increasingly moved towards direct provision of social services and welfare. Da'wa, responding to God's call, must include promoting justice in human affairs.

Some mechanisms that Islam has institutionalized to ensure social justice have been documented. We have seen how a detailed system of religious giving has evolved in Islam under the principles of *zakat*, *sadaka* and *khayraat*. Each has its own significance, guidelines around how to administer it, criteria for selecting the recipients, and rewards. By clearly defining different categories of beneficiaries at different poverty levels, Islam provides for both immediate relief and long-term development work, showing its sensitivity to the need for a multi-pronged approach to addressing issues of social justice and poverty in society. The notion of *waqf* has been critical in Islamic history in supporting much welfare and development work.

In addition to charity, the chapter has examined how both the Christian and Islamic traditions have a long history of political engagement. The boundaries of so-called 'church–state separation' have often been overstepped. Churches have had a significant role in pro-democracy movements worldwide. The mode of engagement of the Christian tradition in politics is extremely varied, ranging from direct involvement in political parties to civil society participation in political advocacy, to diplomacy and moral leadership.

The political involvement of Islam is equally varied. Some Islamic groups have engaged consciously in gaining control over the state to shape society in line with Islamic teachings, while others have been drawn into political engagement by the changing wider political context, especially during the colonial period. Other voices within the Islamic tradition have warned against extensive political involvement for fear that it might lead to the exploitation of religion for political gain. These narratives illustrate the multiplicity of interpretations that exist in each religious tradition, thereby countering the assumption that there is one hegemonic religious interpretation.

From the examples narrated in this chapter, one may observe that the actions of members of religious traditions, based on their fundamental beliefs, have much in common with the basic principles of modern-day development thinking and practice: social justice and securing the basic conditions for people to live in dignity and lead flourishing human lives. Indeed, often the way religious traditions conceive of development, or what constitutes desirable social change, is in tune with the way non-religious traditions, such as secular humanism, conceive the same end. But sometimes differences arise, and these the next chapter discusses.

Notes

1 In her analysis of the Norwegian Mission Society, Hovland (2007) notes that it is not easy to separate its missionary from its development activities. For an exploration of the connections between 'doing theology' and 'doing development', see White and Tiongco (1997).

2 The full text is available at <http://www.vatican.va/holy_father/paul_vi/ apost_exhortations/index.htm> (accessed November 2008).

3 For an electronic copy of the Catholic Church's documents on social justice, from which this quote is taken, see the website of the Office for Social Justice of the Archdiocese of St Paul and Minneapolis at <http://www.osjspm.org/> (accessed November 2008). For an introduction to Catholic social thought, see Hornby-Smith (2006).

4 The following short biography is summarized from Josaphat (2001). See also Gutierrez (1993) for a historical account of Las Casas's defence of the Indians and its relevance for the contemporary situation of the oppressed and marginalized in Latin America. For Las Casas's pioneering work in the human rights movements, see Ruston (2004).

5 The encyclical was the first Catholic official statement on economic and social issues. It condemned unbridled capitalism and urged the lay faithful to take action to protect the rights of the workers, including through political action with trade unions and political parties.

6 It was a Lutheran lay preacher, Friedrich Wilhem Raiffeisen, who started the movement for cooperative banking. He established a system of rural cooperative banks, linked to parishes, in German villages to assist poor farmers with credit. His idea of credit union was strongly linked to his faith and his interpretation of the biblical concern for the poor through helping them help themselves and not through short-term charity. See a history of the Raiffeisen banking system at <http://www.cera.be/brs/en/about/history/raifstelsen> (accessed November 2008).

7 See Tomkins (2007) for a biography of the Anglican evangelical William Wilberforce.

8 See the National Association for Evangelicals at <www.nae.net>. See also Shah (2004) on the misconception regarding evangelicalism.

9 For an account of the engagement of evangelicalism in the cause of social justice, see Hilborn (2004); Smith (1998); Thomas (2003); and Wolffe (2006).

10 See Martin (2002) for an analysis of the Pentecostal movement worldwide.

11 For a study of evangelical Protestantism in Latin America, see, among others, Freston (2008); Lehmann (1996); Martin (1990, 2002); and Stoll (1990).

12 See <http://www.northmeadassembly.org.zm>.

13 See the website of Ghana's Assemblies of God Relief and Development Services at <http://www.agreds.org/> (accessed November 2008).

14 Brouwer *et al.* note in particular that other religions such as Buddhism and Hinduism are not demonized along with Islam as part of 'Evil'.

15 Roman Catholicism is another denomination that the American right is currently using for promoting its own political interests. In a review of church documents on social justice, Verstraeten (2007) observes that there has been a clear shift, from the 1980s onwards, from a focus on structural transformation to individual morality. Some Vatican documents also now directly attack the welfare state, in violation of its earlier teachings.

16 Dayton (1988) and Bebbington (1989) offer an historical account of the involvement of evangelicals in the cause of justice in the context of Britain and the United States.

17 See <http://www.micahchallenge.org/> (accessed November 2008). The website states that such engagement in political advocacy with poor communities might be 'a new step built upon a new understanding of Christ's mission for the church'. The bestselling evangelical book by Rick Warren, *The Purpose Driven Life*, is having a significant impact on transforming the nature of evangelical

churches into greater social and political involvement for the sake of promoting human dignity and greater justice in the world. See, for example, the chapter in Marshall and Van Saanen (2007) which narrates the impact of Warren's book on some evangelical mega-churches in the United States.

18 For an analysis of the role of Christian churches in welfare provision in Britain, see Prochaska (2006).

19 See also the project on *Evangelical Christianity and Democracy in the Global South*, currently being published in a series by Oxford University Press. The first volume, on Latin America, is edited by Paul Freston, and the second, on Africa, by Terence Roger.

20 The short narrative is drawn from Borer's book *Challenging the State: Churches and Political Actors in South Africa* (1998). See also Johnston (1994) and Walshe (1995) for an analysis of the Church's resistance to apartheid.

21 Ian Linden, private communication.

22 See Berryman (1995), Brockman (1989), De Broucker (1979) and MacLean (1999) on the struggles for democracy and justice in El Salvador and Brazil, and the lives of Oscar Romero and Helder Camara.

23 See Clements (1995) and Plant (2004) for a discussion of the Barmen Declaration and the role of Bonhoeffer and Barth in the Church's resistance to Nazism.

24 For the role of the Catholic Church against the Pinochet regime, see Cavanaugh (1998), and in the democratic transition in the Philippines, see Moreno (2007).

25 In a review of books about conflict resolution in Africa, Copson (1997) observes that, more often than not, religion is portrayed as part of identity-based conflict and is systematically dismissed as a force for peace.

26 Talking about Rosa Parks who refused to sit at the back of the bus, an action which generated the US civil rights movement, Thomas (2005, pp. 236–8) writes that such action was not an act of heroic individualism, but the result of years of moral formation at her African Methodist Episcopal Church.

27 Qutb was also a leading critic of Nasser's regime, which led to his imprisonment and execution. See Kepel (1994) for a discussion of Qutb's links with movements demanding the Islamization of Egypt. Qutb's writings continue to influence many present-day Islamist movements.

28 'Invite (all) to the Way of thy Lord with wisdom and beautiful preaching; and argue with them in ways that are best and most gracious: for thy Lord knoweth best, who have strayed from His Path, and who receive guidance' (16: 125). See Walker (1995).

29 For an analysis of the working of Da'wa groups in non-Muslim societies, see Poston (1992).

30 For an analysis of the dominant religious texts influencing Jama'at philosophy, see Metcalf (1993).

31 For further examples of the work of Da'wa organization in nation-state societies, see Piscatori's *Islam in a World of Nation-States* (1986).

32 'The Muslim world seen from the economic angle', article by Ashfaq Ahmad in *Islamic Herald* (Kuala Lumpur), 5, nos. 1 and 2, pp. 27–29 (1981), quoted in Eickelman and Piscatori (1996).

33 For details of the Foundation's programmes, see <http://www.hamdard-foundation.org/index.htm> (accessed November 2008).

34 For a detailed account of the Sanusiya order of Cyrenaica, see Evans-Pritchard (1949).

5 | Conflicts between Traditions

The previous chapter described how development activities, such as political advocacy for social change, provision of social services, and redistribution, lie at the heart of the Christian and Islamic traditions. This may have appeared to some as a puzzle. Surely, there are many examples where religion is not conducive to desirable development outcomes. When religious decrees prohibit women working outside the home; when different religious groups consider each other as enemies to be converted or killed; when women whose partners are HIV-positive are denied the use of contraception on moral grounds; when religious education teaches children to hate those who do not believe in the same religion – surely these are all cases where religion appears to be undermining basic human rights such as the right to dignified work, freedom from discrimination and hatred, and security from an easily preventable death?

There are indeed instances of conflicts between 'religion and development', or what we prefer to call conflicts between the religious and secular traditions regarding some aspects of their respective understandings of the 'good life', of what it means to live well together. This chapter discusses some of these conflicts. Its review of empirical examples of conflict reinforces the argument made earlier. Religions are not to be understood as unchanging belief systems but as dynamic traditions which are continuously searching for the best ways to embody their respective fundamental teachings into particular social, political, economic and cultural contexts. Religious traditions are thus not homogeneous. What Christianity or Islam is about – how it is lived – depends on the interpretation that Christians and Muslims, as individuals or groups, give to it, and it depends on which and whose interpretations prevail.

Methodist Christians have a different interpretation of what a 'just' war is about from Catholic Christians. Even within the Catholic Church, disagreement is the norm about 'just' war – some Catholics saw the British and American intervention in Iraq as just; for others it was radically unjust. Catholic married women will often have another interpretation of the 'justness' of the use of contraception than male clerics who define official Catholic teachings on sexuality. Disagreement in Islam is also the norm. Many practising Muslim women choose not to wear *hijab* because in their view the Islamic injunctions on piety are concerned with inculcating a code of behaviour that entails self-restraint, rather than with the actual act of covering the hair. Ulama from all dominant schools of thought argue otherwise.

Identifying the points of conflict between the religious and secular traditions on development issues involves several difficulties. A first difficulty is that the foundations of the secular tradition can often not be disentangled from its religious roots. If one conceives development as the striving for all societies to respect the rights inscribed in the Universal Declaration of Human Rights, given the religious foundation of the declaration, the secular conception of development appears merely as a religious-based conception shorn of its transcendental elements. A recent book entitled *A Secular Age* by Charles Taylor (2007) provides a historical narrative of the emergence of secular humanism. He argues that atheism, and secular humanism, was only possible because of transformations within the Christian religious tradition from the sixteenth century onwards. Hence, secular humanism cannot be understood without reference to its Christian roots.[1] So, the boundaries between what constitutes the secular tradition and the religious tradition, and how the two understand 'development' and what it means to live well together, are not clear, given the religious foundations of secular humanism.

A second difficulty with identifying areas of conflict between the secular and religious traditions relates to the choice of interpretation. Given the diversity of interpretations, how can one define what the Christian or Muslim traditions as such believe in, and how this conflicts with the secular tradition? A Moroccan Sufi woman will interpret how to live well according to Islam differently from an Iranian Shia imam, or an Afghan Sunni soldier differently from an Afghan Sunni female doctor. Who has the correct interpretation of Allah's message contained in the Qur'an and what it entails for one's life? The problem is reproduced in Christianity. Similarly, interpreting the secular tradition, as it bears on development issues, is subject to controversy, depending on which strand of development thought one follows – whether neo-liberalism, human development, human rights-based approach, human security, the Millennium Development Goals, post-modernist development thought . . . and there are many others. Thus, while some members of a tradition may see conflict between 'religion and development', others will see harmony.

Third is the difficulty of identifying the relevant conflicts, given the innumerable areas of human life where different traditions of thought may meet or conflict. Even within the single area of health, we could review a number of issues – such as vaccination, HIV/AIDS, maternal health and birth attendance, and reproductive health – where traditions conflict in some contexts and meet in others. For example, it has been reported that some clerics in Nigeria have prevented Muslim girls from being vaccinated against polio because the vaccine is believed to make them infertile;[2] while, in other contexts, the vaccination programme might even take place after a religious service next to the place of worship.

Given the above difficulties, we have chosen to limit our discussion to four areas where a secular vision of certain development issues has been popularly perceived to be in conflict with a religion-based understanding of these same issues. All four areas relate to the Millennium Development Goals. Women's reproductive rights have probably been one of the most frequently publicized tensions between 'religion and development'. The 1995 UN Conference on Women in Beijing witnessed a strong alliance between Vatican and Muslim clerics to oppose women's reproductive rights. The area of education has been another point of tension between different traditions. What religious traditions view as the purpose of education and an appropriate curriculum might not be in agreement with a secular view of education held by Western development agencies and international organizations – the particular case of the kind of education offered by Muslim religious schools, the madrasas, has especially received attention in development studies. The third area of significant contention is that of the place of religion in modern liberal democracies. The secular tradition is based on the proposition that religion ought to be kept within certain boundaries and should not interfere in the public sphere, a proposition which is not accepted by religious traditions. These conflicts have their roots in the fundamentally different epistemological foundations of religious traditions from those of the secular tradition of thought. Religions are based on truth and transcendence, from which everything else derives. The secular tradition, which has so far underpinned the social sciences and development studies, rests on radically different premises.

From the review of examples drawn from these four development areas, this chapter shows that, despite similarities, there remain differences between the secular and religious traditions on certain development issues. Neither ignoring these conflicts (and focusing instead on areas of agreement between traditions), nor discarding religion altogether, are desirable or workable solutions. Yet again these examples point to the need to understand religious traditions in their entirety and complexity, to recognize the critical role of interpretation within religious traditions and the contexts in which interpretations are conducted.

Women's reproductive rights

In April 2007, after a period of intense debate, the General Assembly of Amnesty International voted to end the organization's long neutral stance regarding abortion. From now on, Amnesty will actively campaign for women's right to have access to abortion when the pregnancy is a result of rape, incest, or violence, or when the woman's life or health is threatened. That decision spurred a wave of controversy within the religious groups which had so far supported Amnesty's work on human rights. Many felt that their membership of the organization had to be withdrawn as a consequence, for they wished to uphold the right to life of the foetus, regardless of the circumstances in which it was conceived.

Christian denominations disagree about when exactly human life starts. The Catholic tradition maintains that human life starts at the moment of the first division of the fertilized ovum, while other denominations maintain that life starts only with the implantation of the fertilized ovum in the womb – the 'morning after pill' is therefore seen as either a contraceptive by some Christians or as an abortive method by others. Some individual Christians may also disagree about the absolute prohibition of abortion. Some may come to the conclusion that abortion may be the only option left to resolve a desperate situation – such as a woman being gang raped by enemy soldiers – and some may regard the legalization of abortion as a lesser evil than unsafe backstreet abortions, which put the lives of both mother and child in danger. But this does not change the Christian tradition's stance regarding the sacredness of human life. Even if life has emerged because of evil such as rape, as the human being is the image of God, nothing can detract from the inherent dignity and immeasurable worth of human life.[3]

The Christian tradition believes that, like all created things and beings on earth, the human body has been given to humans for stewardship, and one does not have absolute self-ownership over one's body. Therefore, the woman's right to choose over her own body does not extend to the new human life growing in her. In cases where the mother's life is threatened by the pregnancy, termination may occur as a result of treatment to save the mother's life. This is known in Christian theology as the 'doctrine of double effect'; it is permissible to do harm if the harm occurs as an unintentional effect of promoting a good – the life of the foetus has not been violated intentionally.

Some female Christian theologians are increasingly questioning the position that the deliberate killing of an innocent human being can never be justified, however painful and difficult the context is. They advance the claim that in some exceptional circumstances, compassion for the woman's life should take precedence over the absolute right to life of the foetus. In an article published in the Catholic weekly *The Tablet* in October 2007, theologian Tina Beattie argues that a girl in a war-torn zone made pregnant through gang rape by the enemy is also 'among the most defenceless of all humans', like her unborn child. Raising her child may entail life-long humiliation, ostracism and abuse. She may become 'the prisoner of her own body' through the violence of men. Balancing equal right to a flourishing human life when the rights to life of two human beings are incompatible is not easy. And women should be given a voice as to how to solve that moral dilemma, which affects their lives in a unique way.

Beattie argues that the Catholic Church's exclusive male hierarchy and power often taints its moral pronouncements in matters of women's reproductive rights. The male Catholic leadership recognizes that 'there are situations of acute poverty, anxiety or frustration in which the struggle to make ends meet, the presence of unbearable pain, or instances of violence, especially against women, make the choice to defend and promote life so demanding as sometimes to reach the point of heroism' (*Evangelium Vitae*, paragraph 11). It is easy, however, for men to require heroic actions from women when they will never have to face such circumstances themselves.

Within the Islamic tradition, abortion is discouraged but is not forbidden as long as it is carried out within 120 days of the start of the pregnancy. The majority of Muslim schools of thought divide the development of the foetus into two stages: the first 120 days, and the remaining period before childbirth. The Qur'an has also described the process of foetal development, which progresses through stages of differentiation and growth:

> Man We did create from a quintessence [of clay]; then We placed him as [a drop of] sperm in a place of rest, firmly fixed; then We made the sperm into a clot of congealed blood; then of that clot We made a [foetus] lump; then We made out of that lump bones and clothed the bones with flesh; then We developed out of it another creature. So blessed by God the Best to create! (23: 12–14).

It is thus widely permissible, though not encouraged, within Islam to have an abortion for valid reasons during the first stage. These reasons are primarily of a medical order, such as threats to the life of the mother and the strong likelihood of the child being born with abnormalities. Out of the four dominant schools of thought in Islam, Hanafi scholars, who comprised the majority of orthodox Muslims in later centuries, permitted abortion up to the end of the fourth month. According to them, a pregnant woman could have an abortion without her husband's permission, but she should have reasonable grounds for this act (Brockopp, 2003). The Islamic scholarship is extremely strict about the 120 days period, as it is on this day that the angel responsible for the womb blows the breath of life into the lifeless foetus. After the stage of the foetus being endowed with a soul, abortion is prohibited completely except where it is imperative to save the mother's life (al-Akiti, 2004).

Many Shafi'i and Hanbali scholars, on the other hand, agree with the Hanafis in tolerating the practice of abortion, some putting an upper limit of forty days, others eighty or 120 days. The last school of thought, the Maliki jurists, is divided between those who view abortion as completely forbidden and those who disapprove of abortion without a valid reason (Brockopp, 2003). Broadly, their view is that when the semen settles in the womb, it is expected to develop into a living baby and should not be disturbed by anyone. Thus although the right of abortion is recognized by the majority of Islamic scholars, differences of opinion remain.

On the issue of women's right to abortion, the Christian and Muslim traditions seem to be in conflict, though in varying degrees of emphasis, with the secular tradition, especially when a secular vision of the world is coupled with a liberal one – that is, when the prevailing tradition of thought in a given society holds that religion should not influence decisions in the public sphere and that society should be based on the idea of individual freedom. Even if women theologians were given equal voices to develop religious teaching binding the Christian and Muslim communities, one could speculatively conclude that the likely outcome would be a compassionate compromise recognizing abortion as a lesser evil in some very exceptional circumstances, and questioning the imposition of 'heroism' on women by force of law through criminalizing abortion. But the fundamental agreement of both religious traditions, that all human life belongs to God, is in conflict with the secular liberal tradition which holds that human beings are their own masters and that women are owners of their bodies, and the potential life within.

While abortion is a permanent source of conflict between the religious and secular liberal traditions, there is more hope for common ground on the issue of contraception, which has been highly controversial in the context of HIV/AIDS prevention. Most Christian denominations allow for family planning methods other than natural. The Catholic Church remains notoriously opposed to artificial contraception, on the grounds that 'every matrimonial act must remain open to the transmission of life. To destroy even partially the significance of intercourse and its end is contradictory to the plan of God and to his will' (*Humanae Vitae*, paragraph 14).[4] No papal statement has been as controversial. The promulgation of the encyclical *Humanae Vitae* by Paul VI in 1968 created a fury among the Catholic laity and put in question the authority of the Church in binding lay faithful. The history of the encyclical explains why (Keely, 1994; Stourton, 1998).

During the Second Vatican Council (which will be discussed in detail in the next chapter), a commission was set up to discuss the traditional stance of the Church on contraception in the light of the changes that modern society has brought about. The commission included not only bishops and male theologians but also lay physicians and married lay women and men. After surveying more than 3,000 Catholic couples, and three years of discussion, the Commission concluded that using artificial birth control methods was as legitimate as natural ones. Despite this overwhelming support (only 7 out of the 72 members of the Commission opposed artificial contraception) the Pope rejected the conclusion in order to follow the advice of the opposing minority led by a conservative Italian cardinal, Alfredo Ottaviani. This case exemplifies how a minority within a religious community can impose its own interpretation of what it means to live well according to God's commands on the majority through power and authority. Religious traditions, in so far as they are composed of human beings and the institutions they create, are not immune from the disruptive effects of abuses of power and authority that characterize non-religious institutions.

The papacy of John Paul II has reinforced the traditional ban on artificial contraception on the basis of his theology of the body, described in *Love and Responsibility*.[5] For Wotjyla, human sexuality has both a procreative and a unitive dimension. A sexual act which denies one of the two violates the dignity of the person (who is a unity of body and spirit). Given that spousal love has to be lived responsibly, and that welcoming new life ought not to be left to chance but deliberated between the spouses on an equal footing, contraception is needed. However, Wotjyla defends the ban on artificial contraception because it allows one spouse to control unilaterally the procreative dimension of the matrimonial act, and it lacks the discipline of abstinence, which he sees as formative of self-giving love.

The reality of many couples can be quite distant from an ideal situation of love, equality and respect. If a woman suffers from domestic violence at the hands of her alcoholic husband, banning artificial contraception could be seen as furthering her exploitation and abuse. Or if her husband has been unfaithful and contracted HIV/AIDS, the prohibition of the use of a condom could be seen as a death warrant for the woman.

Not all Catholics agree with the Pope's treatment of sexuality and spousal love. Many priests and bishops adopt a pastoral approach, letting the conscience of the spouses judge whether using artificial contraception in their conjugal context was violating God's love and disrespectful of the other person's body – a position paradoxically reinstated in John Paul II's encyclical *Veritatis Splendor* in 1993, which affirms the 'imperative character' of the judgment of conscience (paragraph 60).[6]

Even within the official Catholic teaching on contraception, moral theologians are now justifying the use of condoms when one spouse is HIV-positive, following the doctrine of double effect, which is central to Catholic moral theology. The condom is used to protect the woman's life; the fact that the matrimonial act remains close to procreation is an unintended side effect. At the grassroots level, Catholic groups are urging a more pastoral approach to the epidemics. The NGO of the Catholic Church of England and Wales,

CAFOD, took an explicit position on the issue in January 2005, and saw the distribution of condoms as a pastoral response when it is beyond the person's reach to be faithful or abstain – for example, people forced into sex work to survive given the lack of alternative employment opportunities.[7]

The Islamic tradition, though more open to the use of contraption, shares similar underlying precepts and concerns. Fertility is highly prized in Islam and children are considered a gift of God to bring 'joy to our eyes' (25: 74). The stress Islam places on the value of life is visible in the verse in the Qur'an that states that God 'breathed (his) own spirit' into Adam and distinguished him from the rest of God's creatures (15: 29) (Brockopp, 2003). In addition, many Muslim scholars discourage the use of contraception on economic grounds: 'There is no creeping being on earth but that upon God is its sustenance' (11: 6). Islamic clerics in many mosques often draw on this verse to justify the inappropriateness of family planning. Further, they disapprove of contraception for fear that it may encourage pre-marital and extra-marital sex (Paz, 2007). Finally, because of the belief that life is eventually in the hands of God, they argue that no contraception can prevent a conception that is destined to happen: while approving the use of withdrawal technique to avert conception, Prophet Mohammad explained, 'You do not have to hesitate, for God has predestined what is to be created until the judgement day.'

Contraception has a long history in Islam. Ibn Sina (981–1037), known as Avicenna in Western scholarship,[8] discusses twenty different substances used for birth control. In his view, Islam allows the use of contraception on many grounds: reasons of health, economics, and improving the quality of offspring. The most detailed analysis of Islamic permission of contraception was made by the prominent scholar within the Shafi'i school of thought, Al-Ghazali (1058–1111), who accepted contraception if the motive for the act is any of these: (1) to avoid financial hardship and embarrassment; (2) a desire to preserve a woman's beauty or her health, or save her life; (3) avoidance of other domestic problems caused by a large family (Shaikh, 2003). More recently, Deoband,[9] a leading Islamic seminary which gave rise to the Deobandi tradition in Islam, issued a *fatwa* ('religious decree') in 2008 that allowed the use of contraceptives by Muslims in order to keep a gap between two children and to ensure that 'the children are properly nourished'.[10]

Fazlur Rahman, a leading Islamic scholar, further elaborates this position. He argues that God has shared responsibility for providence with us and that He has gifted us with reason to see problems and do something sensible about them. In Islam, the sexual act is thus not merely a means of procreation. To have sexual intercourse for pleasure is not forbidden; what is required is that it be conducted within marital relationships, that the use of contraception is the result of mutual consent of the partners, and that the methods chosen are not irreversible.

In practice at the grassroots, however, in many mosque networks in Muslim countries, local preachers, who are not trained in Islamic scholarship, encourage the idea of procreation as the preferred option and denounce family planning measures – a message which can have dangerous consequences among Muslim communities in countries with a high prevalence of HIV/AIDS. The resistance to the HIV/AIDS prevention programme of the Islamic Medical Association of Uganda (IMAU) by ulama in madrasas is revealing of this tension. For over a year the ulama refused to give the Association permission to promote the use of condoms among madrasa students as a means to prevent HIV/AIDS, fearing this would promote sex outside marriage (Paz, 2007). The ulama instead preferred other preventive measures: abstain from sex or have sex only within marriage. This clear divide in the reasoning of the Islamic scholars and the actual practice of ulama in the mosques highlights the importance of the role of religious interpreters and theological training in shaping the practical manifestations of religious precepts and teachings. How a religious text is interpreted and permeates society often depends on who within the religious tradition exercises authority over its interpretation. This is something that development practitioners who work from within the secular tradition should recognize when engaging with religion. Apparent conflicts between 'religion and development' could sometimes be mitigated when due attention is given to how a religious tradition interprets its fundamentals, and to the power dynamics which operate within each religious tradition.

Education

Our discussion of Christian mission work in the previous chapter noted its considerable contribution to the education system in the colonized countries. Before the state took over the education system at independence, a large number of schools in the colonized world were faith-based and run by missionaries. While the education effort had initially a strong religious component (reading and writing was important so that people could read the Bible or the Qur'an), it soon evolved to include core skills for children to become empowered citizens. In some contexts, such as tribal areas in India, missionaries saw literacy, numeracy and vocational skills as crucial in resisting the oppression of landlords, and in providing employment and sustainable economic development to the region.

Faith-based schools have recently received a lot of criticism from those advocating 'liberal education'. In the philosophy of education, the evolving debate has turned on the critique that faith-based schools are socially divisive and the breeding ground for intolerance.[11] The discussion has mainly taken place within the context of industrialized countries and has centred on the desirability of state funding for these schools, but it contains interesting insights for interventions by bilateral and multilateral agencies in religious schools in developing countries.

In 2001, the UK government decided to extend its funding of faith-based schools. This unleashed a series of critiques expressing the fear that such public support for faith-based schools would be a threat to social cohesion, for children would no longer mix with people from other faiths and cultures. They would be confined among their peers and not learn to live together with people from different backgrounds. In his review of these critiques, Short (2002) argues that faith-based schools are not *per se* an instrument of social divisiveness. He bases his argument on two grounds. First, social cohesion depends more on what children learn than whether the school is faith-based or not. It is the content of the school curriculum that makes pupils tolerant or prejudiced towards others. Second, he contends, tolerance towards other groups and knowledge of different ways of life does not stem only from mere interaction with other groups but can also be nurtured through reading about other cultures, and media exposure to them. Educational research has shown that there is no link between multicultural interpersonal contact and the reduction of prejudice. Often, faith schools are set up precisely to counteract racial and religious discrimination towards ethnic and religious minorities, and to offer an escape from the institutional racism of the state educational system.[12] Short concludes that, given that it is the content of the school curriculum which makes pupils tolerant or prejudiced towards others, the proper terms of debate should not be as much about government funding as about control of the curriculum.

This account, however, of faith-based education as being conducive to autonomy and social cohesion may not represent the reality of *all* faith schools. Burtonwood (2003) makes the point that the liberal support for faith-based education only applies to one particular strand of faith schools, what he calls the 'moderate' version. What attracts large sections of faith communities is the 'strong' version, which he defines as one that aims at inculcating in children a strong distinct identity from the rest of society throughout their lives. Moderate versions, in contrast, educate pupils in one particular tradition, while equipping them with the tools to examine critically what they have learned and design their own conception of the good life when they reach maturity.

Whereas the central tenets of liberal education – autonomy and critical examination – are wholly at ease within moderate versions of faith schools, Burtonwood argues that it is difficult to make the aims of liberal education compatible with strong versions of faith schools, for their goal is simply to reproduce the vision of the good life of the religious group, and they do not allow pupils to examine their tradition critically. Could the liberal defence of faith-based education be extended to Christian schools which teach creationist science and women's subordination to men, or to Muslim schools which teach every subject from the perspective of the Qur'an and which, according to their critics, do not allow for critical thinking among various possible interpretations of divine revelation?[13]

According to Burtonwood, the strong version of faith schools is precisely what attracts some members of faith communities because what they value most is a sense of belonging and identity that separates them from others. Their vision of education endorses the value of belonging and not that of critical autonomy. He contends that one must recognize that the choice between these two goods, the qualities of community that they bring to children on the one hand and autonomy on the other, is often tragic: that is, it is difficult to pursue these two goods at the same time. The right of parents to sustain their way of life and the right of liberal states to educate children as autonomous citizens may conflict. When they conflict, there is little possibility of resolution, only compromises on both sides. This is particularly manifest in the case of madrasas.

The importance of education and the study and transmission of religious teachings have always been at the heart of the Islamic tradition. Islam is a religion of the Book and of religious commentary. Most Muslims regard religious study as a form of worship in its own right. The very first verse of the Qur'an revealed to the Prophet Mohammad emphasized: 'Read! And your Lord is most generous, who has taught by the pen' (96: 3–4). Every Muslim is required to acquire a basic knowledge of God's words and injunctions as revealed in the Qur'an, the words and the deeds of the Prophet Mohammad. From earliest times, the transmission of Islam from teacher to disciple also created the network of religious leaders who, in the absence of formal clergy and an institutionalized Church like that of Christianity, came to exercise religious authority in the Muslim community.

Central to Islamic learning has been the institution of the madrasa, which has continuously evolved in response to the changing political, social and economic realities. The madrasa system in South Asia provides a good illustration of this. During the Mughal rule in India, madrasas were establishments of higher learning that produced civil servants and judicial officials. The advent of the British Empire in the sub-continent posed serious challenges to the madrasa education system. The madrasas' financial support base disappeared as they traditionally relied on state patronage. Changes in the administration and economy introduced by the English East India Company meant that madrasa education lost its employment utility (Bano, 2007a). The result was that madrasa education became increasingly other-worldly. The rise of Deoband, the Islamic school of thought with the largest affiliation of madrasas in South Asia, was a consequence of this displacement of Muslims from political authority and public offices. Rather than focusing on capturing state power, it focused on developing the individual piety of believers as the best means to resist the colonial hegemony.

In addition to accommodating change in response to external factors, the madrasa education system has engaged in a constant attempt at internal intellectual reform of its curriculum. Historically, a continuing internal struggle has been evident within the madrasa tradition in South Asia to strike the right balance between the rationalist and traditionalist sciences (Robinson, 2007). At the time of the colonial takeover, the absorption of rationalist influences from Persia within leading madrasas in India, like Faranghi Mahal, was at its peak. The displacement of Muslim states by the colonial power did not thaw this process of internal reform but changed its direction from rationalist to traditional sciences as increasingly large numbers of ulama attributed the downfall of Muslim political power to its growing distance from true Islamic principles. Thus, reform progressively came to mean going back to the original Islamic texts rather than engaging with the secular and liberal traditions of thought (Robinson, 2007; Zaman, 1999).

In contrast to this embrace of internal reform, in many Muslim countries madrasas have actively resisted state-led attempts at curricular reforms. This resistance encompasses the tensions inherent in the religious and the secular notions of education and ideal learning. For the ulama, the pursuit of education is to discover God through better understanding of his texts, moral training, and the search for real truth. Education is thus not sought as a means of gaining employment. On the other hand, the modern state has argued that religious education is in itself insufficient for producing productive citizens. It should also enable children to learn modern subjects for vocational purposes. Rather than aiming to strengthen religious learning or to help the ulama gain higher learning of Islam, the state aspires to secularize and commercialize the madrasas. To the senior ulama this has always been offensive and continues to be so. The response of Mawlana Yusuf Ludhianawi, a leading Islamic scholar, to state-led attempts to reform the madrasa system in the 1970s was that the reformed curriculum would not produce men who 'combine the medieval and the modern . . . [rather], the products of such a system would be useless equally for religion and the world'. What the reforms seek to create are not 'ulama' but 'only loyal government servants' (quoted in Zaman, 1999). This kind of response is still widespread today.

Thus, the challenge to reform rests in the very conception of the idea and purpose of knowledge. The result is that most reform attempts by government and international development agencies have failed, and in some cases created hostility between the madrasa leadership and the state. The madrasa leadership in Pakistan, for instance, has actively resisted the USA-sponsored madrasa reform programme initiated by the state after September 11. The five state-recognized *wafaqs* (madrasa boards) in Pakistan strongly advised their members against joining the reform programme. The result is that, five years later, no more than a couple of hundred of the 16,000 registered madrasas in Pakistan have accepted the reform package (Bano, 2007b).

From this discussion, it is clear that the madrasa education system in Islam has its own underlying philosophy of the idea of knowledge. What we observe in the above debate is the clear divergence of views regarding the purpose of education in society between the religious and secular traditions, and that in response to the changing surrounding realities, madrasas either adapt, isolate themselves, or radicalize. The above discussion also demonstrates that the madrasa system is not a static but a constantly evolving institution, which has been shaped by multiple influences including 'religious reform, the ascent of the West, nationalism, the developmentalist state, and mass education' (Hefner and Zaman, 2007). The failure of secular development agencies to recognize this internal dynamic of change – with the result that madrasas are simply regarded as places of learning to be reformed in line with the secular tradition's conception of knowledge – is highly problematic. The conflict surrounding madrasa reform probably illustrates most acutely the need for a deeper mutual understanding between the secular and religious traditions.

Democracy

Tony Blair's press secretary, Alastair Campbell, once said that the Blair government 'didn't do God'. Discussing this statement in a lecture at Westminster Cathedral in London in April 2008, Tony Blair explains the following:[14]

> One of the oddest questions I get asked in interviews is: Is faith important to your politics? It's like asking someone whether their health is important to them or their family. If you are someone 'of faith' it is the focal point of belief in your life. There is no conceivable way that it wouldn't affect your politics. But there is a reason why my former press secretary, Alastair Campbell, once famously said 'We don't do God'. In our culture, here in Britain and in many other parts of Europe, to admit to having faith leads to a whole series of suppositions, none of which are very helpful to the practising politician. Second, there is an assumption that before you take a decision, you engage in some slightly cultish interaction with your religion – 'So, God, tell me what you think of City Academies or Health Service Reform or nuclear power?' i.e. people assume that your religion makes you act, as a leader, at the promptings of an inscrutable deity, free from reason rather than in accordance with it. Third, you want to impose your religious faith on others. Fourth, you are pretending to be better than the next person. And finally and worst of all, that you are somehow messianically trying to co-opt God to bestow a divine legitimacy on your politics. So when Alastair said it, he didn't mean politicians shouldn't have faith; just that it was always a packet of trouble to talk about it.

Although Britain 'does not do God in politics', the political space is regularly filled with the interventions of religious leaders on policy matters, such as the treatment of immigrants and refugees, foreign policy, scientific research and education. Moreover, the faith of political leaders cannot be separated from their public commitments, for it bears on their values. Tony Blair acknowledges that it is inconceivable to think that the faith of a politician will not affect his or her politics. Democratic debate is permeated by voices that base their views on religious traditions. And many public actions in democracies are faith-based. In his lecture, Tony Blair singled out the Jubilee Campaign for debt relief, the presence of faith communities in the care of the sick and marginalized, and their struggle against oppressive regimes such as apartheid South Africa. He argues that faith is a great force for good in the world and that it only turns out problematic 'when it becomes a way of denigrating those who do not share it, as somehow lesser human beings'.

'Speaking from faith in democracy' contains many challenges (Chaplin, 2007).[15] The predominant secular view is that the duties of being a citizen of a state take precedence over duties entailed by religious affiliation. For Muslims and Christians, though, performing the duties of the Qur'an or the Bible takes precedence over the duties of state citizenship if the two are not compatible. Living a good British citizen's life, and a good Christian or Muslim life, do not necessarily always go hand in hand (Rosenblum, 2000). How liberal democracies accommodate religion may sometimes conflict with the way religious traditions themselves conceive their place in democratic politics.

Broadly, in a liberal democracy, the state abides by the principle of neutrality: that is, the state should not impose on its citizens a particular vision of the good. It should remain neutral in defining what the good life is, and should limit itself to providing the resources people need to live a life of their own choosing (Kraut, 1999; Wall, 1998). A liberal democracy cannot limit the freedom of adults to pursue what they consider as good, provided that their actions do not prevent other people from pursuing their conception of the good and living a life of their own choosing.

John Rawls's theory of justice has been by far the most influential recent political theory for Western liberal democracies.[16] It is based on the assumption that, in liberal democracies, citizens have different, incommensurable and irreconcilable conceptions of the good. The goal of Rawls's political liberalism is to find a political conception of justice which people with different conceptions of the good can endorse, a political conception that will be an overlapping consensus between these different conceptions. Using the device of the original position where people are under a veil of ignorance, that is, 'the parties [in the original position] are not allowed to know the social position of those they represent, or the particular comprehensive doctrine of the person each represents' (1993, p. 24), Rawls establishes a list of primary goods, goods which are necessary for people to conceive and pursue, whatever conceptions of the good and of justice they may hold.[17] The role of the state is to provide these primary goods so that each individual is able to pursue his/her chosen conception of the good life.

The political philosopher Martha Nussbaum has been one of the most outspoken proponents of political liberalism in the context of development studies. She argues that the role of governments is to provide some central human capabilities, like Rawls's primary goods. These are the necessary means that people need to pursue whatever conception of the good they choose to adopt. The role of the government is not to advocate any particular conception of the good life for its citizens (Nussbaum, 2000).

Religious traditions do not sit at ease with political liberalism for they are based on a particular conception of good living. Believers are not always prepared to leave behind their religious-based conception of the good life and good society when they enter the public space. When a Christian MP is elected, should s/he represent the views of the church or the views of his/her constituency as a whole? Can s/he strive to be in Rawls's original position when making laws, forget who s/he is and make decisions as if s/he could be Muslim, atheist or agnostic? Some Catholic politicians hold the view that, even if they are personally against abortion, it is their duty to represent the electorate who might be in favour of abortion, and not the position of the church to which they belong. But other Catholic politicians and the Catholic hierarchy think otherwise. Some bishops have sometimes threatened Catholic members of Parliament with excommunication if they voted in favour of laws that would facilitate abortion.

Liberal political theory thus assumes that liberal democracies should make laws which anyone, whatever their conception of the good, can accept. It should never impose a particular view on the whole of society. In that respect, the Bush government decision not to give public funding to organizations that promote abortion violates the fundamental principle of a neutralist liberal democracy. The essence of liberal democracies appears to conflict with the essence of a religious tradition: to live and embody in social practices its fundamental teachings in all spheres of life.

This pessimistic evaluation of the accommodation of religion in liberal democracies rests on the assumption that the role of the state is to be neutral and that its role is limited to providing the conditions for people to pursue whatever they see fit, provided they do not infringe on other's people's pursuit of their own conception of the good. Not all conceptions of liberal democracy subscribe to a neutralist standpoint, however – and not until the publication of Rawls's *Theory of Justice* in 1971 did the claim that the state should be neutral become widely adopted. A large number of democratic theorists still subscribe to what is known as a 'perfectionist' conception of political authority, which affirms that the democratic state cannot remain neutral and refrain from advancing a particular conception of the good life and the good society through its public policies. For example, when a non-discrimination law is voted, the law is based on an implicit recognition that the fundamental equality between human beings is constitutive of a good society.[18]

For some philosophers and theologians, there is a fundamental consistency between the Christian and liberal democratic traditions, for modern liberal democracy has Christian roots.[19] Chaplin (2007) summarizes five core principles of democracy which emerged, among other influences, from a prior articulation in Christian thought.[20] First, the principle of equality, that all human beings are equal in front of the law, stems from the theological understanding of each human being made in the image of God, and hence the radical equality of all in the Judeo-Christian tradition. Second, the principle of freedom and non-coercion originates in the biblical freedom of men and women in front of God (God leaves them free to disobey divine commands). The rights to religious freedom and freedom of conscience were the product of Christianity and not secularism. Third, the principle of justice guiding relations among humans also proceeds from biblical social and political thought. The debt relief campaign in 2000, the Jubilee Campaign, was taken straight from Old Testament teaching. Fourth, the principle of non-absolute state authority relies on a theological conception of temporal political authority submitted to God. This means that government authority is to be limited by other sources, such as civil society association, which are equally submitted to God. Finally, the principle of accountability derives from the four other principles. Human beings have the duty to check whether government actions are compatible with equality, justice, freedom and non-arbitrariness; and, reciprocally, government has a duty to be accountable to its citizens. The role played by churches in supporting democratization in many countries, as described in the previous chapter, is evidence of this intrinsic relationship between Christianity and democracy. Democracy is the political system which accords most respect to the dignity of the human person and her freedom as created by God.

That the state relies on a perfectionist conception of the good, that is, that the state is committed to the above principles as constitutive of what a good society is about, does not entail perfect agreement among citizens. Even if all agree on these fundamental principles of good living – equality, freedom, justice, restricted political authority and accountability – there remain large areas of disagreement. The debates over abortion and unrestricted capital flows, for example, demonstrate that commitment to the above principles does not lead to universal agreement about what decision a democratic state should make in these areas (Chaplin, 2007).

Disagreements lie at the heart of democratic decision-making and religious traditions. All, whether believers or not, should enter the democratic public space and give reasons for their positions in a way that other traditions can understand, and possibly accept. There might be cases where mutual acceptance cannot be achieved, where there is an inherent incompatibility between different positions. The democratic challenge is how to make workable policies in a context of disagreement. There is no solution except an open dialogue between different positions in an environment of mutual respect, tolerance, and understanding of divergent views. Thus again, when conflicts arise between the secular and religious traditions, better knowledge of each other, and recognition of internal dynamics of change, is often, if not always, the most suitable strategy to mitigate conflicts.

One has to note that there is no consensus in the Christian tradition as to whether democratic engagement is the best route to take for Christians to live out their commitments in the public space. The theologian Stanley Hauerwas has been one of the most vocal critics of Christian democratic engagement. He argues that liberal democracy is corrupted by the values of individualism and capitalism, which are incompatible with the gospel values of community and solidarity. According to him and his followers, the task for

Christians is to constitute radical communities where the values of the Gospel are fully embodied in social practices.[21]

The debate on democracy and the exercise of individual choice, and its relationship with religion, becomes more complex in Islam given the limited democratic space visible in the majority of Muslim countries. In the last three decades the world has witnessed a major shift towards democratic norms of governance. Since 1974, the number of democracies in Eastern Europe and the former Soviet Union has gone up from none to 19; in Latin America and the Caribbean, 30 of the 33 states have become democracies; and in sub-Saharan Africa the number of democracies has increased from 3 to 19, about two-fifths of the 48 states. Only in the Middle East and North Africa has democracy failed to take hold (Diamond *et al.*, 2003). The 19 states of the Middle East have by far the lowest average levels of political freedom. On the 7-point combined Freedom House scale of political rights and civil liberties, with 1 being most free and 7 least free, they score on average 5.53 (*ibid.*).

The failure of democratic institutions to flourish in many Muslim societies has led over time to the widespread academic position that Islam and democracy are incompatible. Abu Al-Ala al-Maududi, a leading Islamic thinker, argues that the political system of Islam has been based on three principles: *tawheed* ('unity of God'), *risalat* ('prophethood') and *khilafat* ('caliphate'). He maintains that it is difficult to appreciate different aspects of the Islamic polity without fully understanding these principles (Kramer, 1997; Maududi, 1967).[22]

All schools of thought within Islam agree that acceptance of *tawheed* is the core concept of Islam. Although it may be expressed in many different ways, it is simply defined as 'the conviction and witnessing that "there is no God but God"' and the consequence of this is that at 'the core of the Islamic religious experience, therefore, stands God Who is unique and Whose will is the imperative and guide for all men's lives'. Building on this, Muslim political thought affirms that there can be only one sovereign and that is God (Maududi, 1967).

Critics argue that *tawheed* makes it impossible for Islam to be compatible with democracy because the concept of sovereignty of people, central to democracy, conflicts with the sovereignty of God. Muslim intellectuals like Maududi point out that this does not imply that Islam rejects the idea of a democratic political system; rather, it demands that the system be framed within the worldview of *tawheed.* He argues that in order to understand the significance of *tawheed* for democracy it is important to understand fully the notion of *khalifa* (God's agents on earth). In Maududi's view the association of the notion of the caliphate with monarchical forms of government formation is a misrepresentation of true Islamic principles. Sections of the Qur'an can be interpreted to identify human beings in general as God's agents on this earth (Esposito and Voll, 1996). Thus, humans are all *khalifas,* and it is up to them mutually to select one of their number to lead the others in establishing a society in line with divine wisdom. Such a notion of *khalifa* brings the practice of the caliphate very close to the idea of democracy. Scholars supporting this line of reasoning place much emphasis on utilizing the longstanding Islamic concepts of consultation (*shurah*), consensus (*ijma*) and independent interpretive judgements (*ijtihad*) in the process of state formation in Muslim countries.

These scholars thus argue that Islam and democracy are indeed compatible – taking the debate away from those who consider democracy an alien system, thus prioritizing divine obedience over popular sovereignty and God's law over the man-made laws framed by elected legislative bodies. An increasing number of intellectuals in societies as diverse as Egypt, Jordan, Iran, Turkey, Indonesia and Malaysia are now engaged in translating the values of pluralism, tolerance and civic participation, which in their view are central to Islam, within the political systems of Muslim countries. Fazlur Rahman (1986), a leading Islamic reformist thinker, argues: 'The participatory association of the ummah (the Muslim community) through directly ascertaining the will of the ummah in the political and legislative decisions affecting the life of the community can neither be rejected nor postponed. Those who advocate such a course of action are wittingly or unwittingly guilty of rendering Islam null and void.' Ayatullah Baqir al-Sadr (1982) placed similar emphasis on consultation: 'The people, being the vicegerents of Allah, have a general right to dispose of their affairs on the basis of the principle of consultation.' According to some scholars, such as Ansari (2006), Iran is leading the way in demonstrating this compatibility between Islam and democracy through a mixture of elite and mass politics.

On similar lines, Soroush argues that the idea of an autocratic God who ignores human freedom is a reflection of an autocratic political system (Ansari, 2006). This shows that the way a religious tradition interprets its fundamentals is never free from political influences and the interests of powerful actors. Islam is not alien to the idea of consultation in government formation. Thus, it predetermines the desirable goals for a society, whereby they should be shaped in line with Islamic principles, instead of leaving the identification of those goals to the free choice of individuals. Within these boundaries, people are free to run the affairs of the state as they wish.

Another noticeable dimension of the relationship between Islam and democracy is that many Islamic revolutionary movements have been quite successful in electoral politics. The Islamic Revolution that overthrew the Iranian monarchy in 1979 was one of the first popular revolutions against a modern authoritarian political system in the final quarter of the twentieth century. In the early 1990s, another Islamic movement, the Islamic Salvation Front (FIS), was suppressed when it dramatically challenged the authoritarian regime of the National Liberation Front (FLN) in Algeria after the government had been forced through international pressure to allow open elections. One of the most recent examples of Islamic political movements within electoral politics is the success of Hamas in Palestine. This, however, poses another major dilemma for secular development planners, who fear that a democratic system under control of religious groups may propagate a religious vision of state and society. This, in their view, is incompatible with a liberal secular conception of democracy, which leaves individuals free to define the desirable ends that societies should pursue, and which kind of society they should live in, provided that no explicit reference to God is made.

Even if each religious tradition contains a wide diversity of opinions about how democracies should best accommodate religion within their midst, secular and religious traditions have conflicting views about what the role of religion should be in the public space. These conflicts have to be lived with, and dismissing religion because of these conflicts often only contributes to fuelling conflicts, as the experiences of Algeria and Palestine have testified.

Epistemology

Most research within development studies is based on the belief that no moral judgment should be made on the reality under study: in other words, that the social sciences can be free of normative standpoints. The role of the social sciences is to explain social phenomena – for example, how gender relations affect women's wellbeing, how power affects redistribution, how religion affects people's motivations and actions – without the social scientist introducing his/her opinions on the matter.

One methodology for analysing the world in the social sciences has been positivism, which is based on observing and collecting data.[23] This methodology is the dominant one in economics, and is expressed for example in the econometric studies which analyse the relationship between religion and development. In their review of the literature on economics and religion, Paul Jackson and Christiane Fleischer (2007) summarize many of these econometric studies, such as the impact of Islam on economic growth and unemployment, or the influence of Protestantism on labour productivity, or the effect of the belief in an afterlife on charitable giving.

This positivist methodology has come under considerable criticism. The political philosopher Charles Taylor (1985) has been one of the foremost critics of the way positivist social science has analysed reality. He argues that social sciences 'need to go beyond the bounds of a science based on verification to one which would study the inter-subjective and common meanings embedded in social reality' (Taylor, 1985, p. 52) – for social reality is not constituted by brute data but by social practices and institutions, and the meanings these have for participants. To be a human agent is to experience one's social reality in terms of such meanings. Therefore, social reality is to be *interpreted* in order to be understood.

It is the hermeneutical approach in philosophy (Gadamer, 1976; Ricoeur, 1981) that has brought to the fore the importance of interpretation for understanding social reality. Kanbur and Shaffer (2007, p. 185) define hermeneutics as 'the interpretative understanding of intersubjective meanings'. This means that 'first, understanding entails critical assessment of given beliefs and perceptions involving some underlying conception of truth or validity; and second, emancipation, enlightenment or empowerment is an essential part of the process of inquiry' (*ibid.*).

According to the hermeneutic approach, the purpose of research is to uncover the underlying conception of truth behind people's beliefs and the meanings that people give to their actions. For example, the researcher will observe a difference between female and male literacy in some parts of the world, and will try to interpret the meaning that women themselves give to their poor educational achievements (such as 'the place of a woman is at home and she does not need to be educated', or 'the woman should serve her husband

and he is the one who guides her, therefore it is sufficient for him to be educated'). By uncovering these meanings, the task of research is to validate these in the light of the conception of truth that gave rise to them. The women might base the meanings they give to their low educational status on their Christian or Muslim religion. Believing in God and accepting the authority of the Bible or the Qur'an might have given rise to the belief that women were subordinate to men. But is such a belief consistent with the truth as revealed in the religious texts and the theological interpretation of that truth?

Given that the religious traditions are built on a basic truth, a fundamental agreement – that there is no God but Allah and that Mohammad is his messenger for Muslims, and that there is no other God but the one revealed by his Messiah Jesus Christ for Christians – studying the social reality of religion requires a hermeneutical approach.

The hermeneutical approach in the social sciences highlights that it is impossible to escape value judgments. Even the positivist claim is based on the value judgment that it is possible to study the social reality in an empirical way, free of value judgments. The Harvard philosopher of science Hilary Putnam (1993, 2002) has long argued that the attempt to build a value-free social science has failed. The fact/value dichotomy, which attempts to disconnect scientific statements from value judgments and claims that the former are empirically verifiable and the latter unverifiable, is a fallacy. Facts and value judgments, descriptive and evaluative concerns, are deeply 'entangled'.

To go back to our example of women who refuse to be educated on the grounds of religious teachings, when a social scientist describes this social phenomenon, it is difficult for him or her to understand it without looking at the meanings that these women give to their non-educated status. The description of the 'fact' that women are illiterate is linked to the value judgements that these women have regarding education. And one could add that the very enterprise of looking at these women's illiteracy is made under the implicit value judgement that illiteracy is a social bad and that it is better for women to be educated. It is thus difficult to understand social phenomena without looking at the meanings that social actors give to their actions. The task of the social scientist is therefore to uncover these meanings that people ascribe to their actions on the basis of their underlying conception of what is good. An example of this different epistemological approach to the study of religion in development studies is given in the context of gender in the next chapter, at the end of the 'liberation theology' section.

A difficulty for the social sciences in studying religion is that of the transcendental nature of the conception of the good to which religious traditions adhere. The Christian and Muslim traditions believe that there is a higher reality, which transcends earthly human realities. This entails that the earthly life is not absolute for the believer, for s/he will find fullness of life in sharing the life of God/Allah after death. Life on earth is believed to be only the first phase of a journey that includes a life hereafter, taken to be eternal. This transcendental understanding of the good, and of what a good life in society may be, is a source of potential conflict with the secular tradition, which rules out such transcendental understanding. We related in Chapter 2 an example of a compensation scheme which failed to recognize this transcendental understanding – a displaced community was not compensated for the displacement of its religious site (Vandenberg, 1999).

That a religious tradition is entirely submitted to the basic truth of the existence of God does not entail that there can be no common ground between religious and secular traditions, and that they cannot understand each other. Both the Muslim and Christian traditions emphasize the importance of *reasoning*, and the possibility of reaching agreements despite divergent views. In 1998 Pope John Paul II issued an encyclical on the relationship between faith and reason. Its opening sentence states that 'faith and reason are like two wings on which the human spirit rises to the contemplation of truth'. The encyclical provides a forceful critique of the popularly held opinion that faith and reason cannot be reconciled: 'The Church remains profoundly convinced that faith and reason mutually support each other; each influences the other, as they offer to each other a purifying critique and a stimulus to pursue the search for deeper understanding' (*Fides et Ratio*, paragraph 100).[24]

Within the Islamic tradition, likewise, great emphasis is placed on the use of human reason. The very act of belief and discovering God is attributed to knowledge and reasoning: 'Only the knowledgeable of His slaves fear Allah' (Qur'an 35: 28). Islamic scholarship draws on two main sources: the Qur'an and the *Sunna*. The Qur'an maintains: 'We have indeed revealed to you the Book with the Truth, so that you may judge between mankind' (4: 105). The second source of knowledge is the record of the sayings and doings of the Prophet. The collective memory of these sayings (*Hadith*) and doings came to be known as the *Sunna*, the practices of the Prophet. The core of Islamic teaching was shaped in the first five centuries after the Revelation to Mohammad in 610 AD. To this date, the ulama use many of the texts written by the great Islamic scholars of the Middle Ages. This has led some to argue that Islamic scholarship rests on the unquestioned acceptance of archaic texts. Such critiques, however, ignore the complexity of Islamic scholarship. Islamic scholars do draw on old texts, but the use of reason is viewed as critical to the interpretation and reinterpretation of these texts. The very emergence and persistence of different Islamic sects rest on alternative interpretation of texts where scholars from each sect critically engage with reasoning put forward by scholars of other sects to defend a position. This process of argumentation and refutation – based on logical reasoning, formally referred to as *rad* – is critical to Islamic scholarship.

The basic difference between the Muslim and secular tradition is that Islam recommends the use of the intellect within the boundaries of core Islamic beliefs such as the five pillars of Islam. For example, Islamic scholars are free to deliberate on the various modes of conducting the prayers, but they cannot challenge the need for prayer. The Islamic school of thought known as Ash'aris holds the position that the human mind is unable to know how Allah judges morally responsible acts except by means of His messenger and inspired books. They set such limits on human reason and the power of the human intellect because 'caprice often wins out' over the intellect and human reason, and something might be judged to be good or bad on mere whim (Al-Misri, 1994). In contrast, modern Muslim scholars like Fazlur Rahman (1982, 2000), who have placed much emphasis on *ijtihad* and reinterpretation of Islamic texts, put higher emphasis on the need for reasoning while interpreting Islamic texts (the next chapter examines more closely the practice of *ijtihad* in Islam).

Summary

There are significant areas of encounter between the religious and secular traditions on development issues. Both are committed to human dignity, social justice, poverty relief, concern for the earth, equality and freedom. Yet, the religious traditions cannot be reduced to a mere humanistic moral framework where the concern for all the above issues is cut off from its divine or transcendental roots.

For religious traditions, respect for human dignity and all that it entails stems from the *imago dei*. Each human being has been created in the image of God. Life on earth is a journey which reaches its final stage in the meeting between the creatures and their Creator. The transcendental nature of the humanism of religious traditions, and the religious justification of the respect for human dignity, leads to unavoidable conflicts with secular humanism. Even if the two traditions agree on certain fundamentals (most of the Millennium Development Goals would fit in that category, and most human rights set out in the Universal Declaration of Human Rights constitute common ground between the religious and secular traditions), there remain areas of conflict.

First, despite variations between the Islamic and Christian traditions on abortion and women's reproductive rights, whereby one gives provision for it under certain circumstances, and the other completely rules it out, there is a consensus that abortion ought to be discouraged. The Christian tradition emphasizes particularly that humans do not have absolute self-ownership of their bodies, which means that women do not have decision-making power over the lives they carry, whatever the stage of foetal development. There is also diversity of opinion about the use of contraception and the desirability of welcoming children. Both religious traditions emphasize responsible childbearing, although maintaining that every child is a gift of God. We noted in that respect the role of religious leadership in Islam and the lack of religious education of ordinary imams, who sometimes sideline this notion of responsibility as an aspect of childbearing. In the case of Christianity, especially in its Catholic branch, we emphasized how the power of a minority could impose its vision on the whole body of the Church, which has had significant consequences in the case of HIV/AIDS epidemics.

Second, the task of education, according to religious traditions, is to nurture children within the framework of God's commands for humankind. Again, views diverge about how to educate children. For some, it is a matter of forming children into the conception of the good life that the religious tradition upholds, but leaving them the freedom to make up their own minds, for faith cannot be coerced but must be freely chosen and endorsed. For others, education is about making children reproduce the conception of the good life of the religious tradition throughout their lives. In contrast, according to the secular tradition, the purpose of education is to make children autonomous citizens, and exposing them to one single conception of the good life is not likely to lead to citizenship in a multicultural context.

Third, religious traditions have a specific vision of the good society which derives from their core teachings. This is problematic for the relationship between religion and political authority in liberal democracies. For those in the secular tradition who advocate the principle of state neutrality, religions seem incompatible with modern liberal democracies. Religious traditions sit more easily with those who hold the position that state neutrality is not achievable and that public policies are unavoidably advancing a particular conception of the good. Within that perspective, religious traditions and democracies share some common constitutive elements: freedom, equality, social justice, restricted political authority and accountability. The democratic challenge is to accommodate in the public space divergent conceptions of the good beyond these commonalities. The relationship between Islam and liberal democracies has also been subject to considerable disagreement within the Islamic tradition. Countering the dominant position that Islam and democracy are incompatible, a growing number of Islamic scholars demonstrate the importance of consultation and reasoning in establishing political structures in Muslim countries.

A final area of possible conflict that we have highlighted relates to the different epistemological foundations of religious and secular traditions. Social sciences demand neutrality and objectivity. Yet religious traditions conceive themselves as explicitly based on an idea of truth which displaces any claim to neutrality. Researching the role of religion in development is most adequately supported by the epistemological foundations of the hermeneutical approach, according to which the task of research is to interpret the meanings that people themselves give to their actions in the light of their idea of truth and conception of the good life.

That religious and secular traditions encounter conflicts over certain development issues does not mean that they are set to 'clash'. As this chapter has emphasized, each religious tradition contains a wide diversity of views, and each is dynamic, continually revising the most appropriate ways of embodying its fundamental truth within the context in which those who adhere to this truth live. Despite conflict, dialogue is possible, not for the sake of reaching agreement – for agreement on certain issues can never be achieved given the different transcendental premises of religious and secular traditions – but for the sake of generating greater understanding of each other in order to learn to live peacefully together whatever the differences. The centrality of human reasoning in both the Islamic and Christian traditions offers an important window for dialogue between the secular and religious traditions, and for mitigating conflicts. This is what the next chapter explores.

Notes

1 The question that guides Taylor's historical account is 'Why was it impossible not to believe in God in 1500, while it is now possible?'. He argues that the answer to that question cannot be separated from developments within Christianity.

2 *Islam in Africa Newsletter*, 1 (3) (July 2006).

3 Pope John Paul II's encyclical *Evangelium Vitae* (1995) best summarizes the Christian tradition view on abortion from the Catholic perspective. See <http://www.vatican.va/holy_father/john_paul_ii/encyclicals/> (accessed November 2008).

4 The full text is available at <http://www.vatican.va/holy_father/paul_vi/encyclicals/> (accessed November 2008).

5 A brief summary of the Pope's theology of the body can be read in George Weigel's biography of John Paul II.

6 The full text is available at <http://www.vatican.va/holy_father/paul_vi/encyclicals/> (accessed November 2008).

7 See the various statements on CAFOD's policy on HIV prevention at <www.cafod.org.uk> (accessed November 2008).

8 Avicenne was a Muslim physician, astronomer and philosopher and had a major influence on the thought of Aquinas.

9 Darul Uloom Deoband is the most influential madrasa in South Asia. It was established in response to colonial rule and turned the focus of the Muslim community, displaced from political power, to self-reform and personal piety. These were viewed to be the only means to preserve Muslim identity under foreigner occupiers. Its success and replication across South Asia led to the rise of the Deobandi tradition, which refers to the branch of Islam which draws on the writings of the ulama of Deoband in interpreting Muslim texts.

10 'Muslims can use contraceptives, says Deoband's fatwa', *Express India*, 16 January 2008.

11 For a summary of the debate about faith schools, see Gardner *et al.* (2005). See also Grace (2003), who discusses the lack of evidence-based argument which underpins most of the criticism against faith schools.

12 For another study showing that faith-based schools are not *per se* incompatible with a liberal education emphasizing autonomy, tolerance and respect, see De Jong and Snik (2002).

13 For a discussion of Muslim schools in the British educational context, see Hewer (2001).

14 Tony Blair's lecture, entitled 'Faith and globalisation', can be viewed at <http://www.rcdow.org.uk/lectures/> (accessed November 2008).

15 Inaugural lecture of the Kirby Laing Institute for Christian Ethics, at <http://www.tyndale.cam.ac.uk/KLICE/> (accessed November 2008).

16 *A Theory of Justice* was published in 1971, and revised in 1993 in *Political Liberalism*.

17 The five primary goods are: (1) basic rights and liberties; (2) freedom of movement, freedom of association and freedom of occupational choice against a background of diverse opportunities; (3) powers and prerogatives of office and positions of responsibility in political and economic institutions of the basic structure; (4) income and wealth; and (5) the social bases of self-respect (Rawls, 1993, p. 181).

18 See Raz (1994) for an articulation of a liberal perfectionist view of the state. See Richardson (2002) and Estlund (1997) for a discussion of the 'truth orientation' of liberal democracies.

19 For a discussion of the linkages between democracy and the Christian tradition, see, for example, Courtney Murray (1986); Maritain (1944); O'Donovan (1996); Song (2006); Taylor (1989); and Weithman (1997).

20 See also Maddox (1996) for a discussion of the religious background to the emergence of democratic systems in eighteenth- and nineteenth-century Europe. He argues that religion has not been the only source of the rise of democracy, but that it was nonetheless a very significant one.

21 See Hauerwas (1981) for the seminal exposition of his views on the role of the Christian church in society.

22 Other useful references on the links between Islam and democracy include Ansari (2006); Ayubi, (2006); Eickelman and Piscatori (1996); Lewis (2002); Piscatori (1988); Roy (2006); and Vatikiotis (1987). For a discussion of the influence of Maududi's political thought in India, see Singh (2000).

23 For an overview of qualitative research methodology in the social sciences, see Denzin and Limden (1994).

24 The full text is available at <http://www.vatican.va/holy_father/paul_vi/encyclicals/> (accessed November 2008).

6 | Dialoguing Traditions

This book has argued that the conceptualization of religion in development studies is best understood in terms of traditions, which are politically, socially and historically embedded. Conceiving Christianity and Islam as traditions means that they are based on a fundamental agreement that adherents of the tradition endorse – for Christians, that Christ is God's incarnation in the world and that the Bible is the word of God; for Muslims, that Mohammad is Allah's Prophet and that the revelation contained in the Qur'an is Allah's message to humankind. Yet there is a wide disagreement about how to embody that agreement in the context in which members of these traditions live. How adherents understand individual actions and social practices as fulfilling the fundamental teachings that characterize their tradition is never free from historical, social, political and cultural influences.

This chapter examines further the implications of this for understanding the role of religion in development processes, and for helping development practitioners and policy makers deal with the increasing presence of religion in their work. It starts by analysing the dynamic and non-homogeneous character of religious traditions. This point has been made several times in earlier chapters but now it is examined systematically. By narrating some selected stories within Christianity and Islam, we underline the significance of interpretation and leadership in shaping the way traditions embody their fundamental agreement into certain social practices. The stories serve to illustrate that apparent conflicts between the secular and religious traditions are not to be solved by the secular response of sweeping religion under the carpet, or by engaging only with elements of religion which are compatible with 'development' as the secular tradition understands it, but by active engagement with the religious traditions in their entirety, and especially by engagement with what we have called their interpretive leadership.

Four stories which have had direct bearings on development processes and outcomes – two within Christianity and two within

Islam – demonstrate this dynamic character of religions. The Second Vatican Council shook the foundations of the Roman Catholic Church and reshaped the relationship that Catholicism had with other Christian denominations and with the rest of the world. Another illustration of this two-way relationship between how a religious tradition interprets its fundamentals and the wider social world in which it is embedded is offered by liberation theology – a specific branch of theology which emerged in the Christian tradition in response to the context of Latin America in the late 1960s. Within Islam, we focus on how the Islamic tradition has responded differently in time and space to the capitalistic economic context in which Muslims live. We also discuss the practice of *ijtihad* ('engaging in reasoning') and its impact on processes of social change. While these four stories illustrate the reality of dialogue and exchange between secular and religious traditions, the final section discusses more theoretically how dialogue between traditions can take place. It goes on to propose some concrete guidelines for development practitioners and policy makers who wish to engage with religious communities in the light of the practice of inter-faith dialogue.

The Second Vatican Council

In 1958, Angelo Guiseppe Roncalli was elected Pope and took the name of John XXIII. In 1959, he convoked an ecumenical council, known as the Second Vatican Council, or Vatican II, which took place during 1962–5. A council is a gathering of all the world's Catholic bishops and cardinals, including some expert theologians, to discuss and settle matters of Christian doctrine. The first council dates from 325, when the Council of Nicea settled the doctrine of the Trinity – that God is a communion of three persons, the Father, Son and Holy Spirit. The Council of Ephesus in 431 settled the double nature, divine and human, of Christ, and declared Mary the mother of God. Numerous other councils took place afterwards.

A common characteristic of councils is that they are responses to external events that require the church to take a position on certain matters. The doctrines of the Trinity and the double nature of Christ were set against the background of theological disagreement about the nature of God and Christ. The Council of Trent in 1545 was convened to discuss the Catholic Church's response to the theology developed by Luther and Calvin and the Protestant Reformation. Similarly, the Second Vatican Council (or Vatican II) was convened to revise the Church's doctrine in the light of the new context in which Catholics lived.[1] Vatican II was the first council to gather the universal, global, church, and not only its European centre, and the first one since the Reformation to include observers from the Reformed and Orthodox Churches. More than 2,000 people from all continents participated for three years in the discussions. Vatican II ended under the papacy of Paul VI following the death of John XXIII in 1963.

The world had evolved dramatically since the previous council (Vatican I) in 1869. It had changed politically, economically, socially and technologically. The colonial order had ended. Women had the right to vote and were making their way into the workplace. Education had become compulsory and universal in Western countries. The development of technologies had reshaped relationships between people and with the working environment. Two world wars had happened, and the world had witnessed genocides on unprecedented scales. Economic development and medical advances had brought prosperity and a better quality of life to large populations of the world. Yet many more remained at the margins of the benefits of economic, technological and scientific progress.

How the Catholic Church had interpreted how to live and proclaim God's Word was becoming increasingly out of tune with the way the world was evolving. Within the church, lay people were supposed to be passive and obedient to hierarchical orders. Yet they were now highly educated and empowered to make decisions in the social, economic and political world. Within the church, women had a subordinate role to men – only ordained males were making decisions binding all the faithful. Yet women were now enjoying the same rights as men in the outside world. Within the church, Latin, the Roman imperial language, continued to be the *lingua franca*. Yet, in the world, knowledge was produced in national languages and Latin had long disappeared as the language of the Western intellectual elite.

John XXIII faced two options: either to leave the church and its theology untouched, on the grounds that the modern world was permeated by evil forces and that a 'fortress Church' resisting the modern world was the most adequate response (as Pope Pius IX did at the First Vatican Council, rejecting modern advances in his *Syllabus of Errors*), or to reform the church's theology in the light of the modern world, for the Catholic Church's proper embodiment of the revealed truth is a constant search for a better fit to the world to which the truth is proclaimed. John XXIII chose the latter option, and announced an *aggorniamento* ('readjustment' or 'update') of the Catholic Church to the modern world. Another embodiment of the fundamentals of the Catholic religious tradition in different social practices was needed. As John XXIII put it in his opening speech, 'The Church should never depart from the sacred treasure of truth inherited from the Fathers. But at the same time she must ever look to the present, to the new conditions and the new forms of life introduced into the modern world.'[2] Among the people that the Fathers of the Council – that is, its participants – had in mind as the proceedings opened were those who lived in impoverished conditions:

> We urgently turn our thoughts to all the anxieties by which modern man is afflicted. Hence, let our concern swiftly focus first of all on those who are especially lowly, poor, and weak. . . . We want to fix a steady gaze on those who still lack the opportune help to achieve a way of life worthy of human beings.[3]

The consequences of Vatican II for the Catholic Church, Christianity and the world were far-reaching. The Council had an important influence on development processes and outcomes.[4] The role of religion in development cannot be fully understood without understanding the religious tradition itself. There are three features of Catholicism that became prominent in the Second Vatican Council and which had direct development consequences.

First, there is the emphasis on the duty to 'scrutinize the signs of time and interpret them in the light of the Gospel' (Pastoral Constitution on the Church in the Modern World, *Gaudium et Spes*, paragraph 4). How to respond to the 'signs of time' of massive poverty, growing inequality and social exclusion? The constitutive documents of the Council urged Christians not to neglect their duties in promoting human welfare:

> The Council regards with great respect all the true, good and right elements in the vast variety of institutions which men have founded and continue to found. It declares that the Church wants to help and promote such institutions. . . . She desires nothing more strongly than to serve the general welfare. (*Gaudium et Spes*, paragraph 42)

The documents particularly single out the engagement of all believers in the political, economic and social world to build a more just social order: 'Let there be no false opposition between professional and social activity and the life of religion. The Christian who neglects his temporal duties neglects the duties to his neighbour, neglects God' (*Gaudium et Spes*, paragraph 43). The third chapter of the Pastoral Constitution is entirely devoted to discussing how principles of equity and justice should guide economic and social relations in a world where progress has deepened the divide between the haves and have-nots. The Constitution of the Church especially calls people to share with those in need: 'Each as far as he can must share and spend his wealth in coming to the assistance especially of these suffering individuals or peoples so that they may thereby be enabled to go on to self-help and self-development' (*Gaudium et Spes*, paragraph 69).

A second feature of Catholicism is its particular ecclesiology – that is, the nature and structure of the church – which was reformed at the Council in a way that had profound influences for dialogue with other Christian denominations, other religions and the modern world. At the Council, the Catholic Church defined itself as a communion of human beings united in God, whatever their denominations or religions. The Church is no longer a hierarchical spiritual monarchy under the absolute authority of the Pope, outside which there can be no salvation. Paragraph 8 of the Dogmatic Constitution of the Church, *Lumen Gentium*, opens up the door to ecumenism by affirming that the Christian churches which do not recognize the apostle Peter and his successors (that is, the Pope) as shepherd of the universal church nevertheless contain 'elements of sanctification and of truth'. Paragraph 16 goes further by affirming that Muslims, Jews, agnostics and even atheists 'are related in various ways to the people of God'. The Declaration of the Council *Nostra Aetate* on the relationship between Christianity and non-Christian religions states that there is a 'ray of truth' in every religion. The Declaration was particularly noted for its repudiation of anti-Semitism.

This ecclesiological reform changed the nature and structure of faith-based development work. Roman Catholics could now collaborate with other Christian denominations and even with other religions in the transformation of the world in the light of the Gospel. Catholic organizations could now partner with Muslim ones in order to improve the outreach and effectiveness of poverty reduction activities – Islamic Relief is, for example, an official partner of CAFOD in Muslim countries. In countries where different Christian denominations competed for winning the souls of the locals, co-operation between Churches became the norm. All those who worked for social justice and for improving the lives of the marginalized and oppressed, whatever their creed, were seen by the post-Vatican II Catholic Church as united in the same communion of human beings living under the impulse of the same Spirit. They were the 'people of God' Church. From a fortress church claiming to be the only bearer of truth in the world, the Catholic Church became a 'pilgrim church' (*Lumen Gentium*, Chapter 7), walking alongside other human beings towards their final destination, and being endlessly transformed by the circumstances and encounters along the journey on earth.

A third indelible mark on development left by Vatican II is its Declaration on Religious Freedom, *Dignitatis Humanae*, which is addressed to the whole world, and not only to the Catholic faithful:

> This Vatican Synod declares that the human person has a right to religious freedom. This freedom means that all men are to be immune from coercion on the part of individuals or of social groups and of any human power, in such way that in matters religious no one is to be forced to act in a manner contrary to his own beliefs. . . . This right of the human person to religious freedom is to be recognized in the constitutional law whereby society is governed. Thus it is to become a civil right. (Paragraph 2)

The Catholic Church no longer tries to impose its teachings on others, sometimes through state power, on the grounds that it alone possesses the right path to God or the only truth. Other religions have the right to worship and live according to their religious precepts without hindrance, for they too have access to the truth – even if the Catholic Church believes this access is imperfect. The Declaration establishes clear 'church and state boundaries'. The role of the state is to enable every person to live a life according to his or her religion, without coercion or impediment. This does not mean that religion should be kept separate from political matters, but that all states should inscribe religious freedom as a civil right. This principle of religious freedom is also to be applied within the Catholic Church itself. She should never use coercion, for the faithful 'possess the civil right not to be hindered in leading their lives in accordance with their conscience' (paragraph 13).[5]

These three dramatic changes – the duty of Catholics to make equity and justice guide economic and social progress, the recognition that believers in other denominations and religions possess a ray of truth,[6] and the respect for religious freedom outside and within the Church – illustrate how a religious tradition is not static but shaped by historical influences and political, social and economic realities. All the documents written during the Second Vatican Council were responses to the new context in which Christians tried to translate into social practices the fundamental teachings of Christianity. Because their existing practices had emerged in another context, they no longer embodied the core teachings of Christianity in the world's new context; a reinterpretation of how to live the truth revealed by Jesus Christ was required. The truth had not changed, but the interpretation of how to embody that truth in a concrete historical context certainly had.

In the section on 'fundamentalism and violence' in Chapter 2, we argued that those who have authority over the interpretation of sacred scriptures played a large role in how a religious tradition responds to given situations. Appleby (2000, p. 27) highlighted the 'critical interpreting role of leadership in forming and mobilizing the religious community'. Vatican II illustrates how the leadership of the Catholic community has formed and mobilized the whole community for transforming the world and making it a more just and equitable place to live in accordance with the requirements of human dignity. The specific personality and character of Pope John XXIII played an important role in changing the mode of engagement of the Church with the modern world. Had he not been elected Pope, one might perhaps never have seen such a commitment of the Church to the cause of justice and democracy.[7]

Nor should one underestimate the role of theological investigation in formulating this response to the rapid scientific, economic and social changes that had engulfed the world since the nineteenth century. John XXIII might have taken the initiative of summoning the Council, but there were countless theologians who opened the way to the Council through their work in reshaping Catholic theology in relation to the modern world. Most of these theologians – Yves Congar, Karl Rahner and Edward Schillebeeckx, to name a few – had suffered persecution from the Pope preceding John XXIII (Pius XII), and some had even been banned from teaching, because their theological investigation was deemed by Catholic authorities to be harmful to the Church.

Religious traditions are thus never exempt from power. This predominant influence of a religious leadership and intellectual elite in changing a religious tradition should not sideline the critical role of Christians at the grassroots, who are at the forefront of this engagement with the world. The world's bishops gathered in Vatican II brought with them the struggles of the men and women in their dioceses who were finding it difficult to continue to practise the fundamental Christian teachings in a rapidly changing world. They could no longer see in these practices an adequate interpretation and embodiment of the truth revealed by Christ and contained in the holy scriptures. It is because of these concerns at the grassroots that theologians tried to articulate theologically a more appropriate Christian response to the changing world – despite strong resistance by some factions in the Church who refused to adjust the interpretation of Christ's message of salvation to the modern context.

Another important conclusion for the mode of engagement between religion and development that the story of Vatican II highlights is the crucial need for taking into account the richness and complexities of a religious tradition, and for avoiding stereotypes. This conclusion equally applies to members and non-members of a religious tradition, for there is often ignorance both within and outside a religious tradition of its fundamental teachings. And ignorance, coupled with a lack of dialogue, leads to misunderstanding which sometimes can turn dangerous, as will be illustrated later with the example of the Red Mosque siege in Islamabad in February 2007.

Liberation theology

Among development practitioners, the Catholic Church's involvement in development work is best known through a theological movement that emerged in the late 1960s, liberation theology. Like the above story, the birth, flourishing and demise of liberation theology illustrates that religious traditions cannot be comprehended without looking at the wider social, political, economic and cultural contexts in which members of a religion live. The story also demonstrates that it is not possible to understand the role of one religious tradition in development processes and outcomes without giving a clear account of how a religion interprets its fundamental beliefs and teachings. This includes a full analysis of the power dynamics within a tradition.

On their return from Rome after the Second Vatican Council, Latin American bishops endeavoured to put into practice the contents of the Council documents. The Council gave greater authority to local bishops and placed greater emphasis on episcopal collegiality, which allowed bishops worldwide to make decisions in their own territory through national and regional bishops' conferences. The Latin American bishops had their first regional conference in 1968 in Medellín, Colombia. On the agenda was the orientation of the Latin American Church in the light of the insights of Vatican II and its invitation to scrutinize the signs of the time and enter into dialogue with the world.

The Latin American continent in the 1960s was marked by massive poverty, economic dependency, large inequalities, and non-democratic rule. It was deeply scarred by divergent responses to the Cuban Revolution and divided by Cold War allegiances. The United States did not hesitate to intervene in countries where the political left became too prominent, shoring up right-wing dictatorships with military support when necessary. The Latin American Catholic Church was characterized by a strong bias towards the elite. In many countries, there had been an alliance between the military, the elite and the Church – the heritage of colonial times when Catholicism was brought by the conquistadors to legitimize the colonial and plundering enterprise. The political authorities confined the role of the Church to consoling the souls of the oppressed and comforting the souls of the elite; it was not invited to pronounce any judgement on the economic, social or political order of the time. It took a present-day Bartolomé de las Casas to question this state of affairs.

At the Medellín conference, a Peruvian priest, Gustavo Gutierrez, made a speech where he first articulated his translation of Vatican II into Latin American language. The speech deeply influenced the documents issued at the conference, and was subsequently turned into a book, published in 1971 as *A Theology of Liberation*. Liberation theology can be characterized by the following elements (all straightforwardly inspired by the Vatican II documents).[8] First, religion and life cannot be separated. The question that should guide all Christians is how to live in the light of the Gospel in a concrete historical context. Second, Christians cannot separate discourse about God from the historical process of liberation, for one cannot say that one loves the unseen God if one does not love and help the neighbour that one sees daily (first letter of St John). Third, Christian living is marked by a preferential option for the poor. This option is not a choice among many others but a choice which conditions all other choices in one's life. This option is commanded by God who, throughout the Bible, has a special relationship with the poor, the oppressed and the marginalized. Fourth, salvation is not only a private individual matter that happens at one's death, but a collective and historical process of liberation in the here and now. Economic, social and political structures can be tainted by 'structural sin' and become exploitative and dehumanizing.[9] Challenging, transforming or eradicating such structures is part of human salvation. Living the Gospel means being alongside those who suffer from injustice and participating in the struggle for liberation, not only in the spiritual realm but also in the economic, political and social spheres. Gutierrez was far from being the only theologian who brought theology closer to the conditions in which people live, and tried to talk about God in a world marked by poverty, injustice and racism. Numerous other theologians in Latin America, and throughout the world, followed suit.[10]

It is obvious that the very content of liberation theology made it particularly likely to be in tune with the secular tradition on development issues. To live a full Christian life is a matter of being fully engaged in the transformation of the world and reducing its poverty and injustice. In the Latin American countries which were under military dictatorships, the Church was vocal in defending human rights, as we saw briefly in Chapter 3 when discussing the role of religion in democratization. The Salvadoran archbishop, Oscar Romero, was murdered for his opposition to the military dictatorship. In Brazil, the Church was also instrumental in forming a trade union which later became the Workers' Party. Insights from liberation theology, such as the concept of structural sin, helped to catalyse the anti-racist struggles in apartheid-torn South Africa. Some terms coined by liberation theology, such as 'preferential option for the poor', 'evangelization of social structures' and 'structural sin' became part of Vatican-sanctioned documents such as papal encyclicals.

The above paragraphs have painted a rather triumphant picture of liberation theology, as if the one billion Catholics worldwide suddenly became the champions of the defence of the poor and marginalized against the structures which violate their basic human rights. As earlier chapters have already emphasized, religious traditions are not immune from disagreement, conflict and power. In the 1980s, the Vatican issued two 'instructions' on liberation theology which condemned:[11] its intellectual flirting with atheism (some liberation theologians had borrowed explicitly from Marxism for their social analysis of the Latin American reality); its earthly emphasis (as if the Kingdom of God could fully be achieved here on earth through social justice struggles and as if Christianity could be reduced to a mere social justice agenda cut off from its transcendental roots); and its sanctioning, or at least non-prohibition, of the use of violence to promote justice (some liberation theologians were sympathetic towards guerrillas, and some priests were even fighting with them).

The Catholic hierarchy did not reject liberation theology as such, as it was a mere reflection of the major insights of Vatican II – the non-separation between religion and life, the pursuit of justice as integral to the love of God, the concern for the marginalized and oppressed as orienting one's life, the advent of the Kingdom of God already growing in this world, and the humanization of the world as part of evangelization. John Paul II even used the liberation theologians' concept of 'structures of sin' in his 1986 encyclical *De Rei Socialis* (*On Social Concern*). What the Vatican did reject was some of the excesses at the margins, for it was only a small minority of liberation theology sympathizers who subscribed to a pure Marxist analysis, who reduced the Kingdom of God to the earthly pursuit of justice, and who condoned violent struggles against injustice.[12]

While fully endorsing the ideas of Vatican II, the Roman Curia was less zealous in putting these into practice than in denouncing the deviations of some forms of liberation theology. The misunderstanding regarding the two instructions, which Catholics perceived as denouncing liberation theology altogether rather than some deviations and excesses, led to a considerable climate of suspicion. The Roman Curia progressively removed all Latin American bishops who were openly supportive of liberation theology and replaced them with clerics who did not view political and social engagement against poverty and injustice as being the church's role.

Various explanations are advanced today for the apparent demise of liberation theology, or what was called the 'activist Church' in Latin America: the crackdown by John Paul II for its alleged flirtation with Marxism; the transition to democratic rule and thus the obsolescence of a resistant Church; or the rise of Pentecostalism, which made the Catholic Church seek a new following at the same charismatic, devotional and apolitical level as the Pentecostals. Daudelin and Hewitt (1995) also note that the international outreach of liberation theology across the world never really matched the extent of its implementation in pastoral practice in Latin America. The large number of casualties among the Christians involved in the resistance against authoritarian regimes gave an international impression that the activist Church was hegemonic, but the reality was that large segments of the Church still refrained from fully living the insights of Vatican II in the reality of their lives.

Another explanation that can be advanced for the very limited support offered by the Roman Curia and Church authorities to those trying to implement documents of the Second Vatican Council at the grassroots is that translating Vatican II theology into practice requires a redistribution of power and privilege both within and outside the Church that not all are willing to accommodate.

First, liberation theology directly implemented the more prominent role given to the laity in decision-making processes within the Church. Male clerics in positions of authority are not always willing to accept eagerly a sudden sharing of decision-making power. Moreover, those who came into positions of authority after the death of popes John XXIII and Paul VI may not all have agreed with the content of the Council's documents, such as collaborative ministry between priests and lay people or episcopal collegiality and responsibility. The papacy of John Paul II, for example, has centralized decision making in the Church as opposed to increasing episcopate collegiality. As for the relationship with other Christian denominations and religions, the papacy of Benedict XVI appears to be sending ambiguous messages.

Second, the concern for the marginalized and the injunction of humanizing social structures implied that believers occupying a dominant position in a dehumanizing structure might have to lose their privileged status – something they might not have been ready to do. A big Roman Catholic landowner in El Salvador in the 1980s would probably not have been a major supporter of land reform, and would have accused the Church of inappropriate meddling in politics if it spoke in favour of such a course. This disagreement regarding the role of the Church in politics, depending on whether the believer enjoys a privileged position in the existing social order or suffers from a marginalized one, is perceived by the religious authorities as a threat to the Church's unity. And as in secular politics, those who occupy a more powerful position have a greater opportunity to make their voices and opinions heard, and to impose their own interpretations of scriptures and tradition.[13]

That the interpretation of the fundamental agreement of a

religious tradition depends so much on the role of its interpretative leadership and the power dynamics between its members leaves serious doubts about any idea of truth that is not socially constructed by the most powerful within that tradition. This has especially been a concern regarding the treatment of women.

Discussing the issue of women's reproductive rights, we have already seen that female theologians are often excluded from participating in the development of the Church's teaching on issues which affect women only. As a religious tradition is not immune from the influence of power so it is not immune from the influence of a patriarchal social order. There are never clear boundaries between religion and the wider social, political and economic order in which a religion is practised.

One of the main tasks of what is known as feminist theology has been precisely to uncover the patriarchal layers that have permeated the interpretation of religious texts.[14] The feminist theologian Elizabeth Schüssler-Fiorenza (1983, 1992) argues that the interpretation of Mary's anointment of Jesus before his crucifixion (Mark 14: 9, John 12: 3) has been tainted by patriarchal biases that ignored parallels with Jesus's words at the Last Supper, preventing what she calls a discipleship of equals in mission and ministry.

Reviewing the literature on religion from a gender studies perspective, and discussing the fact that the oppression of women is sometimes seen from the perspective of 'culture not religion' (such as female genital mutilation or stoning of adulterous women), Tomalin (2007) makes the following bold claim:

> The fact that religious texts are open to different, and often opposing, interpretations means that the 'culture not religion' argument is possible to sustain on a range of issues. It relies upon the notion of a pure and original religion that periodically becomes corrupted by cultural influences. This is incompatible with a social science perspective that is interested in the ways the particular views and attitudes are socially constructed. From this perspective, what we have is a series of socially constructed positions that maintain their legitimacy through the argument that 'actual' religion is as it was intended to be. Whether this presents methodological problems is worth considering. I would argue that this research is not concerned to scrutinize the validity of particular positions from a theological perspective: it is not the role of social science to engage in this sort of enterprise. However, we are concerned to investigate and highlight the ways in which different religious positions may be

compatible with a development agenda that is concerned with poverty reduction and the pursuit of human rights. (pp. 26–7)

In the light of our earlier discussion, two comments can be made. First, that the beliefs and practices of a religious tradition can never be separated from the social, cultural and historical context in which that religion is practised. God does transcend human history and culture, but God's revelation to creation occurs in a world inscribed in a particular time and space. That religion, or the idea of truth for that matter, is culturally embedded is different from the claim that religion or truth is socially or culturally constructed. Not that there is a 'pure' view of religion, as if there was ever in human history a view from nowhere, but the truth contained in a religious tradition is always revealing itself in a particular context.

Second, social science research cannot remain neutral and abstain from making value judgements about the validity of certain positions. The concern of the social sciences is therefore not to limit itself to finding meeting points between certain 'social constructions of religion' which are compatible with a development agenda, but to fully engage with a religious tradition as a whole, and to be aware that 'development studies' is also embedded in a certain tradition of thought, namely one that is mainly a secular liberal tradition. A review of two case studies within the Islamic tradition further reinforces this conclusion.

Capitalism and Islam

The response of the Islamic tradition to its surrounding environment – for example, capitalism, along with the rise of the nation-state and democracy – has been a recurrent theme in much of the history of Islam. The way Muslim scholarship and societies have adapted Islamic precepts and institutions to capitalist ideas is well documented by Charles Tripp (2006). His study provides a detailed analysis of the variety of responses to capitalist ideas within Islamic scholarship. He shows that these scholars have devised a range of strategies which have enabled Muslims to remain true to their faith while engaging effectively with their changing societies under increasing exposure to Western influences and its dominant traditions of thought (liberalism and secularism).

One could divide the Islamic response to capitalism into various groups. There are those who have resorted to confrontation or insularity to cope with the challenges of modernity. Most others have aspired to innovate and experiment to ensure fruitful engagement with today's global capitalism. Three different positions are clear: complete replication, intense disengagement and innovation.

Confronted with the colonial powers, the leaders of most Muslim countries aspired to replicate the economic activity of the great European cities and their associated social order. Their evident technological innovation and wealth inspired and challenged Muslim leaders to reflect upon their own societies. The challenge was how best to capture the capitalist advances and to reproduce the visible strengths of European societies through the transformation of their own. Some of the returning Ottoman elites, for example, had been so impressed that they advocated wholesale adoption of European social forms precisely to preserve and strengthen the Ottoman state in the nineteenth century (present-day Turkey). The need was to adapt these developments within the Islamic precepts. This led to reinterpreting many of the religious principles.

First, Islamic discourses about property began to change. The traditional commentary on the understandings and specificities of different kinds of property continued. In addition, however, writings appeared across the Islamic world which increasingly brought together a variety of novel concepts, and created space for individual property ownership. Then, many Islamic scholars, prompted by their concern for social cohesion, social progress and social equity, started to question the standard prohibition of *riba* ('interest'). Ahmad Khan, a leading Islamic scholar in late nineteenth-century India, asserted that this prohibition should only apply to the debts of the poor who borrowed money out of necessity, and not to those whose expanding commercial virtues contributed to the public good (Baljon, 1970).

Other scholars resisted accommodation of capitalist ideas. Their main critique rested on moral grounds. Allama Iqbal, the famous Indian Muslim philosopher of the early twentieth century, gave a powerful indictment of the ruthless competition, egotism and materialism of capitalism and of European civilization, which he believed had encouraged man's 'ruthless egoism and his . . . indefinite gold-hunger which is gradually killing all higher striving in him and bringing in life-weariness in a society motivated by an inhuman competition and civilization which has lost its spiritual unity' (Iqbal, 1968).

Some scholars also resisted the capitalist influences because of their effects on the identity and future of their societies. Hasan al-Banna of the Muslim Brotherhood in Egypt argued that wealth turned people into oppressors, reiterating his belief that Islam had come to 'free the poor from golden idols and their power and tyranny' (al-Banna, 1946). He called for the restoration of brotherly feelings of mutual responsibility among Muslims in order to counteract the divisive nature of wealth disparities. His contemporary, Ayatollah Taleqani in Iran, developed this theme further, dwelling not simply on the ways in which great wealth would lead to indifference to the plight of the poor, but also on the ways in which wealth creation under capitalism was undermining the very fabric of society. These thinkers argued that capitalism, by encouraging private property, isolated individuals. Further, they argued that, with a regime of private property, individuals who do not possess property and only have their labour to offer become exploitable by those who own the property. They were also troubled by class fragmentation within the society, which they saw as an inevitable result of a capitalist economic system. The concerns of many of these Islamic critics of capitalism thus shared many similarities with those of socialist thinkers in the West.

Tripp (2006) also discusses those who, in rejecting capitalism, resorted to violent means to register their protest, which he refers to as the 'symbolic' response, one that targets anything which symbolizes capitalism. Examples include the nineteenth-century *wahhabi* movement in India, which drew on the Islamic idiom in mobilizing people to attack the spinning machines and factories threatening the livelihoods of local weavers; the movement of Al-Jihad in Egypt in the 1980s, which used violence against a state it identified by ubiquitous capitalist symbols; and the Al-Qaida attack on the Twin Towers, which demonstrated the relative weakness of the apparently all-powerful institutions of the West. Tripp notes that, for Muhammad al-Farag, the ideologue of Al-Jihad in Egypt, violence was purposive and was the first step to the formation of an Islamic order; in his view violence was a sign that the idols of this world can only disappear through the power of the sword.

The third main response to capitalism came from scholars who were conscious of the moral dilemma inherent in a capitalist economic system. But rather than recommending disengagement or complete replication, they argued for adapting capitalist ideas in the light of Islamic principles. This response was partly due to the failure of socialist states to deliver prosperity and social services in many Arab countries in the 1960s. Although the interventionist regimes in several Arab states had yielded many dividends for the national economy, by the early 1970s state control of the economy had led to falling productivity, underemployment and stagnating international trade. Alternatives to capitalism, whether secular or Islamic socialist, had not worked. This made some Islamic scholars explore alternative ideas for governing the economy, which would lead to material prosperity as proposed under the capitalist system but would be based on moral principles (Kuran, 1986).

Attempts at developing such an alternative economic system started in the late 1940s and gained momentum from the 1960s onwards. Islamic economics is based on the premise that individuals in making their economic decisions are inspired by behavioural norms established in the light of the Qur'an and the tradition of the Prophet. Such an assumption helps eliminate the exploitative dimensions of the capitalist economic system while harnessing its economically productive principles. Thus, Islamic economics would lead to outcomes where an individual who believes in Islamic norms would engage in trade and profit-making ventures but would refrain from making profit at the cost of others (*ibid.*). This means that he would pay fair wages, charge reasonable prices and be content with normal profits. It would also mean that he would not engage in speculation and monopolization that involved features of gambling and which were exploitative. Further, the surplus generated by the believers in an Islamic society would be redistributed more effectively given the heavy emphasis that Islam places on *zakat* and other forms of giving (*ibid.*).

The central challenge to Islamic economists, however, rests in the apparent prohibition of the practice of charging interest in Islam. It is here that Islamic economists have tried to invent new banking instruments. One solution proposed entails replacing interest-based saving accounts with profit sharing. Rather than receiving a fixed percentage return, which would constitute interest, the depositors, lenders and investors invest in profit-sharing accounts. This means that they get a predetermined share of any income made by the projects financed through their contributions. In this system they also share the losses according to the same predetermined formula. *Mudarabahs*, the lending and borrowing options of Islamic banks, are a prominent example of such a profit-sharing system (*ibid.*). These banks accept deposits from individuals in return for a share of proceeds from them. The ideal banking system, according to Islamic economists, however, remains interest-free banking. Here people earn a return on their money only if they take the risks involved in profit sharing. This implies that an individual who want to make money on his retirement savings will have to face the risks inherent in a *mudarabah* system (*ibid.*).

Thus, while some Islamic scholars have embraced capitalism, others have resisted it, and others have tried to reinterpret innovatively some central teachings of the Islamic tradition in response to certain capitalistic ideas and practices, while also trying to adapt the latter in the light of Islamic teachings. This description of how the Islamic tradition has tried to accommodate within its ranks an economic system that saw the light within another tradition shows that religious traditions need not be incompatible with elements outside them. Islam contains different contested views about how to live the fundamentals of the Islamic faith (revealed at a given time in history) in specific economic contexts that characterize the modern world. Likewise, in case of apparent conflict between Islam and a secular vision of development, there is always scope for dialogue and critical engagement.

Ijtihad

Within the Islamic tradition the instrument of adaptation to the needs of changing times, and to the world, is *ijtihad*, which literally means 'exerting oneself' to engage in individual reasoning. The emphasis is on ensuring that the jurist who practises *ijtihad* is engaged in the process with full intellectual commitment (Codd, 1999); sometimes it is simply called 'opinion' or 'considered opinion' or 'interpretation'. In practice it means that one analyses the unique data of a current moral problem, and argues from Qur'anic principles, using analogy and logic to come to the best and most reasonable solution.

As Islamic jurists and philosophers argue, *ijtihad* gives Islamic ethics great flexibility. The Qur'an clearly states that it provides guidance for all people for all times: 'We have revealed it an Arabic Qur'an, that you may [use your mind], understand [it and become intelligent and wise]' (12: 2). It restricts this guidance to broad principles, however, allowing much flexibility in interpretation of the verses in the light of the *Hadith* and the socio-economic and political context of the time. By resting authority with the Islamic jurists to find fresh solutions to complex problems in the light of the changing needs of time, *ijtihad* is thus critical to defending the claim that Islamic teachings provide guidance to humankind until eternity. The tool of *ijtihad* has not been used widely by Muslim scholars, with contention as to who has the right to use this authority arising as early as the eighth century – many modern scholars attribute the apparent backwardness of some Islamic practices to this fact.[15] It continues to be employed nonetheless by some, and can be a useful instrument to bridge the divide between Islamic principles and the demands of modernity.

How *ijtihad* can be utilized to shape practices among Muslim societies today can be seen in the example of some of the legal reforms in Syria. Islam gives the man a right to four wives. This right, however, comes with serious moral obligations, where the man contemplating second marriage is required to ensure equal treatment of all wives and sufficient economic means to ensure them a comfortable living. The Syrian Law of Personal Status, which was passed in 1953 and came about as a result of a process of *ijtihad*, turned this moral check into a legal requirement. Now the courts can prevent a man marrying a second time if he is not seen as financially fit to support the second wife (Codd, 1999).

Malaysia provides another example of a Muslim country where the process of *ijtihad* is still alive. The process of *ijtihad* has been employed to address issues of national significance ranging from lotteries, attendance of Muslim leaders at non-Islamic religious ceremonies, insurance, use of income from interest-bearing deposit accounts and employees' providence funds and insurance policies (Hooker, 1993). For example, the issue of lotteries has been controversial in Malaysia, since Muslims generally view it as a form of gambling, a forbidden practice in Islam. The fact that proceeds from the government lottery went to numerous social welfare projects, including projects run by mosques and religious schools, made the Islamic response to lottery much more complex. Islamic scholars gave numerous interpretations. Some allowed for government-organized social welfare lottery as long as the proceeds are used to finance public projects, but others ruled out lotteries altogether. These different interpretations by different *ijtihad* bodies demonstrate that the outcomes of the process of *ijtihad* are heavily dependent on the particular training of the jurists involved.

The process of *ijtihad* can also vary in form, between remaining a venture at the individual level and becoming a collective endeavour. A person who practises *ijtihad* is called a *mujtahid*. Traditionally, this person is required to be a scholar of Islamic law, or an *alim*, the majority of them having been trained in madrasas. In many Muslim countries, scholars engaging in *ijtihad* now combine modern and religious education, and have risen to prominence due to their perceived ability to engage better with the challenges confronted by Muslims in modern-day societies.

Javed Ahmed Ghamidi is a good example of a modern Islamic scholar trained in both traditions, who relies on the use of logic and reasoning to reinterpret the Islamic text. He argues for putting the Qur'anic revelations in their historic context in order to grasp their real meaning. This stance often puts him in opposition to traditional ulama. On the issue of the veil where all traditional Islamic schools of thought concur on the need for women to cover their heads, Ghamidi draws upon verses from within the Qur'an to negate these claims. He maintains a prominent presence on the Pakistani cable TV channels and enjoys increasing popularity among upper-middle-class Muslims for his religious interpretations, which make Islamic principles compatible with the demands of modern-day life. He heads a research foundation, the Al-Mawrid Institute of Islamic Sciences, which conducts research on Islam with a view to producing scholars who have the intellectual training to interpret the Islamic texts in the light of the needs of the time.[16]

While other reformist scholars adopt positions verging on the heretical within mainstream Muslim thought and practice, their contributions are noteworthy. Asghar Ali Engineer, a well-known Indian Muslim writer-activist, is one example (Sikand, 2005). Engineer's work aims at developing analytical tools to interpret Islam so that it is more relevant to modern life. From his father, who was a religious leader, he received an Islamic education, but his main educational training took place in non-religious institutions (he took a degree in engineering). Over time, he has challenged many traditional interpretations of the Islamic faith in India and has been part of many reformist struggles including the Bohra reformist movement (an Islamic sect). He has written extensively on Hindu–Muslim conflicts in India and on the need for a renewed understanding of these religions in order to facilitate a process of co-existence. He has established two research centres in Mumbai to promote such research: the Institute of Islamic Studies and the Centre for the Study of Secularism and Society.

In addition to these individual attempts at reinterpretation, whether by traditional ulama or Muslim scholars trained in modern subjects, there is also a tradition of collective *ijtihad*. In many Muslim countries, like Malaysia and Indonesia, Islamic councils are formed with panels of experts in a given field in order to carry out *ijtihad* on a controversial issue. This is referred to as 'collective *ijtihad*' where the responsibility for reasoning and reinterpretation rests not with an individual jurist but is held collectively by a group of jurists acting together (Hosen, 2004). The primary advantage of this method is that it enables Islamic scholars and those trained in modern subjects to draw upon their respective disciplinary trainings to seek mutually acceptable answers to modern-day problems. Nadhah al-'Ulama (NU), one of the largest Islamic organizations in Indonesia, established in 1926, has engaged in collective *ijtihad* for a long time (*ibid.*). Before issuing a *fatwa* ('legal opinion') the scholars of NU discuss the issue in a meeting, which is attended by scholars with training in relevant secular subjects. For example, when writing *fatwas* on family planning the council engages medical experts; when addressing issues related to banking, it includes economists.

The concept of *ijtihad* thus in principle allows Islamic scholars to respond realistically to new problems, which are not clearly addressed in the Qur'an. *Mujtahids* and *ijtihad* councils open great opportunities for genuine dialogue with development practitioners. *Ijtihad* therefore provides a powerful tool for adapting Islamic principles as practised in many Muslims societies to the changing socio-economic and political context, but it remains underutilized. International development agencies, and the secular NGOs which they often support, could employ this tool to win greater credibility for their programmes among Muslim societies. In instances where development ideas and programmes are resisted within Islamic societies, engagement through *ijtihad* offers possibilities in over-coming initial resistance, for Islamic texts might provide the necessary supporting ground.

The gender empowerment programmes of many of these agencies have repeatedly failed to win wide support among women in Muslim societies, who often view the ideas of Western feminism as contradictory to their beliefs (Bano, 2005). A conscious attempt to engage with Islamic jurists who are capable of being open to the demands of the present would bring greater credibility to these development programmes. Such an approach could pay dividends across development sectors such as family planning, environmental preservation and preventive health, for in societies where religion is still a living force, actions supported by religious injunctions are more likely to gain moral legitimacy than those entirely wrapped in secular discourses.

Engagement and dialogue

So far the development community, based mainly on secular principles, has engaged with religious traditions by focusing on areas where the secular and religious traditions meet, as described for example in a series of books published by the World Bank staff member Katherine Marshall which detail successful cases of engagement between secular development agencies and faith communities. In this book, however, we have argued that the development work of a faith community cannot be separated from its identity as a worshipping faith community, with all that this entails. Conflicts can sometimes be unavoidable. If a secular donor partnered with a faith-based organization in order to open a school in a remote area, but made the funding conditional on having a secular orientation (for example, the exclusion of prayer), could such a partnership be viable?

Some studies of partnerships between secular donors and faith-based agencies have reached the conclusion that, given the different terms on which the secular and religious traditions operate, the partnership often ends up with the faith-based agency having to compromise its religious character.[17] This conclusion suggests that, despite apparent convergences on core development issues, a partnership between secular donors and faith-based agencies is not always desirable. It is not our aim to discuss whether such partnerships should take place or not: that would need a careful case-by-case study of specific donors and agencies. What we would like to highlight here is that an apparent conflict between the secular worldviews of donors and the religious worldviews of faith-based agencies should not be an obstacle to fruitful engagement.

We cannot stress it enough: religious traditions are not homogeneous. There is significant disagreement about how best to embody in practices the core beliefs and teachings of a religious tradition. Discussing how religion affects the life of poor women in developing countries, Nussbaum (2000) argues that potential conflict between a woman's right to religious freedom and her other fundamental human rights is best resolved through engagement with the tradition itself. When a certain religion denies women equality in front of the law, there often exist some liberating forces within the religious tradition itself which can challenge that unequal treatment from a religious perspective. Not every Muslim believes that women are unequal to men before the law; not every Christian believes that homosexuality is intrinsically evil and should be forbidden by law. So when religious liberty conflicts with other fundamental human rights, active engagement with those within that religious tradition who can accept the legitimacy of fundamental human rights is often a way to overcome the dilemma.

Nussbaum calls this form of engagement the 'principle of moral restraint'. Each religion contains ideals of compassion and justice; going against them is going against the religion itself. Nussbaum illustrates this by the speech given by Abraham Lincoln regarding slavery (quoted in Nussbaum, 2000, p. 195):

> Both read the same Bible, and pray [to] the same God; and each invokes His aid against the other. It may seem strange that any men should dare to ask a just God's assistance in wringing their bread from the sweat of other men's faces; but let us judge not that we be not judged.

This principle of moral restraint, or engagement with the liberating forces within a religious tradition, could be used in areas where the interpretation of certain teachings of a religion seems to conflict with the values of a secular-based conception of development. Nussbaum reports the case of a young Bangladeshi woman who was told by the mullahs that her religion forbade her to work in the fields. She replied that if this was really the case, if Allah preferred her to stay hungry rather than work so that she could buy food, then Allah had obviously sinned, for a just and good God would not allow one of His beloved creatures to starve to death. What is under question here is not the teachings of Islam but the interpretation that some members of the Islamic tradition have made of its teachings regarding women's role in society.

There is a risk that such engagement between the secular and religious traditions on development issues occurs at a superficial level. In a collection of case studies of partnerships between faith communities and secular development organizations, Marshall and van Saanen (2007, pp. 129–38) narrate an attempt at such engagement which they viewed as a success story. The case is a reform of madrasas in Pakistan initiated by the International Centre for Religion and Diplomacy in Washington, DC. The programme aimed at informing and training madrasa teachers about the values of Islam, especially the values of tolerance, respect for human rights and critical thinking that Islamic civilization upheld at the peak of its power one thousand years ago. In the eyes of the initiators of the programme, the reform was not aimed at imposing 'Western secular values' but at uncovering the very Islamic values of 'tolerance and scholarship'. They claimed that not only were the schools reformed but also the wider community (Candland, 2005). They reported the case of a girl who was caught making a secret phone call to a boy. The sanction was death for the girl, for her mother and sister, and for the boy's mother; and cutting of the ears and nose of the boy. A madrasa leader who attended some of the workshops of the programme challenged the sanction of the tribal leaders on religious grounds – that the Qur'an did not prohibit a boy talking to a girl, and that it emphasized forgiveness and not harsh sanctions.

Such reform programmes and their evaluation are highly problematic, however. They often end up reinforcing existing biases against the religious leaders and communities rather than bridging the divide between religious and secular traditions. The madrasa reform programme run by the International Centre for Religion and Diplomacy makes the apparently innocent claim of reintroducing tolerant Islamic values within madrasa leaders, but in doing so it takes the position that tolerance and respect for difference of opinion existed in Islam only in the Middle Ages, and that the Muslim leaders of today have to be taught these values all over again. Such a position contains a biased portrayal of the other – that today's ulama are intolerant; it also makes the intellectual error of ignoring the huge diversity in ulama training in Pakistan and the complexity of the madrasa education system (Bano, 2007b). In the same way, the example of a Pakistani girl and her family being punished for daring to call a boy through her mobile phone seems to exhibit a selection bias – given that the majority of students, even in female madrasas, travel from remote regions to reside in the madrasas in the cities, and many have mobile phones through which they stay in contact with their families. No one could possibly monitor all their calls. To quote such extreme cases without the necessary qualification (their isolated nature) not only puts into question the academic integrity of the researchers but actually risks widening the gulf between secular and religious traditions. Engagement between secular donors and religious traditions requires a careful approach.

Genuine engagement between different traditions requires dialogical skills, and knowledge of the other tradition's language. The philosopher Alasdair MacIntyre suggests the following mode of dialogue when there is controversy between rival traditions:

> The first is that in which each characterizes the content of its rival in its own terms, making explicit the grounds for rejecting what is incompatible with its own central theses. . . . A second stage is reached if and when the protagonists of each tradition, having considered in what ways their own tradition has by its own standards of achievement in enquiry found it difficult to develop enquiries beyond a certain point, or has produced in some area insoluble antinomies, ask whether the alternative and rival tradition may not be able to provide resources to characterize and to explain the failings and defects of their own tradition more adequately than they, using the resources of that tradition, have been able to do. (MacIntyre, 1988, p. 166)

In other words, when two traditions of thought conflict on certain issues, the first step is to try to understand the other tradition on its own terms. So, when the secular and religious traditions conflict in terms of what women's empowerment means, for example, the secular tradition should try to articulate why it rejects a religious-based conception of women's empowerment, and a religious tradition should articulate why it rejects a secular-based conception of women's empowerment. Once each tradition has understood why it rejects the other's position on women's empowerment, each tradition has then to examine whether, within itself, it is possible to articulate its rival understanding of women's empowerment.

An example of such conflict between traditions, and the failure of successful engagement between them when they conflict on certain development issues, is the tension between the secular and the religiously inspired women's empowerment movements in Pakistan: women's rights NGOs and female madrasas. The former emerged in the late 1970s and soon found support from the international development community, with an influx of development aid. The 1980s and 1990s saw a massive expansion in the number of women's rights NGOs. The birth and expansion of female madrasas, interestingly, followed similar time lines. Female madrasas are a recent phenomenon in Pakistan, where they only started to appear in the late 1970s (male madrasas are more than a millennium old; some Muslim countries like Malaysia and Indonesia adopted female madrasas much earlier than Pakistan). Despite their relatively late creation, their number has grown dramatically, especially since the early 1980s.

The discourse and the practice of the two groups show a strikingly different notion of women's empowerment. The NGOs ask for individual liberty, including sexual liberty, and participation of women in economic and political affairs. They argue for women's freedom to make choices, but such choices are strongly encouraged to prioritize the woman herself and not her family. When women make choices which sacrifice their own wellbeing for that of their families, their choices are viewed as the result of patriarchal structures which need to be challenged. The work of the leading women's rights NGOs ranges from creating economic opportunities for women through provision of micro-credit to ensuring legal protection through legal aid, or drawing them into political activity. Most of these NGOs focus on awareness programmes for women rather than the actual delivery of services.

The female scholars at the madrasas promote a different vision of female wellbeing. In their thought, a woman's interests are best served in a stable family unit. The emphasis is not on equality but on equity. They assume that men and women have different dispositions and that their respective interests are guaranteed by a clear division of labour. They view women's economic empowerment or sexual liberty as counter-productive to women's wellbeing. They argue that economic independence increases women's burden and that sexual liberty makes women vulnerable to unstable relations which are more detrimental to women than men. They often mention the breakdown of the family unit in the West, the economic burden on the woman, and the problems of single motherhood and illegitimate children as arising from such a vision of women's empowerment. In their eyes, Western feminism actually further burdens women rather than liberating them. Piety, self-restraint and interdependence between sexes are thus seen to be in women's best interests. They insist that women in Islam also have the right to free choice, but this choice has to be informed by the awareness that it is in women's interest not to damage the family unit.

These two groups are thus based on fundamentally different premises: one prioritizes the woman as an individual, the other the family on the ground that the woman's individual interest is best preserved within a family unit. A dialogue between the two would be critical to developing understanding between the two positions, but the two groups show strong resistance to such engagement and to articulating to each other why each rejects the other's position. If such engagement occurred, one group would have to try to articulate the other's position in its own terms, that is, to articulate an Islamic-based conception of women's empowerment that may come close to the secular vision, or vice versa.

Paramount to initiating such a dialogue is the recognition that both groups have to co-exist in the same society and that their growing polarization is in neither group's interest. A genuine desire to engage would be the precondition for overcoming that polarization. The two groups have much to learn from each other and from the exercise of negotiating a balance between extreme feminist views and the notion of women's rights in Islam. Initiating such a dialogue requires dynamic leaders within the two groups, who recognize the importance of engagement and are capable of understanding their different languages. These leaders are likely to come from the most influential women's rights NGOs in Pakistan and leaders of top-ranking female madrasas, as deliberations at the top of the hierarchy trickle down to the lower ranks.

Dialogue and translation

Genuine dialogue requires not only engagement but also capacities for understanding and translating each other's language. MacIntyre notes that being open to the conflicting tradition and its resources in order to enrich one's own 'requires a rare gift of empathy' (1988, p. 167). Members of one tradition, especially those intellectuals who contribute to constructing a tradition of thought, such as theologians or political theorists, should be able to understand the other tradition's theses, arguments and concepts. Basically, the language of another tradition has to become like a 'first second language' (MacIntyre, 1988, p. 387).[18] Successful translation between two spoken languages, say French and English, occurs when someone possesses a mastery of both; so it is in the case of translation between traditions of thought or inquiry. It is only when one begins to master the language of another tradition that one is able to start to understand it, that is, one is able to understand the system of meanings that articulate the tradition coherently around its fundamental agreement.

This is precisely what the Catholic theologians of Vatican II have done. The language of secular modernity and liberalism had become their first second language, and they were able to make translations between the religious and secular liberal traditions. In that mode, dialogue between secular development agencies and religious bodies would require them to learn each other's language and make translations between the two. In the example we have used, Western feminists would need to understand the meaning that Muslim women give to women's empowerment from the perspective of Islam, and vice-versa. Such an occurrence is indeed a 'rare gift' enjoyed far too seldom by those engaged in development work or in dialogue between religious communities. Pessimists might even conclude that such an outcome as a widespread reality is merely utopian wishful thinking. MacIntyre shares a degree of pessimism regarding the possibility of dialogue and understanding between conflicting traditions:

> The perspective of a tradition . . . does not permit of any generalized confidence about the potential hospitality of other languages and cultures to the articulated statement of, let alone allegiance to, that particular tradition. And that is to say that the standpoint of tradition is necessarily at odds with one of the central characteristics of cosmopolitan modernity: the confident belief that all cultural phenomena must be potentially translucent to understanding, that all texts must be capable of being translated into the language which adherents of modernity speak to each other. (MacIntyre, 1988, p. 327)

Despite the difficulty of translation and dialogue, such an exercise is absolutely *paramount* to development work. We argue that, without it, the development process risks alienating religious communities who might distort the development process. So far, Western donors and multilateral and international agencies have tended to deal with religion by (1) focusing on the common elements between secular and religious traditions, such as the concern for human dignity, care for the environment, equity and redistribution, and using religion instrumentally to attain these goals within a secular project; (2) pushing religion aside in the private sphere as if it did not exist when views on certain development issues conflict; and (3) avoiding areas of conflict when engagement occurs. For example, some UK-based Muslim FBOs have refrained from participating in development projects in controversial areas such as gender equality and women's reproductive health, or projects which directly involve people's religious values, in order not to hurt the secular sensitivity of major government donors.[19]

These strategies that secular development agencies have adopted for engaging with religious traditions are not sustainable in the long run. Conflicting views cannot be ignored for they are bound to resurface in one way or another. Selective partnerships between secular donors and 'secularized' FBOs (that is, faith-based organizations whose principles bear no religious references) risk alienating religious communities and FBOs which refuse to tone down the religious foundations of their development work, a point rightly made by Clarke (2006).

In her review of case studies of religion-based development initiatives from the World Faith Development Dialogue, Wendy Tyndale (2007) argues that a dialogue about major aspects of development, such as its aims, how to measure progress and how to understand the 'good life', is urgently needed in development work. One cannot assume that the conception of development of major secular international organizations will be in tune with that of religious traditions. Without such open dialogue on these issues, the result risks being either a secularization of religious traditions (forcing them to abide by the secular vision of development) or their marginalization – which is likely to fuel violent resistance.

Dealing with religion within a secular-based conception of development could take some inspiration from dialogues that are already taking place between religious traditions themselves. In a book which summarizes their experience of decades of inter-faith dialogue, Michael Fitzgerald (the previous head of the Pontifical Commission for Inter-Religious Dialogue and Islam specialist) and John Borelli (2006, pp. 27–8) note, first, that dialogue is about 'relations', which means that it is between people and not systems of thought. It is an exercise in human interaction. Second, it is for 'mutual understanding', which means that each party should strive to understand the other in its own terms (what MacIntyre called the other tradition's language becoming like one's second first language). This requires a significant amount of openness, distance from one's prejudices and willingness to enter the other person's world. Third, the goal of dialogue is 'mutual enrichment', which means that dialogue is not about proving that one's own position is better, but about understanding all the views in play, including one's own.

Fitzgerald and Borelli distinguishes four forms of dialogue (2006, p. 28):

(1) Dialogue of life: where people strive to live in an open and neighbourly spirit, sharing their joys and sorrows, their human problems and preoccupations;

(2) Dialogue of action: in which Christians and others collaborate for the integral development and liberation of people;

(3) Dialogue of theological exchange: where specialists seek to deepen their understanding of their respective religious heritage, and to appreciate each other's spiritual values (this dialogue becomes one of discourse if it does not bear on theological issues);

(4) Dialogue of religious experience: where persons rooted in their own religious traditions share their spiritual riches, for instance with regard to prayer and contemplation, faith and ways of searching for God or the Absolute.

In the development community, there is already a lot of 'dialogue of action' taking place, with organizations from different religious traditions working together for the sake of poverty reduction and social justice; and probably also a widespread 'dialogue of life', where people from different religions work alongside each other in secular development organizations, or even faith-based ones (some Christian NGOs have Muslim staff and Muslim NGOs Christian staff), and form friendships. But there seem to be few reports of 'dialogue of discourse', where different traditions seek to understand differences in their shared concepts of 'freedom', 'equality', 'justice' or 'human dignity'.

Such dialogue between secular and religious traditions requires openness, receptivity and respect. It is not possible if one is convinced that one's position is the right one. It also requires patience and perseverance. These latter qualities are not easily squared with development projects and their log-frames, which impose the priority of quick returns and results. From their experience of inter-religious dialogue, Fitzgerald and Borelli (2006, p. 35) conclude that dialogue between religious traditions encounters many obstacles (ignorance, prejudice, suspicion, self-sufficiency and socio-political factors) which may lead to failures or disappointments, but this, they note, should not be a source of discouragement. Perseverance is crucial. Similar conclusions apply for a dialogue between secular and religious traditions as they bear on development issues. We may not expect an immediate harmony between Western secular feminist and Pakistani Muslim views on what it means for a woman to be empowered.

Inter-religious dialogue does not take place for the sake of agreement (Muslims will never agree with the Christian view that God is Trinity, for example, just as Christians will never agree with the Muslim view that Jesus was only a very important prophet and not God made human). Likewise, secular–religious dialogue on development issues should not propose the aim of agreement. Dialogue might lead to greater awareness of commonalities, upon which 'dialogue of action' can take place, such as common action regarding environmental protection (as witnessed for example by the inter-religious ecological initiative led by the Ecumenical Patriarch of Constantinople, Bartholomew II),[20] but agreement on commonalities should not be the closing point of dialogue. Within the context of inter-faith relations, dialogue occurs first and foremost for the sake of mutual understanding and mutual enrichment. Internal change within one tradition may follow, but dialoguing with the other so that s/he may be influenced by one's views, or even come to endorse them, is a recipe for disaster. The engagement between religious and secular traditions on development issues undoubtedly has a lot to learn from inter-faith dialogue.[21]

An example of the potential dangers of non-engagement can be observed through the confrontation between the Pakistani state, on the one hand, and the *ulema* and female students of the Red Mosque in Islamabad on the other. In February 2007, these students launched a resistance against the state to prevent activities that they perceived to be part of a forced secularization agenda and to protest against a corrupt system of governance. Clad in their black dresses (with head and face covered) and holding brown sticks as weapons, they argued for establishing Sharia law. Their activism came as a surprise given that they were known to believe that a woman's role was primarily at home.

This confrontation apparently started when these students occupied a public library for school children next to the madrasa as a protest against the government decision to demolish all the mosques and madrasas in Islamabad which had expanded beyond their original allocated state land. Supported by the male *ulema* of the Red Mosque, the female students rose not only to preserve their madrasa building but also to demand imposition of Sharia in the country. With this in mind, they conducted some protest actions between February and early July 2007. They went around advising CD shop owners to stop such business. They kept a brothel owner in the madrasa by force for three days, pressing her to leave her profession. They captured six Chinese workers at a spa in Islamabad for a day, asking the government to close down such parlours where women massaged the opposite sex.

The government first reacted to these actions by issuing several ultimatums to the madrasa leadership not to break Pakistani law. The madrasa leadership remained open to dialogue and gave easy access to the media, but refused to concede to the government without acceptance of their core demands. What followed was a highly controversial move: the military surrounded the madrasa on 4 July and, without giving them sufficient time for negotiations, launched a violent assault. Phosphorous bombs were used against the stick-holding madrasa students. Government admitted fewer than 100 deaths, but according to the students who left the madrasa before the start of the assault, more than 1,500 students remained in the building. The response of the women's rights NGOs to this incident is symptomatic of the current lack of engagement between traditions.

From the beginning, their response to the resistance of the female students was highly critical and intolerant. They twice protested outside the madrasa, asking the government to take serious action against them. In the past some women's rights activists had accused the female students of this madrasa as having no brains: 'Just like these girls look like ninja turtles – in that all encompassing veil, just like they look like that, their brains are like that. They're atrophied. Totally rusted.'[22] None of the women's rights NGOs tried to go inside the madrasa and negotiate with the female students, despite their openness to talks. The NGOs assumed that the introduction of Sharia would entail enforcing the will of a few on the majority. This could not be tolerated. They viewed the movement as purely ideological and opted for head-on confrontation. Even after the military assault and the heavy casualty list, with a few exceptions most NGO leaders argued that this action was inevitable. Most did not condemn it, and some even defended the government's intervention.

Adopting a more engaging approach the women's rights NGOs could have helped avert this tragedy. Dialogue with the teachers and students inside the madrasa could have led the latter to adopt more acceptable means in making their demands on the state. The NGOs could also have used their influential connections with the state institutions to encourage the state to use dialogue rather than force to end the crisis. Unwillingness to do either of the above resulted in a lost opportunity to resolve a national crisis through peaceful means. A genuine openness to dialogue with the other side and ability to relate to the other's viewpoint, even when that view differs dramatically from one's own, is critical to averting such clashes between religious and secular traditions. Greater burden for initiating such a dialogue rests on the development community, as its very purpose is to enact positive social change.

We have tried to initiate such dialogue in this book by providing detailed examples of how the Christian and Muslim religious traditions understand themselves and act. We have insisted that religions have a dynamic character, and that the way they interpret their fundamental beliefs and teachings, and embody them into concrete realities, is always renewing itself in the light of a changing context. The secular tradition has attempted to account for the role of religion in development processes and outcomes in its own terms – that is, it has tended to conceive religion as a set of static beliefs in the minds of individuals which can have a positive effect on outcomes that the secular tradition sees as valuable (such as protection of the environment, reduction of poverty, or greater equity in social relations). The numerous examples reviewed in this book suggest that another script is needed to account for the presence of religion in development. We have attempted to sketch such a script here. Its basic words are *openness to the other*, without which there can be no genuine dialogue or mutual enrichment, or indeed any engagement at all between 'religion and development'.

Notes

1 For a short introduction to the history of the Church's councils, see Tanner (2001).

2 Extract from the Pope's opening speech to the Second Vatican Council at St Peter's Cathedral on 11 October 1962. The quote is taken from <http://www.vatican2voice.org/> (accessed November 2008). The website provides useful material on the background and significance of Vatican II for Christianity and the world.

3 From the 'Message to humanity', issued at the beginning of the Second Vatican Council by its Fathers, with the endorsement of the Supreme Pontiff, 20 October 1962, in Abbott (1966, p. 5).

4 For a discussion of Vatican II within the context of Catholic social thought, see Dorr (1983, Chapter 6) and Hollenbach (2004). Hollenbach emphasizes the social, economic and intellectual context to which Vatican II responds.

5 For a discussion on the context and significance of *Dignitatis Humanae*, see Griffin (2004). See also Grasso and Hunt (2006) for a reflection on the contemporary significance of the Declaration for the engagement between Christianity and human rights.

6 This recognition does not entail religious relativism (in the light of which all religions are equal), however. The Catholic Church continues to maintain that it possesses the Truth, as Muslims profess that Allah, as revealed to Mohammad, is the only true God.

7 For a biography of John XXIII and how his life shaped his vision of the Church, see Hebblethwaite (1984).

8 See McGovern (1989), Medhurst (1992) and Rowland (1999) for a discussion of liberation theology, and Dorr (1983, Chapter 8) for a discussion of the impact of the Medellín conference for Catholic social thought.

9 For a discussion of the concept of structural sin within the social sciences, see Deneulin *et al.* (2006); and, within theology, see Nebel (2006).

10 To name a few: Leonardo and Clodovis Boff in Brazil, Jon Sobrino in El Salvador, Ernesto and Fernando Cardenal in Nicaragua, Juan Luis Segundo in Uruguay. In Asia, the Sri Lankan Aloyisus Pieris published his *Asian Theology of Liberation* in 1988. Among African-Americans, liberation theology was already practised before its Latin American dawn during the US civil rights movement, and theorized in the publication in 1969 of James Cone's *Black Theology and Black Power*.

11 Cardinal Joseph Ratzinger wrote the first instruction. Pope John Paul II and Cardinal Etchegaray wrote the second.

12 For the response of the Catholic Church's authorities to liberation theology, see Hebblethwaite (1999).

13 In the Catholic Church, authority derives both from scripture and from what is known as 'tradition', that is, the whole of the Church's doctrine and teachings, as found in the documents of the councils, the writings of saints and theologians, and other sources. For an account of the authority of tradition, see Congar (2004).

14 In a review article on feminist theology, Mary Grey (1999) defines feminist theology as 'a critical theology of liberation engaged in the reconstruction of theology and religion in the service of this transformation process [i.e., the struggle for justice for women], in the specificity of the many contexts in which women live' (p. 89).

15 For a detailed discussion of the reasons why Islamic scholars have underutilized the tools of *ijtihad*, see Rahman (1982, 2000).

16 For details on the Al-Mawrid Institute of Islamic Sciences, see <http://www.al-mawrid.org/> (accessed November 2008).

17 For a critical discussion of government/FBO partnerships, see Glenn

(2000) in the United States, and Bretherton (2006) and Orton (2007) in the United Kingdom. See Hovland (2007) for the difficult engagement between the Norwegian Development Ministry (NORAD) and the Norwegian Lutheran Mission.

18 'A condition of discovering the inaccessible is in fact a matter of two stages, in the first of which we acquire a second language-in-use as a second first language and only in the second of which can we learn that we are unable to translate what we are now able to say in our second first language into our first language' (MacIntyre, 1988, p. 387).

19 Personal communication with a senior member of a leading UK Muslim NGO.

20 Documents of that initiative can be accessed on the 'ecological activities' section of the website of the Greek Ecumenical Patriarchate at <http://www.ec-patr.org> (accessed November 2008).

21 In the United Kingdom, inter-faith activities take place, among others, at the St Ethelburga church in the City of London (<http://www.stethelburgas.org>), at the government-initiated network Interfaith Network (<http://www.interfaith.org.uk>), or at the Three Faiths Forum Initiative (<http://www.threefaithsforum.org.uk>). In October 2007, more than 138 Muslim leaders worldwide sent a letter to the leaders of the major Christian denominations entitled 'A common word between us and you'. Stating that 'the future of the world depends on peace between Muslims and Christians', the letter urges more dialogue (<http://www. acommonword.com>) (all websites accessed November 2008).

22 'Pakistan's Islamic girl schools', BBC report by Jannat Jalil, 19 September 2005.

References

Abbott, Walter M. (ed.) (1966), *The Documents of Vatican II*, London: Geoffrey Chapman.

al-Akiti, Afifi M. (2004), *Furu' of Abortion: Down Syndrome Abortion at the Last Minute?* Living Islam website, <http://www.livingislam.org/maa/fads_e. html>.

al-Banna, Hassan (1946), *Hadith al-juma*, Asnam: Al-Ikhwan al-Muslimun.

al-Misri, Ahmad ibn Naqib (1994), *Reliance of a Traveller: a Classical Manual of Islamic Sacred Law*, trans. N. H. M. Keller, Beltsville: Amana Publications.

al-Sadr, Ayatullah Baqir (1982), *Introduction to Islamic Political System*, trans. M. A. Ansari, Accra: Islamic Seminary/World Shia Muslim Organization, pp. 78–9.

Ali-Karamali, Shaista P. and Fiona Dunne (1994), 'The Ijtihad Controversy', *Arab Law Quarterly*, 9 (3): 238–57.

Alkire, Sabina (2002), *Valuing Freedoms*, Oxford: Oxford University Press.

—— (2005), 'Why the Capability Approach?', *Journal of Human Development*, 6 (1): 115–33.

—— (2006), 'Religion and Development', in David A. Clark (ed.), *The Elgar Companion to Development Studies*, Cheltenham: Edward Elgar.

—— (2008), 'Using the Capability Approach: Prospective and Evaluative Analyses', in F. Comim, M. Qizilbash and S. Alkire (eds), *The Capability Approach: Concepts, Measures and Applications*, Cambridge: Cambridge University Press.

Almond, Gabriel A., R. Scott Appleby and Emmanuel Sivan (eds) (2003), *Strong Religion: the Rise of Fundamentalism around the World*, Chicago, IL: University of Chicago Press.

Ansari, Ali M. (2006), *Iran, Islam and Democracy: the Politics of Managing Change*, London: Chatham House.

Appleby, Scott R. (2000), *The Ambivalence of the Sacred: Religion, Violence and Reconciliation*, London: Rowan and Littlefield.

Aristotle (1995), *Politics*, revised Oxford translation, Jonathan Barnes (ed.), Princeton, NJ: Princeton University Press.

Armstrong, Karen (2000), *The Battle for God: Fundamentalism in Judaism, Christianity and Islam*, London: Harper Collins.

Asad, Talal (1993), *Genealogies of Religion: Discipline and Reasons of Power in Christianity and Islam*, Baltimore, MD: Johns Hopkins University Press.

Ayubi, Nazih N. M. (2006), *Political Islam: Religion and Politics in the Arab World*, Abingdon: Routledge.

Baljon, Johannes M. S. (1970), *The Reforms and Religious Ideas of Sir Sayyid Ahmad Khan*, Lahore: Muhammad Ashraf, pp. 34–49.

Bano, Masooda (2005), 'Self-interest, Rationality and Cooperative Behaviour: Aid and Problems of Cooperation within Voluntary Groups in Pakistan', unpublished DPhil thesis, University of Oxford.

—— (2007a), 'Beyond Politics: the Reality of a Deobandi Madrasa in Pakistan', *Journal of Islamic Studies*, 18 (1), pp. 43–68.

—— (2007b), 'Contesting Ideologies and Struggle for Authority: State Madrasa Engagement in Pakistan', mimeograph, London: UK Department for International Development (DfID).

Beattie, Tina (2007), 'Life in All Its Reality', *The Tablet*, 27 October, pp. 6–7.

Bebbington, David (1989), *Evangelicalism in Modern Britain: a History from the 1730s to the 1980s*, London and Boston, MA: Unwin Hyman and Routledge.

Belshaw, D., R. Calderisi and C. Sugden (eds) (2001), *Faith in Development: Partnership between the World Bank and the Churches of Africa*, Oxford: Regnum Books.

Beneditti, Carlo (2006), 'Islamic and Christian Inspired Relief NGOs: between Tactical Collaboration and Strategic Difference', *Journal of International Development*, 18: 849–56.

Berger, Peter (ed.) (1999), *The Desecularization of the World: Resurgent Religion and World Politics*, Grand Rapids, MI: Eerdmans Publishing.

——— (2001), 'Reflections on the Sociology of Religion Today', *Sociology of Religion*, 62 (4): 443–54.

Berryman, Phillip (1995), *Stubborn Hope: Religion and Revolution in Central America*, Maryknoll, NY: Orbis Books.

Borer, Anne Tristan (1998), *Challenging the State: Churches as Political Actors in South Africa, 1980–1994*, Notre Dame, IN: University of Notre Dame Press.

Bosch, David J. (2004), *Transforming Mission: Paradigm Shifts in Theology of Mission*, Maryknoll, NY: Orbis Books.

Bradley, Tamsin (2006), *Challenging the NGOs: Women, Religion and Western Dialogues in India*, London: I. B. Tauris.

Bretherton, Luke (2006), 'A New Establishment?: Theological Politics and the Emerging Shape of Church–State Relations, *Political Theology*, 7 (3), pp. 371–92.

Brockman, James R. (1989), *Romero: a Life*, Maryknoll, NY: Orbis Books.

Brockopp, Jonathan E. (2003), *Islamic Ethics of Life: Abortion, War and Euthanasia*, Columbia, SC: University of South Carolina Press.

Brouwer, Steve, Paul Gifford and Susan D. Rose (1996), *Exporting the American Gospel: Global Christian Fundamentalism*, London: Routledge.

Bruce, Steve (2000), *Fundamentalism*, Cambridge: Polity Press.

Burtonwood, Neil (2003), 'Social Cohesion, Autonomy and the Liberal Defence of Faith Schools', *Journal of Philosophy of Education*, 37 (3), pp. 415–25.

Candland, Christopher (2005), 'Pakistan's Recent Experience in Reforming Islamic Education', in Robert Hathaway (ed.), *Education Reform in Pakistan: Building the Future*, Washington, DC: Woodrow Wilson International Centre.

Casanova, José (1993), 'Church, State, Nation and Civil Society in Spain and Poland', in Said Amir Arjomand (ed.), *The Political Dimensions of Religion*, New York, NY: State University of New York Press.

——— (1994), *Public Religions in the Modern World*, Chicago: University of Chicago Press.

Cavanaugh, William (1998), *Torture and Eucharist*, Oxford: Blackwell.

——— (2003), *Theopolitical Imagination*, London: T. and T. Clark.

Chaplin, Jonathan (2007), 'Speaking from Faith in Democracy', inaugural lecture of the Kirby Laing Institute for Christian Ethics, 27 January, available at <http://www.tyndale.cam.ac.uk/ KLICE/>.

Chenery, Hollis *et al.* (1974), *Redistribution with Growth*, New York, NY: World Bank and Oxford University Press.

Church of England (1985), *Faith in the City: a Call for Action by Church and Nation*, London: Church House.

Clarke, Gerard (2006), 'Faith Matters: Faith-Based Organisations, Civil Society and International Development', *Journal of International Development*, 18: 835–48.

——— (2007a), 'Agents of Transformation? Donors, Faith-Based Organisations and International Development', *Third World Quarterly*, 28 (1): 77–96.

——— (2007b), 'Faith-Based Organisations and International Development: an Overview', in G. Clarke, M. Jennings and T. Shaw (eds), *Development, Civil Society and Faith-Based Organisations*, Basingstoke: Palgrave MacMillan.

Clarke, Gerard and Michael Jennings (2007), 'Introduction', in G. Clarke, M. Jennings and T. Shaw (eds), *Development, Civil Society and Faith-Based Organisations*, Basingstoke: Palgrave MacMillan.

Clements, Keith (1995), *Learning to Speak: the Church's Voice in Public Affairs*, Edinburgh: T. and T. Clark.

Codd, Rachel Anne, (1999), 'A Critical Analysis of the Role of Ijtihad in Legal Reforms in the Muslim World', *Arab Law Quarterly*, 14 (2): 112–31.

Cone, James (1997), *Black Theology and Black Power*, Maryknoll, NY: Orbis Books.

Congar, Yves (2004), *The Meaning of Tradition*, New York, NY: Ignatius Press.

Copson, Raymond W. (1997), 'Review Essay', *African Studies Review*, 40 (2): 209–25.

Cornwall, Andrea and Célestine Nyamu-Musembi (2004), 'Putting the "Rights-Based Approach" to Development into Perspective', *Third World Quarterly*, 25 (8): 1415–37.

Courtney Murray, John (1986), *We Hold These Truths*, second edition, Kansas City, MO: Sheed and Ward.

Cowen, M. P. and R. W. Shenton (1996), *Doctrines of Development*, London: Routledge.

Dale, Graham (2000), *God's Politicians: the Christian Contribution to 100 Years of Labour*, London: Harper Collins.

Daudelin, Jean and W. E. Hewitt (1995), 'Churches and Politics in Latin America: Catholicism at the Crossroads', *Third World Quarterly*, 16 (2): 221–36.

Davie, Grace (1994), *Religion in Britain since 1945: Believing without Belonging*, Oxford: Blackwell.

——— (2002), *Europe – the Exceptional Case: Parameters of Faith in the Modern World*, London: Darton, Longman and Todd.

Davie, Grace, Paul Heelas and Linda Woodhead (eds) (2003), *Predicting Religion: Christian, Secular and Alternative Futures*, Aldershot: Ashgate.

Dayton, Donald (1988), *Discovering an Evangelical Heritage*, Peabody, MA: Hendrickson Publishers.

de Broucker, José (1979), *Dom Helder Camara: the Conversions of a Bishop*, London: Harper Collins.

de Gruchy, John (1995), *Christianity and Democracy: a Theology for a Just World*, Cambridge: Cambridge University Press.

de Jong, J. and G. Snik (2002), 'Why Should States Fund Denominational Schools?' *Journal of Philosophy of Education*, 36 (4): 573–87.

Deneulin, Séverine (2005), 'Development as Freedom and the Costa Rican Human Development Story', *Oxford Development Studies*, 33 (3/4): 493–510.

Deneulin, Séverine, Mathias Nebel and Nick Sagovsky (eds) (2006), *Transforming Unjust Structures: the Capability Approach*, Dordrecht: Springer.

Denzin, N. K. and Y. Limden (eds) (1994), *Handbook of Qualitative Research*, London: Sage.

Diamond, Larry, Marc F. Plattner and Daniel Brumberg (2003), *Islam and Democracy in the Middle East*, Baltimore, MD: Johns Hopkins University Press.

Donovan, Vincent J. (2004), *Christianity Rediscovered*, 25th anniversary edition, Maryknoll, NY: Orbis Books.

Dorr, Donald (1983), *Option for the Poor: a Hundred Years of Vatican Social Teaching*, Maryknoll, NY: Orbis Books.

Eickelman, D. F. and James Piscatori (1996), *Muslim Politics,* Princeton, NJ: Princeton University Press.

Eisenstadt, S. N. (2000), 'The Reconstruction of Religious Arenas in the Framework of "Multiple Modernities"', *Millennium*, 29 (3): 591–612.

Ellis, Stephen and Gerrie Ter Haar (2003), *Worlds of Power: Religious Thought and Political Practice in Africa*, London: Hurst and Company.

Emmerij, Louis, Richard Jolly and Thomas Weiss (2001), *Ahead of the Curve? UN Ideas and Global Challenges*, Bloomington, IN: University of Indiana Press.

Escobar, Arturo (1995), *Encountering Development*, London: Zed Books.

Esposito, John L. and John Obert Voll (1996), *Islam and Democracy*, New York, NY: Oxford University Press.

Estlund, David (1997), 'Beyond Fairness and Deliberation: the Epistemic Dimension of Democratic Authority', in J. Bohman and W. Rehg (eds), *Deliberative Democracy: Essays on Reason and Politics*, pp. 173–204.

Evans-Pritchard, Edward (1949), *The Sanusi of Cyrenaica*, Oxford: Clarendon University Press.

Fitzgerald, Michael L. and John Borelli (2006), *Interfaith Dialogue: a Catholic View*, Maryknoll, NY: Orbis Books.

Freston, Paul (2001), *Evangelicals and Politics in Asia, Africa and Latin America*, Cambridge: Cambridge University Press.

—— (ed.) (2008), *Evangelical Christianity and Democracy in Latin America*, Oxford: Oxford University Press.

Fukuda-Parr, Sakiko and Shiv Kumar (eds) (2003), *Readings in Human Development*, New Delhi: Oxford University Press.

Gadamer, Hans-Georg (1976), *Philosophical Hermeneutics*, trans. David E. Linge, Berkeley, CA: University of California Press.

Gardner, R., J. Cairns and D. Lawton (eds) (2005), *Faith Schools: Consensus or Conflict?* London: Routledge.

Geertz, Clifford (1973), 'Religion as a Cultural System', in C. Geertz, *The Interpretation of Culture*, New York, NY: Basic Books.

Giddens, Anthony (1987), *Capitalism and Modern Social Theory: an Analysis of the Writings of Marx, Durkheim and Max Weber*, Cambridge: Cambridge University Press.

—— (2001), *Sociology*, fourth edition, Cambridge: Polity Press.

Gifford, Paul (1998), *African Christianity: Its Public Role*, London: Hurst and Company.

—— (2004), *Ghana's New Christianity: Pentecostalism in a Globalizing African Economy*, Bloomington, IN: Indiana University Press.

Gilani, Syed Irfan Munawar (2006), 'The Institution of Zakat in Pakistan', Masters thesis, Roskilde University.

Glenn, Charles L. (2000), *The Ambiguous Embrace: Government and Faith-Based Schools and Social Agencies*, Princeton, NJ: Princeton University Press.

Goulet, Denis (1980), 'Development Experts: the One-Eyed Giants', *World Development*, 8 (7/8): 481–9.

Grace, Gerald (2003), 'Educational Studies and Faith-Based Schooling: Moving from Prejudice to Evidence-Based Argument', *British Journal of Educational Studies*, 51 (2): 149–67.

Grasso, Kenneth L. and Robert P. Hunt (eds) (2006), *Catholicism and Religious Freedom: Contemporary Reflections on Vatican II's Declaration on Religious Liberty*, London: Rowman and Littlefield.

Gray, John (2003), *Al Qaeda and What It Means to Be Modern*, London: Faber.

Grey, Mary (1999), 'Feminist Theology: a Critical Theology of Liberation', in C. Rowland (ed.), *The Cambridge Companion to Liberation Theology*, Cambridge: Cambridge University Press.

Griffin, Leslie (2004), 'Commentary on Dignitatis Humanae', in Kenneth R. Himes (ed.), *Modern Catholic Social Teaching*, Washington, DC: Georgetown University Press.

Griffiths, Paul J. (2001), *Problems of Religious Diversity*, Oxford: Blackwell.

Gutierrez, Gustavo (1993), *Las Casas: in Search of the Poor of Jesus Christ*, trans. Robert R. Barr, Maryknoll, NY: Orbis Books.

—— (2001), *A Theology of Liberation*, revised edition, London: SCM Press.

Harb, Mona (2007), 'Faith-Based Organizations as Effective Development Partners? Hezbollah and Post-War Reconstruction in Lebanon', in G. Clarke, M. Jennings and T. Shaw (eds), *Development, Civil Society and Faith-Based Organisations*, Basingstoke: Palgrave Macmillan.

Hastings, Adrian (1994), *The Church in Africa: 1450–1950*, Oxford: Clarendon Press.

—— (1997), *The Construction of Nationhood: Ethnicity, Nationalism and Religion*, Cambridge: Cambridge University Press.

Hauerwas, Stanley (1981), *A Community of Character: Toward a Constructive Christian Social Ethic*, Notre Dame, IN: Notre Dame University Press.

—— (1994), *Dispatches from the Front: Theological Engagements with the Secular*, Durham, NC: Duke University Press.

Haynes, Jeff (1998), *Religion in Global Politics*, Harlow: Longman.

—— (2007), *Religion and Development: Conflict or Cooperation?* Basingstoke: Palgrave Macmillan.

Hebblethwaite, Peter (1984), *John XXIII: Pope of the Council*, London: Chapman.
—— (1999), 'Liberation Theology and the Roman Catholic Church', in C. Rowland (ed.), *The Cambridge Companion to Liberation Theology*, Cambridge: Cambridge University Press.
Hefner, Robert W. and Mohammad Q. Zaman (2007), *Schooling Islam: the Culture and Politics of Modern Muslim Education*, Princeton, NJ: Princeton University Press.
Hewer, C. (2001), 'Schools for Muslims', *Oxford Review of Education*, 27 (4): 515–27.
Hilborn, David (ed.) (2004), *Movement for Change: Evangelical Perspectives on Social Transformation*, Carlisle: Paternoster Press.
Hollenbach, David (2004), 'Commentary on Gaudium et Spes', in Kenneth R. Himes (ed.), *Modern Catholic Social Teaching*, Washington, DC: Georgetown University Press.
Hooker, Barry (1993), 'Fatawa in Malaysia 1960–1985: Third Coulson Memorial Lecture', *Arab Law Quarterly*, 8 (2): 93–105.
Hornby-Smith, Michael (2006), *An Introduction to Catholic Social Thought*, Cambridge: Cambridge University Press.
Hosen, Nadirsyah (2004), 'Nahdlatul Ulama and Collective Ijtihad', *New Zealand Journal of Asian Studies*, 6 (1): 5–26.
Hovland, Inge (2007), 'Who's Afraid of Religion? Tensions between "Mission" and "Development" in the Norwegian Mission Society', in G. Clarke, M. Jennings and T. Shaw (eds), *Development, Civil Society and Faith-Based Organisations*, Basingstoke: Palgrave MacMillan.
Hussain, Haqqani (2005), *Pakistan: between Mosque and Military*, Lahore: Vanguard Books.
Iqbal, Muhammad, (1968), *The Reconstruction of Religious Thought in Islam*, Lahore: Muhammad Ashraf, 187–9.
Jackson, Paul and Christiane Fleischer (2007), 'Religion and Economics: a Literature Review', Working Paper No. 3, Religions and Development Research Programme, University of Birmingham, <www.rad.bham.ac.uk>.
Jenkins, Philip (2007), *The Next Christendom: the Coming of Global Christianity*, Oxford: Oxford University Press.
Johnston, Douglas (1994), 'The Churches and Apartheid in South Africa', in D. Johnson and C. Sampson (eds), *Religion, the Missing Dimension of Statecraft*, Oxford: Oxford University Press.
Johnston, Douglas (ed.) (2003), *Faith-Based Diplomacy*, Oxford: Oxford University Press.
Jolly, Richard, Louis Emmerij, Dharam Ghai and Frédéric Lapeyre (2004), *UN Contributions to Development Thinking and Practice*, Bloomington, IN: University of Indiana Press.
Josaphat, Carlos (2001), 'Las Casas: Prophet of Full Rights for All', in John Orme Mills (ed.), *Justice, Peace and the Dominicans: 1216–2001*, Dublin: Dominican Publications.
Kanbur, Ravi and Paul Shaffer (2007), 'Epistemology, Normative Theory and Poverty Analysis', *World Development*, 35 (2), pp. 183–96.
Keely, Charles B. (1994), 'Limits to Papal Power: Vatican Inaction after *Humanae Vitae*', *Population and Development Review*, 20 (Supplement: 'The New Politics of Population'): 220–40.
Kepel, Gilles (1994), *The Revenge of God: the Resurgence of Islam, Christianity and Judaism in the Modern World*, Oxford: Polity Press.
—— (2006), *Jihad: the Trail of Political Islam*, trans. Anthony F. Roberts, fourth edition, London: I. B. Tauris.
Kramer, G. (1997), 'Islamist Notions of Democracy', in J. Beinin and J. Stork (eds), *Political Islam: Essays from Middle East Report*, London and New York, NY: I. B. Tauris.
Kraut, Richard (1999), 'Politics, Neutrality and the Good', *Social Philosophy and Policy*, 16: 315–32.
Kroessin, Mohammad R. and Abdufatah S. Mohamed (2007), 'Saudi Arabian NGOs in Somalia: "Wahabi" Da'wah or Humanitarian Aid?', in G. Clarke, M. Jennings and

T. M. Shaw (eds), *Development, Civil Society and Faith-Based Organisations: Bridging the Sacred and the Secular*, Basingstoke: Palgrave Macmillan.

Kuran, Timur (1986), 'The Economic System in Contemporary Islamic Thought: Interpretation and Assessment', *International Journal of Middle East Studies*, 18 (2): 135–64.

Lehmann, David (1996), *Struggles for the Spirit: Religious Transformation and Popular Culture in Brazil and Latin America*, Oxford: Polity Press.

—— (2006), 'Secularism and the Public–Private Divide: Europe Can Learn from Latin America', *Political Theology*, 7 (3): 273–93.

Lewis, Arthur W. (1955), *The Theory of Economic Growth*, London: George Allen and Unwin.

Lewis, Bernard (2002) *What Went Wrong? Western Impact and Middle Eastern Response*, New York, NY: Oxford University Press.

Lincoln, Bruce (2003), *Holy Terrors: Thinking about Religion after September 11*, Chicago, IL: University of Chicago Press.

Linden, Ian (2007), 'The Language of Development: What Are International Development Agencies', in G. Clarke, M. Jennings and T. Shaw (eds), *Development, Civil Society and Faith-Based Organisations*, Basingstoke: Palgrave Macmillan.

MacIntyre, Alasdair (1988), *Whose Justice? Which Rationality?* Notre Dame, IN: University of Notre Dame Press.

MacLean, Iain, S. (1999), *Option for Democracy? Liberation Theology and the Struggle for Democracy in Brazil*, New York, NY: Peter Lang Publishers.

Maddox, Graham (1996), *Religion and the Rise of Democracy*, London: Routledge.

Mann, E. A. (1989), 'Religion, Money and Status: Competition for Resources at the Shrine of Shah Jamal, Aligarh', in C. W. Troll (ed.), *Muslim Shrines in India: Their Character, History and Significance*, New Delhi: Oxford University Press.

Manslow, Abraham (1954), *Motivation and Personality*, New York, NY: Harper.

Mansour, Khalid (2002), *War and Peace in Sudan: a Tale of Two Countries*, London: Paul Kegan.

Maritain, Jacques (1944), *Christianity and Democracy*, New York, NY: Scribners and Sons.

Marshall, Katherine and Lucy Keough (eds) (2004), *Heart, Mind and Soul in the Fight against Poverty*, Washington, DC: World Bank.

Marshall, Katherine and R. Marsh (eds) (2003), *Millennium Challenges for Development and Faith Institutions*, Washington, DC: World Bank.

Marshall, Katherine and Marisa van Saanen (2007), *Development and Faith: Where Mind, Heart and Soul Work Together*, Washington, DC: World Bank.

Martin, B. G. (1969), 'Muslim Politics and Resistance to Colonial Rule: Shaykh Uways B. Muhamad Al-barawi and the Qadiriya Brotherhood in East Africa', *Journal of African History*, 10 (3): 471–86.

Martin, David (1990), *Tongues of Fire: the Explosion of Protestantism in Latin America*, Oxford: Basil Blackwell.

—— (2002), *Pentecostalism: the World their Parish*, Oxford: Blackwell.

Marty, Martin E. and Scott R. Appleby (1991), 'Conclusion: an Interim Report on a Hypothetical Family', in Marty and Appleby (eds), *Fundamentalisms Observed*, Chicago, IL, University of Chicago Press.

Masud, M. K. (1995), 'Da'wah – Modern Usage', in J. L. Esposito (ed.), *The Oxford Encyclopedia of the Modern Islamic World*, Vol. 1, New York, NY: Oxford University Press.

Maududi, Sayyid Abul A'la (1967), *Islamic Way of Life*, trans. Khurshid Ahmad, Delhi: Markazi Maktaba Islami.

McGovern, Arthur (1989), *Liberation Theology and its Critics*, Maryknoll, NY: Orbis Books.

Medhurst, Kenneth (1992), 'Politics and Religion in Latin America', in George Moyser (ed.), *Politics and Religion in the Modern World*, London: Routledge.

Mernissi, Fatima (1993a), *The Forgotten Queens of Islam*, Cambridge: Polity Press.

—— (1993b), *Women and Islam: an Historical and Theological Enquiry*, New Delhi: Kali for Women.

Metcalf, Barbara D. (1993), 'Living Hadith in the Tablighi Jama'at', *Journal of Asian Studies*, 52 (3): 584–608.

Miller, David (2003), *Political Philosophy: a Very Short Introduction*, Oxford: Oxford University Press.

Moreno, Antonio F. (2007), 'Engaged Citizenship: the Catholic Bishops' Conference of the Philippines in the Post-Authoritarian Philippines', in G. Clarke, M. Jennings and T. Shaw (eds), *Development, Civil Society and Faith-Based Organisations*, Basingstoke: Palgrave MacMillan.

Munson, Ziad (2001), 'Islamic Mobilization: Social Movement Theory and the Egyptian Muslim Brotherhood', *Sociological Quarterly*, 42 (4): 487–510.

Narayan, Deepa, R. Chambers, M. Shah and P. Petesch (2000), *Voices of the Poor: Crying Out for Change*, New York, NY: Oxford University Press.

Nasr, Seyyed Vali Reza (1994), *The Vanguard of the Islamic Revolution: the Jama'at-I-Islami of Pakistan*, Berkeley and Los Angeles, CA: University of California Press.

—— (1996), *Mawdudi and the Making of Islamic Revivalism*, New York, NY and Oxford: Oxford University Press.

Nebel, Mathias (2006), *La Catégorie Morale de Péché Structurel*, Paris: Cerf.

Norris, Pippa and Ronald Inglehart (2004), *Sacred and Secular: Religion and Politics Worldwide*, Cambridge: Cambridge University Press.

Nurser, John (2005), *For All People and All Nations: the Ecumenical Church and Human Rights*, Washington, DC: Georgetown University Press.

Nussbaum, Martha (2000), *Women and Human Development*, Cambridge: Cambridge University Press.

O'Donovan, Oliver (1996), *The Desire of Nations*, Cambridge: Cambridge University Press.

Orton, Andrew (2007), 'Contesting "Good Practice" in Faith-Based Action for Social Change: Diversity, Dialogue and Dilemmas in Christian Community Work', *Journal of Faith, Spirituality and Social Change*, 1 (1): 20–33.

Ottaway, Marina (2005), 'Civil Society', in Peter Burnell and Vicky Randall (eds), *Politics in the Developing World*, Oxford: Oxford University Press.

Paz, Reuven (2007), *PRIM Papers on Islamist Social Affairs*, No. 2, Global Research in International Affairs Centre, <http://www.e-prism.org/images/Radical_Islam_ and_AIDS_-_social_affairs_-_no_2_-_May_07.pdf>.

Pieris, Aloyisus (1988), *An Asian Theology of Liberation*, New York, NY: Orbis Books.

Pieterse, Jan Nederveen (2001), *Development Theory: Deconstructions/Reconstructions*, London: Sage.

Piscatori, James (1988), *Islam in a World of Nation-States*, Cambridge: Cambridge University Press.

Plant, Stephen (2004), *Bonhoeffer*, London: Continuum.

Poston, Larry (1992), *Islamic Dawah in the West: Muslim Missionary Activity and the Dynamics of Conversion in Islam*. New York, NY and Oxford: Oxford University Press.

Preston, P. W. (1996), *Development Theory: an Introduction*, Oxford: Blackwell.

Prochaska, Frank (2006), *Christianity and Social Service in Modern Britain*, Oxford: Oxford University Press.

Putnam, Hilary (1993), 'Objectivity and the Science–Ethics Distinction', in M. Nussbaum and A. Sen (eds), *The Quality of Life*, pp. 143–57.

—— (2002), *The Collapse of the Fact/Value Dichotomy*, Cambridge, MA: Harvard University Press.

Qutb, Sayyid, (2000), *Social Justice in Islam*, trans. by John B. Hardie and Hamid Algar, Oneonta, NY: Islamic Publications International.

Rahman, Fazlur, (1982), *Islam and Modernity: Transformation of an Intellectual Tradition*, Chicago, IL: Chicago University Press.

—— (1986), 'The Principle of Shura and the Role of the Ummah in Islam', in M. Ahmed (ed.), *State, Politics, and Islam*, Indianapolis, IN: American Trust Publications, 1406/1986, pp. 90–1, cited in Esposito and Voll (1996).

—— (2000), *Revival and Reform in Islam: a Study of Islamic Fundamentalism*, Oxford: Oneworld Publications.

Rakodi, Carole (2007), 'Understanding the Roles of Religions in Development: the Approach of the RaD Programme', Working Paper No. 9, Religions and Development Research Programme, University of Birmingham.

Rawls, John (1971), *A Theory of Justice*, Cambridge, MA: Harvard University Press.

—— (1993), *Political Liberalism*, New York, NY: Columbia University Press.

Raz, Joseph (1994), *Ethics in the Public Domain*, Oxford: Clarendon Press

Richardson, Henry S. (2002), *Democratic Autonomy: Public Reasoning about the Ends of Policy*, Oxford: Oxford University Press.

Ricoeur, Paul (1981), *Hermeneutics and the Human Sciences*, trans. John B. Thompson, Cambridge: Cambridge University Press.

Rist, Gilbert (1997), *The History of Development: from Western Origins to Global Faith*, London: Zed Books.

Robeyns, Ingrid (2005), 'The Capability Approach – a Theoretical Survey', *Journal of Human Development*, 6 (1): 93–114.

Robinson, Francis, (2003) 'Religious Change and Self in Muslim South Asia Since 1800', in F. Robinson, *Islam and Muslim History in South Asia*, New Delhi: Oxford University Press.

—— (2007), *Islam, South Asia, and the West*, New Delhi: Oxford University Press.

Roger, Terence A. (ed.) (2008), *Evangelical Christianity and Democracy in Africa*, Oxford: Oxford University Press.

Rosenblum, Nancy L. (ed.) (2000), *Obligations of Citizenship and Demands of Faith: Religious Accommodation in Pluralist Democracies*, Princeton, NJ: Princeton University Press.

Rostow, William W. (1960), *The Stages of Economic Growth*, Cambridge: Cambridge University Press.

Rowland, Christopher (ed.) (1999), *The Cambridge Companion to Liberation Theology*, Cambridge: Cambridge University Press.

Roy, Olivier (2006), *Globalised Islam: the Search for a New Ummah*, London: Hurst and Company.

Ruston, Roger (2004), *Human Rights and the Image of God*, Canterbury: SCM Press.

Sachs, Wolfgang (ed.) (1992), *The Development Dictionary*, London: Zed Books.

Scholte, Jan (2002), 'Civil Society and Democracy in Global Governance', *Global Governance*, 8 (3): 281–304.

Schulze, R. (1995), 'Da'wah – Institutionalization', in J. L Esposito (ed.), *The Oxford Encyclopedia of the Modern Islamic World*, Vol. 1, New York, NY: Oxford University Press.

Schussler-Fiorenza, Elisabeth (1983), *In Memory of Her: a Feminist Theological Reconstruction of Christian Origins*, New York, NY: Crossroad.

—— (1992), *But She Said: Feminist Practices of Biblical Interpretation*, Boston, MA: Beacon Press.

Sen, Amartya (1999), *Development as Freedom*, Oxford: Oxford University Press.

—— (2006), *Identity and Violence*, London: Allen Lane.

Shah, Timothy S. (2004), 'The Bible and the Ballot Box: Evangelicals and Democracy in the "Global South"', *SAIS Review of International Affairs*, 24 (2): 117–32.

Shaikh, Sadiyya, (2003), 'Family Planning, Contraception and Abortion in Islam – Undertaking Khilafah: Moral Agency, Justice and Compassion', in D. Maguire (ed.) *Sacred Choices: the Case for Contraception and Abortion in World Religions*, Oxford: Oxford University Press.

Shaw, John D. (2002), *Sir Hans Singer: the Life and Work of a Development Economist*, Basingstoke: Palgrave Macmillan.

Short, Geoffrey (2002), 'Faith-Based Schools: a Threat to Social Cohesion', *Journal of Philosophy of Education*, 36 (4): 559–72.

Sikand, Yoginder, S. (1999), 'The Tablighi Jama'at in Bangladesh', *South Asia: Journal of South Asia Studies*, 22 (1): 101–23.

—— (2005), 'Asghar Ali Engineer's Quest for a Contextual Islamic Theology', *Studies in Interreligious Dialogue*, 15 (2).

Singh, David Emmanuel (2000), 'Integrative Political Ideology of Mawlana Mawdudi and Islamisation of the Muslim Masses in the Indian Subcontinent', *South Asia*, 23 (1): 129–48.

Smith, David W. (1998), *Transforming the World? The Social Impact of British Evangelicalism,* Carlisle: Paternoster Press.

Song, Robert (2006), *Christianity and Liberal Society,* Oxford: Oxford University Press.

Stewart, Frances (1985), *Basic Needs in Developing Countries,* Baltimore, MD: Johns Hopkins University Press.

—— (ed.) (2007), *Horizontal Inequalities and Conflict,* Basingstoke: Palgrave.

Stjernø, Steinar (2005), *Solidarity in Europe: the History of an Idea,* Cambridge: Cambridge University Press.

Stoll, David (1990), *Is Latin America Turning Protestant?,* Berkeley, CA: University of California Press.

Stourton, Edward (1998), *Absolute Truth: the Catholic Church in the Twentieth Century,* Harmondsworth: Viking.

Streeten, Paul with S. Burki, M. ul Haq, N. Hicks and F. Stewart (1982), *First Things First: Meeting Basic Human Needs in Developing Countries,* New York, NY: Oxford University Press.

Tanner, Norman P. (2001), *The Councils of the Church: a Short History,* New York, NY: Crossroad.

Taylor, Charles (1985), *Philosophy and the Human Sciences. Philosophical Papers 2,* Cambridge: Cambridge University Press.

—— (1989), *Sources of the Self,* Cambridge, MA: Harvard University Press.

—— (2007), *A Secular Age,* Cambridge: Cambridge University Press.

Ter Haar, Gerrie and Stephen Ellis (2006), 'The Role of Religion in Development: towards a New Relationship between the European Union and Africa', *European Journal of Development Research,* 18 (3): 351–67.

Thomas, Jacob (2003), *From Lausanne to Manila – Evangelical Social Thought: Models of Mission and the Social Relevance of the Gospel,* Delhi: ISPCK.

Thomas, Scott (2005), *The Global Resurgence of Religion and the Transformation of International Relations,* New York: Palgrave.

—— (2007), 'Outwitting the Developed Countries? Existential Security and the Global Resurgence of Religion', *Journal of International Affairs,* 61 (1): 21–45.

Todaro, Michael (2006), *Economic Development,* ninth edition, Harlow: Pearson Addison-Wesley.

Tomalin, Emma (2007), 'Gender Studies Approaches to the Relationship between Religion and Development', Working Paper No. 8, Religions and Development Research Programme, University of Birmingham.

Tomkins, Stephen (2007), *William Wilberforce: a Biography,* London: Lion.

Tripp, Charles (2006), *Islam and the Moral Economy: the Challenge of Capitalism,* Cambridge: Cambridge University Press.

Tyndale, Wendy (ed.) (2007), *Visions of Development: Faith-Based Initiatives,* Aldershot: Ashgate.

UNDP (2004), *Human Development Report: Cultural Liberty in Today's Diverse World,* New York, NY: United Nations Development Programme.

UNGASS (United Nations General Assembly Special Session on HIV/AIDS) (2005), 'India Progress Report on the Declaration of Commitment on HIV/AIDS', New Delhi: Ministry of Health and Family Welfare, Government of India.

Van Hoyweghen, Saskia (1996), 'The Disintegration of the Catholic Church in Rwanda', *African Affairs,* 95 (380): 379–401.

Vandenberg, Todd (1999), 'We Are Not Compensating Rocks: Resettlement and Traditional Religious Systems', *World Development,* 27 (2): 271–83.

Vatikiotis, Panayiotis J. (1987), *Islam and the State,* London: Routledge.

Ver Beek, Kurt Allan (2000), 'Spirituality: a Development Taboo', *Development in Practice,* 10 (1): 31–43.

Verstraeten, Johan (2007), 'A Ringing Endorsement of Capitalism? The Influence of the Neo-Liberal Agenda on Official Catholic Social Teaching and its Implications for Justice', mimeograph, Faculty of Theology, Catholic University of Leuven.

Vikor, Knut S. (1995), *Sufi and Scholar on the Desert Edge: Muhammad b. Ali al-Sanusi and his Brotherhood,* London: Hurst and Company.

Violett, Edward A. (2003), 'Faith-Based Development: the Social Development

Perspective in Catholic Social Teaching (with an Illustrative Case Study of the Ranchi Archdiocese, India)', unpublished PhD dissertation, London School of Economics and Political Science.

Walker, P. E. (1995), 'Da'wah', in J. L Esposito (ed.), *The Oxford Encyclopedia of the Modern Islamic World*, Vol. 1, New York, NY: Oxford University Press.

Wall, Stephen (1998), *Liberalism, Perfectionism and Restraint*, Cambridge: Cambridge University Press.

Walsh, Michael J. (2004), 'A Biography of Barbara Ward, Baroness Jackson of Lodsworth', in the *Oxford Dictionary of National Biography*, Oxford: Oxford University Press.

Walshe, Peter (1995), 'Christianity and Democratisation in South Africa', in Paul Gifford (ed.), *The Christian Churches and the Democratisation of Africa*, Leiden: Brill.

Warren, Heather A. (1998), *Theologians of a New World Order*, Oxford: Oxford University Press.

Weber, Max (1992), *The Protestant Ethic and the Spirit of Capitalism*, introduction by A. Giddens, London: Routledge (first published 1930).

Weigel, George (1999), *Witness to Hope: a Biography of John Paul II*, New York, NY: Harper Collins.

Weithman, Paul. J. (ed.) (1997), *Religion and Contemporary Liberalism*, Notre Dame, IN: Notre Dame University Press.

Westerlund, David (ed.) (1996), *Questioning the Secular State: the Worldwide Resurgence of Religion in Politics*, London: Hurst and Company.

White, Sarah and Romy Tiongco (1997), *Doing Theology and Development: Meeting the Challenge of Poverty*, Edinburgh: Saint Andrew Press.

Wilber, Charles and Kenneth Jameson (1980), 'Religious Values and the Social Limits to Development', *World Development*, 8 (7/8): 467–79.

Wojtyla, Karl (1993), *Love and Responsibility*, New York, NY: Ignatius Press.

Wolffe, John (2006), *The Expansion of Evangelicalism: the Age of Wilberforce, More, Chalmers and Finney*, Nottingham: InterVarsity Press.

Woodberry, Robert D. and Timothy S. Shah (2004), 'Christianity and Democracy: the Pioneering Protestants'. *Journal of Democracy*, 15 (2), pp. 47–61.

Zaman, Mohammad Q. (1999), 'Religious Education and the Rhetoric of Reform: the Madrasa in British India and Pakistan', *Society for Comparative Study of Society and History*, 41: 2.

Index